WILLIAM HOGARTH:

Painter, Engraver, and Philosopher.

MR. GAMBLE'S APPRENTICE.

WILLIAM HOGARTH

Painter, Engraver, and Philosopher.

ESSAYS ON

The Man, the Work, and the Time.

BY

GEORGE AUGUSTUS SALA.

WITH ILLUSTRATIONS.

This edition published by
WARD LOCK REPRINTS · 1970

This work was originally published by
SMITH, ELDER & CO., 1866

Reproduced and Printed by
Redwood Press Limited
Trowbridge & London

CONTENTS.

———◆◆———

LIST OF ILLUSTRATIONS.

———◆◆◆———

WILLIAM HOGARTH:

PAINTER, ENGRAVER, AND PHILOSOPHER.

I.

Little Boy Hogarth.

"THE Life and Adventures of William Hogarth,"—that would be a taking title, indeed! To do for the great painter of manners that which Mr. Forster has done for their great describer, would be a captivating task; and, successfully accomplished, might entitle a man to wear some little sprig of laurel in his cap, and rest, thenceforth, on his oars. It is not my fortune to have the means of writing such a book; and, for many reasons, this performance must be limited to a series of Essays upon the genius and character of the MAN Hogarth; upon the WORK he was permitted, by a healthful, sanguine constitution, and by great powers of will and self-reliance backboning an unflagging industry, to get through in his appointed span here below; and upon the curious quaint TIME in which he lived and did his work.

I

Hogarth's life, away from his works and times, would be
but a barren theme.   Those old Italian painting men
had strange adventures and vicissitudes.   Rafaelle's life
was one brief glorious romance.   Leonardo had a king's
arms to die in.   Buonarotti lived amidst battles and
sieges, and held flouting matches with popes.   Titian's
pencil was picked up by an emperor.   The Germans
and Dutchmen, even, were picturesque and eventful in
their careers.   Was not Rubens an ambassador?   Are
there not mysterious dealings between Rembrandt and
the Jews that have not yet been fathomed?   Did not
Peter de Laar kill a monk?   But in what manner is the
historian to extract exciting elements from the history
of a chubby little man in a cocked hat and scarlet roquelaure, who lived at the sign of the " Painter's Head " in
Leicester Fields, and died in his bed there in competence
and honour; who was the son of a schoolmaster in the
Old Bailey, and the descendant of a long line of north-
country yeomen, of whom the prime progenitor is pre-
sumed to have kept pigs and to have gone by the rude
name of " Hogherd "—whence Hogard and Hogart, at
last liquefied into Hogarth?   Benvenuto Cellini worked
for the silversmiths, but at least he had poniarded his
man and lain for his sins in the dungeons of St. Angelo;
our Hogarth was a plain silversmith's apprentice, in
Cranbourn Alley.   He kept a shop afterwards, and
engraved tankards and salvers, and never committed a
graver act of violence than to throw a pewter pot at the
head of a ruffian who had insulted him during an outing
to Highgate.   Honest man! they never sent him to
Newgate or the Tower.   Only once he was clapped up
for an hour or so in a Calais guardhouse, and, coming

home by the next packet-boat, took a stout revenge on the frog-eaters with his etching needle upon copper. He was no great traveller; and beyond the Calais ship just spoken of, does not appear to have undertaken any journeys more important than the immortal excursion to Rochester, of which the chronicle, illustrated by his own sketches, is still extant (those doughty setters-forth from the Bedford Head were decidedly the first Pickwickians), and a jaunt to St. Alban's after Culloden, to sketch the trapped fox Simon Fraser Lord Lovat, as he sate in the inn-room under the barber's hands, counting the dispersed Highland clans and their available forces of caterans and brae-men on his half-palsied, crooked, picking and stealing fingers.

William Hogarth did but one romantic thing in his life, and that was, to run away with Sir James Thornhill's pretty daughter; and even that escapade soon resolved itself into a cheery, English, business-like, housekeeping union. Papa-in-law—who painted cathedral cupolas at forty shillings a yard—forgave William and Jane. William loved his wife dearly—she had her tempers, and he was not a man of snow—took a country house for her, and set up a coach when things were going prosperously and he was Sergeant Painter to King George; and when William (not quite a dotard, as the twin-scamps Wilkes and Churchill called him) died, Jane made a comfortable living by selling impressions of the plates he had engraved. These and the writing of the *Analysis of Beauty*, the dispute concerning Sigismunda, the interest taken in the welfare of the Foundling Hospital, the dedication [in a pique against the king who hated " boets and bainters,"] of the *March to Finchley* to

Frederick the Great, and the abortive picture auction scheme, are very nearly all the notable events in the life of William Hogarth. And yet the man left a name remembered now with affection and applause, and which will be remembered, and honoured, and glorified when (to quote the self-conscious Unknown who used the *Public Advertiser* as a fulcrum for that terrible lever of his,) " kings and ministers are forgotten, the force and direction of personal satire are no longer understood, and measures are felt only in their remotest consequences."

By the announcement, then, that I do not contemplate, here, a complete biography of Hogarth : that I do not know enough to complete a reliable and authentic life : " *nec, si sciam, dicere ausim :* " these papers are to be considered but as " *Mémoires pour servir ;* " little photographs and chalk studies of drapery, furniture, accessories of costume and snuff-box, cocked hat and silver buckle detail, all useful enough in their place and way, but quite subordinate and inferior to the grand design and complete picture of the hero. I am aware that high critical authorities have been inveighing lately against the employment of the costumiers and *bric a brac* shopkeepers and inventory takers' attributes in biography ; and writers are enjoined, under heavy penalties, to be, all of them, Plutarchs, and limn their characters in half a dozen broad vigorous dashes. It can conduce little, it has been argued, towards our knowledge of the Seven Years' War to be told that Frederick the Great wore a pigtail, and that to his jackboots " Day and Martin with their soot-pots were forbidden to approach ; " and it has been asked whether any likelihood exists of our knowing more of the character of Napoleon Bonaparte from the sight of his cocked hat and tooth-brush at Madame Tussaud's. Presuming to run counter to the opinion of the high critical authorities, I would point out that the very best biographies that have ever been written—those of Samuel Johnson, Samuel Pepys [his diary being eminently biographical], Lord Herbert of Cherbury, and Jean Jacques Rousseau [in the *Confessions*, and bating the lies and madnesses with which that poor crazed wanderer disfigures an otherwise limpid narrative]—are full of those little scraps and fragments of minute cross-hatching, chronicles of " seven livres three sols, parisis," lamentable records of unpaid-for hose, histories of joyous carouses, anecdotes of men and women's meannesses and generosities, and the like. On the other hand, how cold, pallid, unhuman, is the half-dozen-line character, with all its broad vigorous dashes! Certain Roman emperors might have come out far better fellows from the historian's alembic if their togas and sandals had been more scrupulously dwelt upon. Is our awful veneration for St. Augustine one whit diminished by the small deer he condescends to hunt in the history of his youth ? The heaviest blow and greatest discouragement to the composition of admirable biographies, are in the fact that strength and delicacy, vigour and finish, are seldom combined ; and that a Milton with a dash of the macaroni in him is a *rara avis* indeed. Now and then we find an elephant that can dance on the tight-rope without being either awkward or grotesque ; now and then we find a man with a mind like a Nasmyth's steam hammer, that can roll out huge bars of iron, and anon knock a tin-tack into a deal board with gentle accurate taps. These are the men who can describe a Revolution, and by its side the corned beef and carrots which country parsons were once glad to eat ; who can tell us how the Bastile was stormed, and, a few pages on, what manner of coat and small-clothes wore Philip Egalité at his guillotining. When we find such men we christen them Macaulay or Carlyle.

The latitude, therefore, I take through incapacity for accuracy, saves me from inflicting on you a long prolegomena ; saves me from scoring the basement of this page with foot-notes, or its margins with references ; saves me from denouncing the "British Dryasdust," from whom I have culled the scanty dates and facts, the mile and year stones in William Hogarth's life. Indeed, he has been very useful to me, this British Dryasdust, and I should have made but a sorry figure without him. He or they—Nichols, Steevens, Trusler, Rouquet, Ireland, Ducarel, Burn—have but little to tell ; but that which they know they declare in a frank, straightforward manner. Among commentators on Hogarth, Ireland is the best ; Trusler, the worst. T. Clerk and T. H. Horne also edited (1810) a voluminous edition of Hogarth's works, accompanied by a sufficiently jejune *Life*. Allan Cunningham, in the *British Painters*, has given a lively, agreeable adaptation of all who have come before him, spiced and brightened by his own clear appreciation of, and love for, art and its professors. Half a day's reading, however, will tell you all that these writers know. Horace Walpole for criticism on Hogarth is admirable ; lucid, elegant, and—a wonder with the dilettante friend of Madame du Deffand—generous. The mere explicatory testimony as to the principal Hogarthian series or engraved dramas by the Sire Rouquet [he was a Swiss]

cited above, is valuable ; the more so that he was a
friend of the painter, and, it is conjectured, took many
of his instructions *viva voce* from William Hogarth
himself. The Germans have not been indifferent to
the merits of the great humoristic painter ; and a
certain Herr Von Fürstenburg has found out some odd
things connected with suggestive objects in one of the
most famous scenes of the first series—the *Kate Hackabout, Mother Needham,* and *Colonel Charteris epopœiæ*—
never dreamt of previously in the good people of England's philosophy. Occasionally, too, in a French *Revue,*
you meet with an *Etude* on *La vie et les ouvrages de
Hogarth,* giving us little beyond a fresh opportunity to
be convinced that, if there exist on earth a people of
whose manners and customs the French know consider-
ably less than about those of the man in the moon, that
people are the English.

By his own countrymen William Hogarth has ever
been justly and honourably treated. He was an out-
spoken man, and his pencil and graver were as unbridled
as his tongue. His works have a taint of the coarseness,
but not of the vice of his age. Most at home would be
many of his works, perhaps, in low tap-rooms and skittle-
alleys ; but he was no Boucher or Fragonard to paint
alcoves or *dessus de portes* for the contemporary Cotillons I. and Cotillons II., for the Pompadours and
Dubarrys of Louis the well-beloved. He was vulgar
and ignoble frequently, but the next generation of his
countrymen forgave him these faults—forgave him for
the sake of his honesty, his stern justice, his unbending
defence of right and denunciation of wrong. This philosopher ever preached the sturdy English virtues that

have made us what we are. He taught us to fear God and honour the King ; to shun idleness, extravagance, and dissipation ; to go to church, help the poor, and treat dumb animals with kindness ; to abhor knavery, hypocrisy, and avarice. For this reason is it that Sectarianism itself (though he was hard against tub-thumping) has raised but a very weak and bleating voice against Hogarth's "improprieties ; " that cheap and popular editions of his works have been multiplied, even in this fastidious nineteenth century ; that in hundreds of decorous family libraries a plump copy of Hogarth complete may be found [yes : I have heard the stateliest old ladies chat about the history of *Kate Hackabout,* and I have seen age explaining to youth and beauty—that came in a carriage to Marlborough House—the marvellous *Marriage à la Mode* in the Vernon collections] ; that, finally —and which may be regarded as a good and gratifying stamp of the man's excellence and moral worth—the Church of England have always been favourable to William Hogarth. An Anglican bishop wrote the poetic legends to the *Rake's Progress ;* and Hogarth has been patronized by the beneficed and dignified clergy ever since.

So come, then, William Hogarth, and let me in these essays strive to glorify thy painting, thy engraving, and thy philosophy. Let me stand over against thee, and walk round thee—yea, and sometimes wander for a little while quite away from thee, endeavouring to explore the timeous world as thou knew it. But be thou always near : the statue on the pedestal, the picture on the wall, the genius of the place, to recal me when I stray, to remind me when I am forgetful, to reprove me when I err !

Born in the Old Bailey, and the ninth year of William the Dutchman, that should properly be my starting point; but the reader must first come away with me to Westmoreland, and into the Vale of Bampton—to a village sixteen miles north of Kendal and Windermere Lake. In this district had lived for centuries a family of yeomen, called Hogart or Hogard: the founder of the family, as I have hinted, may have been Hogherd, from his vocation—a guardian of swine. *His* father, perchance, was that Gurth, the son of Beowulph, erst thrall to Cedric the Saxon, and who, after his emancipation by the worthy but irascible Franklin for good suit and service rendered in the merry greenwood, gave himself, or had given to him in pride and joy, that which he had never had before—a surname; and so, emigrating northwards, became progenitor of a free race of Hogherds. In this same Bampton Vale the Hogarts possessed a small freehold; and of this tenement, the other rude elders being beyond my ken, the grandfather of the painter was holder in the middle of the seventeenth century. To him were three sons. The eldest succeeded to the freehold, and was no more heard of, his name being written in clods. He tilled the earth, ate of its fruits, and, his time being come, died. The two remaining sons, as the custom of Borough English did not prevail in Bampton, had to provide for themselves. Son intermediate—my William's uncle—was a genius. Adam Walker, writer on natural philosophy, and who was the friend and correspondent of Nichols of the *Anecdotes*, called him a " mountain Theocritus ; " his contemporaries, with less elegance but more enthusiasm, dubbed him " Auld Hogart." He was a poet, humorist, satirist, and

especially a dramatist; and coarse plays of his, full of
coarse fun, rough and ready action, and sarcastic hard
hitting, yet linger, more by oral tradition than by any
manuscript remains of his, among the Westmoreland
fells. These were all written, too, in the very hardest,
thickest, and broadest Westmoreland dialect; a patois
to which Tim Bobbin's Lancashire dialect is as melli-
fluous as the *langue d'oc;* a patois which has been compared to the speech of Demosthenes before his course of
pebbles, but which, to my ears, offers more analogy to
that which may have proceeded from the famous Anti-
Philippian orator *during* the pebble probation; and in
order to speak which patois fluently (after the pebbles),
an admirable apprenticeship is to fill your mouth as full
as possible of the gritty oatcake, or "clapt bread," which
is kept in the "cratch," or rack suspended from the
ceiling in Westmoreland farmhouses. In this Scythian
speech, however, "auld Hogart" concocted a famous
drama, quite in the Lope de Vega's manner, called *Troy
Taken.* I do not compare the play unadvisedly with
those of the prolific Spanish playwright. You know
how artfully Lope's plays begin: with what immediate
action and seduction of its audience to a foregone conclusion. The curtain draws up. A man in a cloak
crosses the stage. A masked cavalier rushes after him
with a drawn sword. There is a *rixe* at once established;
the audience begin to imagine all sorts of terrible things,
and the success of the piece is half assured. So "auld
Hogart's" play of *Troy Taken* begins with a *rixe.* Paris
is seen in the very act of running away with Helen; and
Menelaus runs after them, calling "Stop thief!" With
such an auspicious commencement, and plenty of good

boisterous episodes throughout : Hector dragged about by
the heels ; Thersites cudgelled within an inch of his life ;
Achilles storming for half an hour at the loss of Patrocles,
and a real wooden horse to finish up with ; the whole spiced
with "auld Hogart's" broadest jokes : who can wonder
that *Troy Taken* achieved immense popularity, and that
years after the death of the facetious author, natural
philosopher Adam Walker saw the piece performed from
recollection by the Troutbeck rustics, the stage a green-
sward, the auditorium a grassy knoll, the canopy,
Heaven ? The proceedings were inaugurated by a grand
cavalcade, headed by the minstrels of five parishes, and
a lusty yeoman mounted on a bull's back and playing
on the fiddle ; and as a prologue to *Troy Taken*, there
was a pilgrimage of the visitors to a stone dropped by
the enemy of mankind in an unsuccessful attempt to
build a bridge across Windermere !

The brother of the "auld" dramatist of the *Iliad*,
and third son of the Bampton yeoman, was Richard
Hogart. Without being dogmatical, I trust that I am
justified in the assumption that the "liquefaction" of the
patronymic into Hogarth was due partly to the more
elegant education of this yeoman's son, partly to our
painter's formation of a "genteel" connection, when he
married Jane Thornhill. I have not seen his indentures ; and take the authority of Ireland for the registry
of his birth ; but it is certain that he was at one
period called,—ay, and pretty well known as—Hogart :
witness Swift, in his hideously clever satire of the *Legion
Club* :—

> " How I want thee, hum'rous Hogart,
> Thou, I hear, a pleasant rogue art "—

Now Swift wrote this in Ireland, at a distance from means of accuracy, and the " pleasant rogue's " name was not likely to be found in a calendar of the nobility and gentry. If Bolingbroke or Pope had written to the dean about the rogue and his pleasantries, it is very probable that they might have spelt his name " Hogart," " Hogard," " Hoggert," or " Hogarth." You must remember that scores of the most distinguished characters of the eighteenth century were of my Lord Malmesbury's opinion concerning orthography, that neither the great Duke of Marlborough, nay, nor his duchess, the terrible " old Sarah," nay, nor Mrs. Masham, nay, nor Queen Anne herself, could spell, and that the young Pretender (in the Stuart papers) writes his father's name thus : " Gems " for " James." Again, Swift may have suppressed the " *th* " for mere rhythmical reasons ; just as Pope, *aux abois* between dactyls and spondees, barbarized a name which undeniably before had been pronounced " Saint John " into " Sinjin." But, on the other hand, Jonathan Swift was not so dizzy when he wrote the *Legion Club* as to have lost one pin's point of his marvellous memory ; and he was too rich in rhymes to have resorted to the pusillanimous expedient of cutting off a letter : if ever a man lived who could have found an easy rhyme to " Hippopotamus," it was the Dean of St. Patrick's. I opine, therefore, that when Swift first heard of Hogarth—in the early days of George I.—he was really called " Hogart ;" that such a name was carried by the dean with him to Dublin, and that the change to " Hogart " only took place when the great Drapier was dying " in a rage, like a poisoned rat in a hole."

Richard Hogart—whatever he callèd himself in the scholastic Latinity that converted "Saumaise" into "Salmasius," and a Dutch logician, "Smygel" into "Smeglesius,"—was educated at St. Bees' College, in Westmoreland ; was too poor, it is thought, after his college course to take orders, and kept school for a time in his native county. His classical accomplishments were considerable. In the manuscript department of the British Museum are preserved some Latin letters by him ; and he wrote besides a Latin-English dictionary, and a school-book entitled *Grammar Disputations*, which has not attained the fame or immortality of the works of Cocker and Walkingame. It is stated that Richard Hogart was occasionally employed as a corrector of the press ; an office then frequently discharged by trustworthy scholars quite extraneous to the recognized staff of the printing-office.

It is certain that, William and Mary reigning, Dominie Hogart came to London, and established himself as a schoolmaster, in Ship Court, Old Bailey. He had married, as it is the wont of poor schoolmasters to do, and his wife bare him two daughters and one son. The girls were Mary and Anne ; and have only to be mentioned to pass out of this record :—Who cares about Joseph Mallard Turner's nephews and nieces ? The boy, WILLIAM HOGARTH, was born on the 10th of November, 1697, and stands in the parish register of St. Bartholomew the Great, as having been baptized, November the 28th.

You do not expect me to tell who nursed little chubby-baby Hogarth, whether he took to his pap kindly, and at what age he first evinced an affection for sweet-stuff? Making, however, a very early halt in his nonage, I am compelled to shake my head at a very pretty legend about him, and as prettily made into a picture, some years ago. According to this, little boy Hogarth was sent to a dame's school, where he much vexed the good woman who boasted " unruly brats with birch to tame," by a persistence in drawing caricatures on his slate. The picture represents him in sore disgrace, mounted on the stool of repentance, crowned with the asinine tiara of tribulation, holding in one hand the virgal rod of anguish, and in the other the slate which has brought him to this evil estate : a slate much bechalked with libellous representations of his dame. In the background is that Nemesis in a mob-cap, inflexible; around, an amphitheatre of children-spectators ; the boys, as suits their boisterous character, jeering and exultant ; the girls, as beseems their softer nature, scared and terrified. A very pretty naïve picture, but apocryphal, I fear. There were no slates in dame-schools in those days. The hornbook, *Pellucïd*, with its Christ Cross Row, was the beginning of knowledge, as the " baleful twig " that " frayed " the brats was the end thereof. If little boy Hogarth had been born at Kirby Thore, I would have admitted the dame-school theory in an instant ; but it is far more feasible that he learnt his hornbook at his mother's knee, and in due time was promoted to a bench in the school his father taught, and an impartial share in the stripes which the good pedagogue distributed. Nor need Dominie Hogart have been by any means a cruel pedagogue. In none of his pictures does Hogarth display any rancour against scholastic discipline (what school-scenes that pencil might have drawn !), and it generally happens that he who has suffered much in the flesh as a boy, will have a fling at the rod and the ferule when he is a man ; even if he have had Orbilius for his father. And be it kept in mind, that, although the awful Busby, who called the birch " his sieve," through which the cleverest boys must pass, and who of the Bench of Bishops taught sixteen mitred ones, was but just dead. Mr. John Locke was then also publishing his admirable treatise on *Education*, a treatise that enjoins and inculcates tenderness and mercy to children.

Ship Court, Old Bailey, is on the west side of that ominous thoroughfare, and a few doors from Ludgate Hill. By a very curious coincidence, the house No. 67,* Old Bailey, corner of Ship Court, was occupied, about forty years ago, by a certain William Hone, an odd, quaint, restless man, but marvellously bustling and ener-getic : a man not to be "put down" by any magnates, civic, Westmonasterian, or otherwise ; and who, at 67, had a little shop, where he sold prints and pamphlets, so very radical in their tendencies as to be occasionally seditious, and open to some slight accusation of ribaldry and scurrility. Here did Hone publish, in 1817, those ribald parodies of the Litany and Catechism for which he stood three trials before the then Lord Ellenborough, who vehemently assumed the part of public prosecutor (staining his ermine by that act), and tried his utmost to have Hone cast, but in vain. As to William Hone,

---

* Ship Court, and the adjoining houses, formerly Nos. 65, 66, and 67, Old Bailey, were pulled down in 1862, and the warehouse of Messrs. John Dickinson & Co., Paper-makers, stands on the site.

the man drifted at last, tired, and I hope ashamed, out of sedition and ribaldry, and, so far as his literary undertakings went, made a good end of it. To him we owe those capital Table-books, Every-day-books, and Year-books, full of anecdote, quaint research, and folk-lore, which have amused and instructed so many thousands, and have done such excellent service to the book-making craft. Be you sure that I have Mr. Hone's books for the table, day, and year, before me, as I write, and shall have them these few months to come. Without such aids; without Mr. Cunningham's *Handbook* and Mr. Timbs' *Curiosities of London;* without Walpole, Cibber, and " Rainy-day Smith ; " without Ned Ward and Tom Brown ; without the Somers Tracts and the Sessions Papers ; without King and Nichols' anecdotes and the lives of Nollekens and Northcote ; without a set of the *British Essayists*, from Addison to Hawkesworth ; without the great *Grub Street Journal* and the *Daily Courant;* without Gay's *Trivia* and Garth's *Dispensary;* without Aubrey, Evelyn, and Luttrell's diaries ; without the *London Gazette* and Defoe's *Complete English Trades-man;* without Swift's *Journal to Stella*, and Vertue and Faithorne's maps, and Wilkinson, Strype, Maitland, Malcolm, Gwynn, and the great Crowle Pennant ; without plenty of small deer in the way of tracts, broadsides, and selections from the bookstall-keepers' sweepings and the cheesemongers' rejected addresses ; without these modest materials, how is this humble picture to be painted ?

After this little glance behind the scenes of a book-maker's workshop, you will be wondering, I dare say, as to what was the curious coincidence I spoke of in con-

nection with William Hone's sojourn in Ship Court, Old
Bailey. Simply this. Three years after his Litany
escapades, the restless man went tooth and nail into the
crapulous controversy between George IV. and his
unhappy wife; who, though undoubtedly no better than
she should be, was undoubtedly used much worse than
she or any other woman, not a Messalina or a Frédé-
gonde, should have been. From Hone's shop issued
those merry, rascally libels against the fat potentate late
of Carlton House, and which, under the titles of "The
Green Bag," "Doctor Slop," the "House that Jack
built," and the like, brought such shame and ridicule
upon the vain, gross old man, that all Mr. Theodore
Hook's counter-scurrilities in the high Tory *John Bull*
could not alleviate or wipe away the stains thereof.
Ah! it was a nice time—a jocund, Christian time.
Reformers calling their king "knave, tyrant, and de-
bauchee;" loyalists screaming "hussey," and worse
names, after their queen. That was in the time of the
Consul *Un*manlius I should think. Hone's clever ras-
calities sold enormously, especially among the aristocracy
of the "Opposition." But Mr. Hone's disloyal facetiæ
from Ship Court were relieved and atoned for by the
illustrations, engraved from drawings executed with
quite an astonishing power of graphic delineation and
acuteness of humour, by a then very young artist named
GEORGE CRUIKSHANK: a gentleman whose earliest
toys, I believe, had been a strip of copper and an etching-
needle; who has, since those wild days of '21, achieved
hundreds of successes more brilliant, but not more notorious, than those he won by working for restless Mr.
Hone; and whom I am proud to speak of here, with

2

Hogarth's name at the head of my sheet, now that he, our George, is old, and honoured, and famous. Do I attach too much importance to the works of these twin geniuses, I wonder, because I love the style of art in which they have excelled with a secret craving devotion, and because I have vainly striven to excel in it myself? Am I stilted or turgid when I paraphrase that which Johnson said of Homer and Milton *in re* the *Iliad* and the *Paradise Lost*, and say of Hogarth and Cruikshank that George is not the greatest pictorial humorist our country has seen, only because he is not the first? At any rate, you will grant the coincidence—won't you?— between the lad George Cruikshank and little boy Hogarth, toddling about Ship Court and perchance scrawling caricatures on the walls, exaggerating in rollicking chalk (I allow him as many brick walls as you like, but no slates) the Slawkenbergian nose of William the Deliverer, or adding abnormal curls to the vast wig of the detested clerical statesman, Burnet.

Little boy Hogarth is yet too young to see these things; but he may be at Gilbert Burnet's turbulent funeral yet. First, we must get him out of the Old Bailey, where he dwells for a good dozen years at least. Dominie Hogarth has the school upstairs, where he drums *Lily's Accidence*, or perhaps his own *Grammatical Disputations* into his scholars. Of what order may these scholars have been? The gentry had long since left the Bailey; and you may start, perhaps, to be told that British Brahmins had ever inhabited that lowering precinct of the gallows, and parvise of the press-room. Yet, in the Old Bailey stood Sydney House, a stately mansion built for the Sydneys, Earls of Leicester, and which they abandoned [*circa* 1660] for the genteeler locality of Leicester Fields. I don't know what Sydney House could have been like, or by whom it was inhabited when Hogarth was a little boy ; but it was to all likelihood in a tumbledown, desolate condition : in Pennant's time it was a coachmaker's shop. The keeper of Newgate may have had children, too, for schooling, but his corporation connections would probably have insured his boy's admission to Christ's Hospital, or to Paul's, or Merchant Taylors' School, for the keeper of Newgate was then a somebody ; and it was by times his privilege to entertain the sheriffs with sack and sugar. Dominie Hogarth's pupils must have been sons of substantial traders in the Bailey itself—where were many noted booksellers' shops—or from the adjacent Ludgate, whilom Bowyers Hill, and from Fleet Street, or, perchance, Aldersgate Street ; which, not then purely commercial or shopkeeping, was the site of many imposing mansions superbly decorated within, formerly the property of the nobility, but then (1697) occupied by stately Turkey and Levant merchants. And to the dominie's may have come the offspring of the wealthy butchers of Newgate Market, whose rubicund meat-wives are libellously declared to have been in the habit of getting " overtaken by burnt sherry " by eight o'clock in the morning ; and while in that jovial but prematurely matutinal condition, rivalling the flat-caps of the Dark House, Billingsgate, and the pease-pottage sellers of Baldwin's Gardens—to say nothing of the cake and comfit purveyors to the Finsbury archers—in voluble and abusive eloquence. Bonny dames were these butchers' wives ; lusty, rotund, generous to the poor, loud, but cheery with their apprentices and journeymen, great (as now) in making fortunes for their beast-buying-and-killing husbands; radiant in gold-chains, earrings, and laced aprons, and tremendous at trades-feasts and civic junketings.

And I am yet in the year 1697, and in the Old Bailey with a child in my arms. Were this an honest plain-sailing biography, now, what would be easier for me than to skip the first twelve or thirteen years of the boy's life, assume that he got satisfactorily through his teething, thrush, measles, and chicken-pox perils, and launch him comfortably, a chubby lad, in the midst of the period of which the ruthless Doctor Swift will write a history—the last four years of the reign of Queen Anne—and make up his little bundle for him, ready for his apprenticeship to Mr. Ellis Gamble, silver-plate engraver of Cranbourn Alley, Leicester Fields. He may have been sent out to nurse at Tottenham or Edmonton, or, may be, distant Ware, as children of his degree were wont to be sent out (Mr. John Locke's *Education*, and Mr. Daniel Defoe's *Family Instructor*, *passim*). But, in good sooth, I am loth to turn over my William to the tender mercies of the eighteenth century and the Augustan age. I fear great "Anna" and her era, and for a double reason: first, that people know already so much about the reign of Queen Anne. No kindly book a' bosom but can follow Sir Roger de Coverley and his tall silent friend the *Spectator* in their rambles; but has seen Swift walking across the park in mighty fear of the Mohocks; but has taken a dish of coffee at Miss Vanhomrigh's; but has lounged in the elegant saloon, among the China monsters and the black

boys, with Belinda or Sir Plume ; but has accompanied
Steele from coffee-house to coffee-house, and peeped
over his shoulder while he scribbled those charming
little billets to his wife ; but has seen Queen Anne
herself, the "stately lady in black velvet and diamonds,"
who touched little Sam Johnson for the evil, and hung
round his neck that broad piece of angel gold, which in
its more earthly form of a guinea the poor doctor wanted
so often and so badly at a subsequent stage of his career.
The humorists and essayists of Queen Anne's days have
made them as crystal-clear to us as Grammont and
Pepys made those of the Second Charles ; and—there !
bah ! it is mock modesty to blink the truth because my
pen happens to be enlisted under such a banner.*   I
could have gone swaggeringly enough into all the
minutiæ of Anne's days, all the glories and meannesses
of John Churchill, all the humours, and tyrannies, and
quarrels of Pope, and Gay, and Harley, and St. John, if
a book called *Esmond* had never been written.   Yet
finding myself in this cleft stick, between the historian
who wrote of the state of manners at the close of the
reign of Charles II., and the novelist, who has made the
men and women of Queen Anne's court and city and
army live again, I feel slightly relieved.   There is just
one little niche left for me.   Just three years to dwell
upon, while little boy Hogarth is in his swaddling clothes,
or is consorting with divers other little brats as diminutive
as he, on the doorsteps or the pavement of Ship Court.
Three years,—'97, '98, '99.   *Ah ! laissez-moi pleurer ces*

---

* This work first appeared in the *Cornhill Magazine*, of which Mr. W.
M. Thackeray was then editor.

années mortes. Let me linger over these three ignored years. They were a transition time. They are lost in the deeper shadow cast by the vicious bonfire that Charles's *roués* and beauties lighted up—a shadow shortly to be dispelled by the purer radiance of an Augustan era of literature. Pepys and Evelyn are so minute, so lifelike, that between their word-paintings, and those of the *Spectator* and *Tatler*, there seems a great black blank.

No seven-league boots are necessary for me to stride back to my subject, and to the time when my little-boy-hero is forming his earliest acquaintance with the Old Bailey stones. I said that I wanted those last three dying years of the seventeenth century. Let me take them, and endeavour to make the best of them, even when I compress some of their characteristics within the compass of a single London day.

The century, then, is on its last legs. The town seems to have quite done with the Stuarts, socially speaking, although politically another Stuart will reign : a dethroned Stuart is actually at St. Germains, maunder-ing with his confessors, and conspiring with his shabby refugee courtiers ; thinking half of assassinating the abhorred Dutchman and making Père la Chaise Arch-bishop of Canterbury *in partibus*, and half of slinking away to La Trappe, wearing a hair shirt, and doing grave-digging on his own account, for good and all. Politically, too, this crooked-wayed, impracticable Stuart's son and grandson will give the world some trouble till the year 1788, when, a hundred years after the Revolution, a worn-out, *blasé* sensualist, called the Young Pretender, dies at Rome, leaving a brother, the Cardinal of York, who survived to be a pensioner of George the Third, and bequeathed to him those Stuart papers, which, had their contents been known at the Cockpit, Westminster, half a century before, would have caused the fall of many a head as noble as Derwentwater's, as chivalrous as Charles Ratcliffe's, and broken many a heart as loving and true as Flora Macdonald's or Lady Nithisdale's. But with the Restoration-Stuart period, London town has quite done. Rochester has died penitent, Buckingham bankrupt and forlorn. Archbishop Tenison has preached Nelly Gwynn's funeral sermon; Portsmouth, Davies, are no more heard of; Will Chiffinch can procure for kings no more: the rigid Dutchman scorns such painted children of dirt; Barbara, Duchess of Cleveland, has married one Fielding, a swindling caricature of a "beau;" Wycherley is old and broken, and the iron of the Fleet has entered into his soul; and poor noble old John Dryden, twitted as a renegade, neglected, unpensioned, and maligned, is savagely writing the finest "copy" that has issued yet from that grand fertile brain, writing it with a Spartan fortitude and persistence, and ever and anon giving left-legged Jacob Tonson a sound verbal trouncing, when the publisher would palm on the poet clipped moidores for milled Jacobuses. Ah, little boy Hogarth, you will see Johnson fifty years hence, listen to him behind the curtain in the twilight room, as the Jacobite schoolman raves against the cruelty of government in hanging Doctor Cameron; but you will never behold John Dryden in the flesh, little boy, or hear him at Wills's on golden summer afternoons, the undisputed oracle of wits, and critics, and poets. The horrible Chancellor Jeffreys (however could the ruffian

have found patience and temper to deliver a decree in
Chancery!) is dead, but he has a son alive, a rake-hell,
Mohock Lord Jeffries, who, four years hence, will be
implicated in a scandalous disturbance at Dryden's
house, in Gerrard Street; the poet's corpse lying there.
There are brave men hard at work for the nineteenth
century. Isaac Newton is working; in '95 he was
appointed Master of the Mint. Pope is beginning to
feel his poetic feet. Mr. Joseph Addison is at college.
Swift has had the run of Temple's library. Lely has
thrown down the pencil; Kneller has taken it up; and
James Thornhill is preparing for vast sprawlings on
ceilings, after the model of Verrio and Laguerre.

Away with Restoration reminiscences, for the more
decent century that is to come. By 8th and 9th
William III., Alsatia is ruined, and its privileges of
sanctuary wholly taken away. A dreadful outpouring
and scattering of ragged rogues and ruffians, crying out
in what huff-cap cant and crambo they can command,
that *delenda est Carthago*, takes place. Foul reeking
taverns disgorge knavish tatterdemalions, soddened with
usquebaugh and spiced Hollands, querulous or lachry-
mose with potations of "mad dog," "angel's food,"
"dragon's milk," and "go-by-the-wall." Stern catchpoles seize these inebriated and indebted maltbugs, and
drag them off to the Compters, or to Ludgate, "where
citizens lie in durance, surrounded by copies of their
freedom." Alewives accustomed to mix beer with rosin
and salt deplore the loss of their best customers; for
their creed was Pistol's advice to Dame Quickly, "Trust
none;" and the debased vagabonds who crowded the
drinking-shops—if they drank till they were as red as

cocks and little wiser than their combs, if they occasionally cut one another's throats in front of the bar, or
stabbed the drawer for refusing to deliver strong waters
without cash—could sometimes borrow, and sometimes
beg, and sometimes steal money, and then they drank
and paid. No use was there in passing bad money in
Alsatia, when every sanctuary man and woman knew
how to coin and to clip it. You couldn't run away from
your lodgings in Alsatia, for so soon as you showed your
nose at the Whitefriars' gate, in Fleet Street, the Philistines were upon you. Oh! for the ruffianly soldados,
the copper captains, the curl'd-pate braggarts, the
poltroons who had lost their ears in the pillory, and
swore they had been carried off by the wind of a cannon-
shot at Sedgemóor! Oh! for the beauteous slatterns,
the Phrynes and Aspasias of this Fleet Street Athens,
with their paint and their black visor masks; their
organ-pipe head-dresses, their low stomachers, and their
high-heeled shoes; the tresses of dead men's hair they
thatched their poor bald crowns withal; the live fools'
rings and necklaces they sported between taking out and
pawning in! Beggars, cut-purses, swindlers, tavern-
bilks, broken life-guardsmen, foreign counts, native
highwaymen, and some poor honest unfortunates, the
victims of a Draconic law of debtor and creditor, all
found their Patmos turn out to be a mere shifting quick-
sand. The town does not long remain troubled with
these broken spars and timbers of the wrecked ship—
once a tall caravel—Humanity. Don't you remember
when the "Holy Land" of St. Giles's was pulled down
to build New Oxford Street, what an outcry arose as to
where the dispossessed Gilesians were to find shelter?

and don't you remember how quickly they found congenial holes and corners into which to subside—dirt to
dirt, disease to disease, squalor to squalor, rags to rags?
So with the Alsatians. A miserable compensation is
made to them for their lost sanctuary by the statute
which quashes all foregone executions for debts under
fifty pounds; but they soon get arrested again—often
for sums not much more than fifty pence—and, being
laid up in hold, starve and rot miserably. There are
debtors in Newgate, there are debtors in Ludgate; in
the Clink, the Borough, Poultry, and Wood Street
Compters, the Marshalsea, the King's Bench, and at
Westminster Gate houses, besides innumerable spunging-
houses, or "spider's webs," with signs like inns, such as
the " Pied Bull" in the Borough, and the "Angel" in
Cursitor Street. Little boy Hogarth will have much to
observe about prisons and prisoners when he is grown to
be a man. Many Alsatians take refuge in the Southwark Mint, likewise and by the same statute deprived
of its sanctuary ; but which, in some underhand manner
—perhaps from there being only one bridge into Southwark, and that rotten—contrives to evade it till late in the
reign of George I. Coining flourishes thenceforth more
than ever in the Mint; the science of Water Lane being
added to the experience of St. Mary Overy, and both
being aided, perhaps, by the ancient numismatic traditions of the place. More of the Alsatians are caught up
by alguazils of the criminal law, and, after a brief sojourn
at Newgate, " patibulate " at Justice Hall, and eventually
make that sad journey up Holborn Hill in a cart, stopping for a refresher at the Bowl House, St. Giles's Pound
—alas! it is not always staying for his liquor that will

save the saddler of Bawtree from hanging—and so end at Tyburn. Some, too, go a-begging in Lincoln's Inn, and manufacture some highly remunerative mutilations and ulcers. And some, a very few, tired of the draff and husks in Alsatia, go back to their fathers, and are forgiven. In this hard world, whose members only see the application of parables that teach us love and mercy on Sundays, it is easier to find prodigals to repent than fathers to forgive. But for our hope and comfort, *that* parable has another and a higher meaning.

Alsatia was linked hand in glove with the Court of the Restoration. 'Twas often but a chapel of ease to the backstairs of Whitehall, and many a great courtier, ruined at basset with the king and his beauties the night before, found his level on the morrow in this vile slum playing butt, playing cards on a broken pair of bellows. But now, 1697, Whitehall itself is gone. The major part of the enormous pile went by fire in '91 ; now the rest, or all but Holbein's Gate and the blood-stained Banqueting-house, has fallen a prey to the " devouring element."

Whitehall, then, has gone by the board. In vain now to look for Horn Chamber, or Cabinet Room, or the stone gallery that flanked Privy Garden, where the imperious, depraved Louise de la Quérouaille, Duchess of Portsmouth, lived amid " French tapestry, Japan cabinets, screens, pendule clocks, great vases of wrought plate, table stands, chimney furniture, sconces, branches, braseners, all of massive silver, and out of number." All these things, worthy Master Evelyn, of Sayes Court, Deptford (who about this time has let his said mansion and ground to Peter Velikè, czar of Muscovy, and thinks

him but an evil tenant, with his uncouth, uncleanly
Russian fashions, his driving of wheelbarrows through
neatly-trimmed hedges, and spitting over polished and-
irons, and gorging himself with raw turnips sliced in
brandy)—worthy, sententious Evelyn shall see these
things no more. Nay, nor that "glorious gallery,"
quoted from his description innumerable times, where
was the dissolute king "sitting toying with his con-
cubines, Portsmouth, Cleveland, and Mazarine, &c. ;
a French boy singing love-songs, whilst about twenty
of the great courtiers and others were at basset round
a large table, a bank of at least 2,000*l.* in gold
before them. Six days after, all was in the dust." And
worse.

Little boy Hogarth, you shall often pass by the
banqueting-house—ay, and admire Hans Holbein's
wondrous gate of red brick, tesselated in quaint and
beauteous design ; of which the fragments, when the
gate was pulled down in 1760, were begged by William,
Duke of Cumberland, and the pieces numbered, with the
project of having them transferred to Windsor Park, and
there re-erected as a royal ducal lodge. But the project
was never carried out, and the duke probably forgot all
about it, or found something more worth begging for
than a lot of old building materials. So exit Whitehall
palace : buttery, bakehouse, wood and coal yards, spicery,
charcoal-house, king's privy cellar, council chamber,
hearth-money office, and other fripperies in stone. It
must have been a grand place, even as the heterogeneous
pile that existed in William Dutchman's time ; but if
James or Charles had possessed the funds to rebuild it
according to Inigo Jones's magnificent plan, of which the

banqueting-house is but an instalment, the palace of Whitehall would have put to the blush the Baths of Diocletian, the golden house of Nero—yea, and the temple which Erostratus burnt, to prove that all things were vanity, even to incendiarism.

Will it please you to walk into the city, now that we have done with Westminster, any day in these three years of the moribund seventeenth century? London is busy enough, noisy enough, dirty enough; but not so smoky. There is little or no foot pavement; but there are plenty of posts and plenty of kennels—three hundred and eleven, I think, between Newgate and Charing Cross. When the humorous operation, resorted to with ugly frequency about this time, of whipping a man at the cart's tail, takes place, the hangman gives the poor wretch a lash at every kennel the near wheel of the cart grates against. Newgate to Ludgate, Charing Cross to the "Cockpit" at Westminster, are considered the mildest pilgrimages to be undergone by those poor flagellated knaves; but Charing to Newgate is the real *via dolorosa* of stripes. That pilgrimage was reserved for the great objects of political hatred and vengeance in James II.'s reign—for Titus Oates and Thomas Dangerfield. The former abominable liar and perjurer, stripped of his ambrosial periwig and rustling silk canonicals, turned out of his lodgings in Whitehall, and reduced to the very last of the last, is tried and sentenced, and is very nearly scourged to death. He is to pay an enormous fine besides, and is to lie in Newgate for the remainder of his life. I wonder that like " flagrant Tutchin," when shuddering under a sentence almost as frightful, he did not petition to be hanged: yet there seems to be an

indomitable bull-headed, bull-backed power of endurance
about this man Oates—this sham doctor of divinity, this
Judas spy of Douai and St. Omer, this broken chaplain
of a man-of-war, this living, breathing, incarnate Lie—
that enables him to undergo his punishment, and to get
over its effects somehow.   He has not lain long in Newgate, getting his seared back healed as best he may,
when haply, in "pudding-time," comes Dutch William
the Deliverer.   Oates's scourging was evidently alluded
to when provision was made in the Bill of Rights against
"cruel and unusual punishments."   The heavy doors of
Newgate open wide for Titus, who once more dons his
wig and canonicals.   Reflective persons do not believe
in the perjured scoundrel any more, and he is seldom
sworn, I should opine, of the common jury or the
crowner's quest.   He has "taken the book in his right
hand," and kissed it once too often.   By a section of the
serious world, who yet place implicit faith in all Sir
Edmondsbury Godfrey's wounds, and take the inscription
on the Monument of Fish Street Hill as law and gospel,
Titus Oates is regarded as a species of Protestant martyr
—of a sorry, slippery kind, may be, but, at all events, as
one who has suffered sorely for the good cause.   The
government re-pension him ; he grows fat and bloated,
and if Tom Brown is to be believed (*Miscellanies*, 1697),
Doctor Oates, about the time of Hogarth's birth, marries
a rich city widow of Jewin Street.

Different, and not so prosperous, is the end of the
assistant villain, Dangerfield.   He, too, is whipped nearly
out of his skin, and within a tattered inch of his miserable life ; but his sentence ends before Newgate is
reached, and he is being taken to that prison in a

hackney-coach, when the hangman's assistants stop the vehicle at the Gray's Inn Coffee-house, to give the poor, tired, mangled wretch a drink. Steps out of the coffee-house one Mr. Francis, a counsel learned in the law of Gray's Inn aforesaid, and who has probably been taking a flask too much at the coffee-house. He is an ardent anti-plot man, and in a railing tone and Newmarket phrase asks Dangerfield whether he has " run his heat, and how he likes it." The bleeding object in the coach, revived to pristine ruffianism by the liquor his gaolers have given him, answers with a flood of ribald execrations—bad language could surely be tolerated in one so evilly intreated as he had been that morning—whereupon the barrister in a rage makes a lunge at Dangerfield's face with a bamboo cane, and strikes one of his eyes out. In the fevered state of the man's blood, erysipelas sets in, and Dangerfield shortly afterwards gives the world a good riddance (though it were better the hangman had done it outright with a halter) and dies. The most curious thing is, that Francis was tried and executed at Tyburn for the murder of this wretched, scourged, blinded perjurer. He was most likely tried by a strong Protestant jury, who (very justly) found him guilty on the facts, but would very probably have found him guilty against the facts, to show their Protestant feeling and belief in the Popish plot ; but I say the thing is curious, seeing that the Crown did not exercise its prerogative of mercy and pardon to Francis, who was a gentleman of good family, and manifestly of the court way of thinking. The conclusion is : either that there was more impartial justice in the reign of James II. than we have given that bad time credit for, or that the court

let Francis swing through fear of the mob. You see
that the mob in those days did not like to be baulked of
a show, and that the mob derived equal pleasure from
seeing Francis hanged as from seeing Dangerfield
whipped. The moral of this apologue is, that Oates and
Dangerfield being very much alike in roguery, especially
Oates, one got not quite so much as he deserved, and
the other not quite enough ; which has been the case in
many other instances that have occurred in society, both
vulgar and polite, since the days of William III.

There, I land you at Temple Bar, on whose gory
spikes are the heads of the last conspirators against
William the Dutchman's life. "*Forsitan et nobis,*" whispered Goldsmith slyly to Johnson, as they gazed up at
the heads which, late in the reign of George III., yet
rotted on those fatal spikes. We will not linger at
Temple Bar now. Little boy Hogarth, years hence,
will take us backwards and forwards through it hundreds
of times. The three last years of century seventeen
glide away from me. Plumed hats, ye are henceforth to
be cocked. Swords, ye shall be worn diagonally, not
horizontally. Puffed sleeves, ye must give place to
ruffles. Knickerbocker breeches, with rosettes at the
knees, ye must be superseded by smalls and rolled
stockings. Shoe-bows, the era of buckles is coming.
Justaucorps, flapped waistcoats will drive you from the
field. Falling bands, your rivals are to be cravats of
Mechlin lace. Carlovingian periwigs, the Ramillies'
wig is imminent. Elkanah Settles, greater city poets are
to sing the praise of city custards. Claude du Val and
Colonel Jack, greater thieves will swing in the greater
reign that is to come. And wake up, little boy Hogarth,

for William the Dutchman has broken his collar-bone, and lies sick to death at Kensington. The seventeenth century is gone and passed. In 1703 William dies, and the Princess of Denmark reigns in his stead. Up, little boy Hogarth! grow stout and tall—you have to be bound 'prentice and learn the mystery of the cross-hatch and the double cypher. Up, baby Hogarth, there is glorious work for you to do!

II.

Mr. Gamble's Apprentice.

HOW often have I envied those who—were not my envy
dead and buried—would now be sixty years old! I
mean the persons who were born at the commencement
of the present century, and who saw its glories evolved
each year with a more astonishing grandeur and brilliance, till they culminated in that universal "transformation scene" of '15. For the appreciation of things
began to dawn on me only in an era of internecine frays
and feuds—theological controversies, reform agitations,
corporation squabbles, boroughmongering debates, and
the like : a time of sad seditions and unwholesome social
misunderstandings ; Captain Rock shooting tithe-proc-
tors in Ireland yonder ; Captain Swing burning hayricks
here ; Captains Ignorance and Starvation wandering up
and down, smashing machinery, demolishing toll-bars,
screeching out "Bread or blood!" at the carriage-
windows of the nobility and gentry going to the drawing-room, and otherwise proceeding the wretchedest of
ways for the redress of their grievances. Surely, I
thought, when I began to think at all, I was born in
the worst of times. Could that stern nobleman, whom
the mob hated, and hooted, and pelted—could the

detested " Nosey," who was beset by a furious crowd in
the Minories, and would have been torn off his horse,
perchance slain, but for the timely aid of Chelsea Pensioners and City Marshalmen,—and who was compelled
to screen his palace windows with iron shutters from
onslaughts of Radical stone-throwers—could *he* be that
grand Duke Arthur, Conqueror and Captain, who had
lived through so much glory, and had been so much
adored an idol? Oh, to have been born in 1800! At
six, I might just have remembered the mingled exultation and passionate grief of Trafalgar; have seen the
lying in state at Greenwich, the great procession, and
the trophied car that bore the mighty admiral's remains
to his last home beneath the dome of Paul's. I might
have heard of the crowning of the great usurper of
Gaul : of his putting away his Creole wife, and taking an
emperor's daughter; of his congress at Erfurt,—and
Talma, his tragedian, playing to a pit full of kings ; of
his triumphal march to Moscow, and dismal melting
away—he and his hosts—therefrom ; of his last defeat
and spectral appearance among us—a wan, fat, captive
man, in a battered cocked hat, on the poop of an English
war-ship in Plymouth Sound—just before his transporta-
tion to the rock appointed to him to eat his heart upon.
I envied the nurse who told upon her fingers the names
of the famous victories of the British army under WEL-
LINGTON in Spain ; Vimieira, Talavera, Vittoria, Salamanca, Ciudad Rodrigo, Badajos, Fuentes d'Onore,—
mille e tre ; in fine—at last, WATERLOO. Why had I
not lived in that grand time, when the very history itself
was acting? Strong men there were who lived before
Agamemnon ; but for the accident of a few years, I

3—2

might have seen, at least, Agamemnon in the flesh.
'Tis true, I knew then only about the rejoicings and
fireworks, the bell-ringings, and thanksgiving sermons,
the Extraordinary Gazettes, and peerages and ribbons
bestowed in reward for those deeds of valour. I do not
remember that I was told anything about Walcheren, or
about New Orleans; about the trade driven by the
cutters of gravestones, or the furnishers of funeral urns,
broken columns, and extinguished torches; about the
sore taxes, and the swollen national debt. So I envied;
and much disdained the piping times of peace descended
to me; and wondered if the same soldiers I saw or heard
about, with scarcely anything more to do than lounge on
Brighton Cliff, hunt up surreptitious whisky-stills, expec-
torate over bridges, and now and then be lapidated at
a contested election, could be the descendants of the
heroes who had swarmed into the bloody breach at
Badajos, and died, shoulder to shoulder, on the plateau
of Mont St. Jean.

Came 1848, with its revolutions, barricades, states of
siege, movements of vast armies, great battles and victories, with their multiplied hecatombs of slain even;
but they did not belong to us; victors and vanquished
were aliens; and I went on envying the people who had
heard the Tower guns fire, and joybells ring, who had
seen the fireworks, and read the Extraordinary Gazettes
during the first fifteen years of the century! Was I
never to live in the history of England? Then, as you
all remember, came the great millennium or peace
year '51. Did not sages deliberate as to whether it
would not be better to exclude warlike weapons from
the congress of industry in Hyde Park? By the side of

Joseph Paxton with his crystal verge there seemed to
stand a more angelic figure, waving wide her myrtle
wand, and striking universal peace through sea and land.
It was to be, we fondly imagined, as the immortal blind
man of Cripplegate sang :—

> No war or battle's sound
> Was heard the world around :
>   The idle spear and shield were high uphung,
> The hooked chariot stood
> Unstain'd with hostile blood,
>   The trumpet spake not to the armed throng ;
> And kings sate still with awful eye,
> As if they surely knew their Sovereign Lord was by.

O blind man ! it was but for an instant. The trodden
grass had scarcely begun to grow again where nave and
transept had been, when the wicked world was all in a
blaze ; and then the very minstrels of peace began to
sharpen swords and heat shot red-hot about the Holy
Places ; and then the Guards went to Gallipoli, and
farther on to Bulgaria, and farther on to Old Fort ; and
the news of the Alma, Inkermann, Balaklava, the Redan,
the Tchernaya, the Mamelon, the Malakhoff came to us,
hot and hot, and we were all living in the history of England.   And lo ! it was very much like the history of any
other day in the year—or in the years that had gone before.   The movements of the allied forces were discussed
at breakfast, over the sipping of coffee, the munching of
muffins, and the chipping of eggs.   Newspaper-writers,
parliament-men, club-orators took official bungling or
military mismanagement as their cue for the smart leader
of the morrow, the stinging query to Mr. Secretary at
the evening sitting, or the bow-window exordium in the
afternoon ; and then everything went on pretty much as

usual. We had plenty of time and interest to spare for
the petty police case, the silly scandal, the sniggering
joke of the day. The cut of the coat and the roasting
of the mutton, the non-adhesiveness of the postage-
stamp, or the misdemeanors of the servant-maid, were
matters of as relative importance to us as the great and
gloomy news of battle and pestilence from beyond sea.
At last I lived in actual history, and my envy was
cured for ever.

I have often thought that next to Asclepiades, the
comic cynic,* Buonaparte Smith was the greatest philosopher that ever existed. B. Smith was by some thought
to have been the original of Jeremy Diddler. He was
an inveterate borrower of small sums. On a certain
Wednesday in 1821, *un sien ami* accosted him. Says
the friend : " Smith, have you heard that Buonaparte
is dead ? " To which retorts the philosopher : " Buonaparte be——! " but I disdain to quote his irreverent
expletive—" Buonaparte be somethinged. *Can you lend
me ninepence ?* " What was the history of Europe or its
eventualities to Buonaparte Smith ? The immediate
possession of three-fourths of a shilling was of far more

---

* According to Tertullian, Asclepiades, the comic cynic, advocated
riding on cowback as the most healthful, and especially the most inde-
pendent means of locomotion in the world ; for, said he, she goes so slowly
that she can never get tired. Wherever there is a field, there is her banquet ; *and you may live on her milk all the way.* But I think that the most
economical and the merriest traveller on record was the Giant Hurtali
(though the Rabbins will have that it was Og, King of Basan), who sat
astride the roof of Noah's ark *à la* cockhorse, steering that great galleon
with his gigantic legs, getting his washing for nothing, and having his
victuals handed up to him through the chimney.—See *Menage* and *Le
Pelletier : l'Arche de Noê*, c. 25.

importance to him than the death of that tremendous
exile in his eyrie in the Atlantic Ocean, thousands of
miles away.   Thus, too, I daresay it was with a certain
small philosopher, who lived through a very exciting
epoch of the history of England : I mean LITTLE BOY
HOGARTH.   It was his fortune to see the first famous
fifteen years of the eighteenth century, when there were
victories as immense as Salamanca or Waterloo ; when
there was a magnificent parallel to Arthur Wellesley,
Duke of Wellington, existent, in the person of John
Churchill, Duke of Marlborough.   I once knew a man
who had lived in Paris, and throughout the Reign of
Terror, in a second floor of the Rue St. Honoré.   " What
did you do ? " I asked, almost breathlessly, thinking to
hear of tumbrels, Carmagnoles, gibbet-lanterns, conven-
tions, *poissarde*-revolts, and the like.   " *Eh ! parbleu*,"
he answered, "*je m'occupais d'ornithologie.*"   This philosopher had been quietly birdstuffing while royalty's
head was rolling in the gutter, and Carrier was drowning
his hundreds at Nantes.   To this young Hogarth of
mine, what may Marlborough and his great victories,
Anne and her " silver age " of poets, statesmen, and
essayists, have been ?   Would the War of the Succession
assist young William in learning his accidence ?   Would
their High Mightinesses of the States-General of the
United Provinces supply him with that fourpence he
required for purchases of marbles or sweetmeats ?   What
had Marshal Tallard to do with his negotiations with
the old woman who kept the apple-stall at the corner of
Ship Court ?   What was the Marquis de Guiscard's
murderous penknife compared with that horn-handled,
three-bladed one, which the Hebrew youth in Duke's

Place offered him at the price of twentypence, and which
he could not purchase, *faute de quoi*?   At most, the
rejoicings consequent on the battles of Blenheim or Ramillies, or Oudenarde or Malplaquet, might have saved
William from a whipping promised him for the morrow ;
yet, even under those circumstances, it is painful to re-
flect that staying out too late to see the fireworks, or
singeing his clothes at some blazing fagot, might have
brought upon him on that very morrow a castigation
more unmerciful than the one from which he had been
prospectively spared.

Every biographer of Hogarth that I have consulted—
and I take this opportunity to return my warmest thanks
to the courteous book distributor at the British Museum
who, so soon as he sees me enter the Reading Room,
proceeds, knowing my errand, to overwhelm me with
folios, and heap up barricades of eighteenth century lore
round me—every one of the biographers, Nichols,
Steevens, Ireland, Trusler, Phillips, Cunningham, the
author of the article " Thornhill," in the *Biographia
Britannica*—the rest are mainly copyists from one another, often handing down blunders and perpetuating
errors—every Hogarthian Dryasdust makes a clean leap
from the hero's birth and little schoolboy noviciate to
the period of his apprenticeship to Ellis Gamble the
silversmith.   Refined Mr. Walpole, otherwise very appreciative of Hogarth, flirting over the papers he got from
Vertue's widow, indites some delicate manuscript for the
typographers of his private press at Strawberry Hill,
and tells us that the artist, whom he condescends to
introduce into his *Anecdotes of Painting*, was bound
apprentice to a " mean engraver of arms upon plate."

I see nothing mean in the calling which Benvenuto
Cellini (they say), and Marc Antonio Raimondi (it is
certain), perhaps Albert Durer, too, followed for a time.
I have heard of great artists who did not disdain to paint
dinner plates, soup tureens, and apothecary's jars. Not
quite unknown to the world is one Rafaelle Sanzio
d'Urbino, who designed tapestry for the Flemish weavers,
or a certain Flaxman, who was of great service to Mr.
Wedgwood, when he began to think that platters and
pipkins might be brought to serve some very noble uses.
Horace Walpole, cleverest and most refined of *dilettanti*
—who could, and did say the coarsest of things in the
most elegant of language—you were not fit to be an
Englishman. Fribble, your place was in France. Puta-
tive son of Orford, there seems sad ground for the scandal
that some of Lord Fanny's blood flowed in your veins ;
and that Carr, Lord Hervey, was your real papa. You
might have made a collection of the great King Louis's
shoes, the heels and soles of which were painted by
Vandermeulen with pictures of Rhenish and Palatinate
victories. *Mignon* of arts and letters, you should have
had a *petite maison* at Monçeaux or at the Roule. Surrounded by your *abbés au petit collet*, teacups of *pâte
tendre*, fans of chicken-skin painted by Leleux or Lan-
tara, jewelled snuff-boxes, handsome chocolate girls,
gems and intaglios, the brothers to those in the Museo
Borbonico at Naples, *che non si mostrano alle donne*, you
might have been happy. You were good enough to
admire Hogarth, but you didn't quite understand him.
He was too vigorous, downright, virile for you ; and
upon my word, Horace Walpole, I don't think you
understood anything belonging to England—nor her

customs, nor her character, nor her constitution, nor her laws. I don't think that you would have been anywhere more in your element than in France, to make epigrams and orange-flower water, and to have your head cut off in that unsparing harvest of '93, with many more noble heads of corn as clever and as worthless for any purpose of human beneficence as yours, Horace.

For you see, this poor Old Bailey schoolmaster's son—this scion of a line of north-country peasants and swineherds—had in him pre-eminently that which scholiast Warton called the "'ΗΘΟΣ," the strong sledge-hammer force of Morality, not given to Walpole—not given to you, fribbles of the present as of the past—to understand. He was scarcely aware of the possession of this quality himself, Hogarth; and when Warton talked pompously of the *Ethos* in his works, the painter went about with a blank, bewildered face, asking his friends what the doctor meant, and half-inclined to be angry lest the learned scholiast should be quizzing him. It is in the probabilities, however, that William had some little Latin. The dominie in Ship Court did manage to drum some of his grammar disputations into him, and to the end of his life William Hogarth preserved a seemly reverence for classical learning. Often has his etching-needle scratched out some old Roman motto or wise saw upon the gleaming copper. A man need not flout and sneer at the classics because he knows them not. He need not declare Parnassus to be a molehill, because he has lost his alpenstock and cannot pay guides to assist him in that tremendous ascent. There is no necessity to gird at Pyrrha, and declare her to be a worthless jade, because she has never braided her golden hair for you. Of Greek I imagine W. H. to have been destitute ; unless, with that ingenious special pleading, which has been made use of to prove that Shakspeare was a lawyer, apothecary, Scotchman, conjuror, poacher, scrivener, courtier—what you please—we assume that Hogarth was a Hellenist because he once sent, as a dinner invite to a friend, a card on which he had sketched a knife, fork, and pasty, and these words, " Come and Eta Beta Pi." No wonder the ῎ΗΘΟΣ puzzled him. He was not deeply learned in anything save human nature, and of this knowledge even he may have been half unconscious, thinking himself to be more historical painter than philosopher. He never was a connoisseur. He was shamefully disrespectful to the darkened daubs which the picture-quacks palmed on the curious of the period as genuine works of the old masters. He painted " Time smoking a picture," and did not think much of the collection of Sir Luke Schaub. His knowledge of books was defective ; although another scholiast (not Warton) proved, in a most learned pamphlet, that he had illustrated, *sans le savoir*, above five hundred passages in Horace, Virgil, Juvenal, and Ovid. He had read Swift. He had illustrated and evidently understood Hudibras. He was afraid of Pope, and only made a timid, bird-like, solitary dash at him in one of his earliest *charges ;* and, curiously, Alexander the Great of Twickenham seemed to be afraid of Hogarth, and shook not the slightest drop of his gall vial over him. What a quarrel it might have been between the acrimonious little scorpion of " Twitnam," and the sturdy bluebottle of Leicester Fields ! Imagine Pope *versus* Hogarth,

pencil against pen ; not when the painter was old and
feeble, half but not quite doting indeed, as when he
warred with Wilkes and Churchill, but in the strength
and pride of his swingeing satire.   Perhaps William and
Alexander respected one another ; but I think there
must have been some tacit " hit me and I'll hit you "
kind of rivalry between them, as between two cocks
of two different schools who meet now and then on
the public promenades — meet with a significant half-
smile and a clenching of the fist under the cuff of the
jacket.

To the end of his life Hogarth could not spell ; at
least, his was not the orthography expected from educated persons in a polite age.   In almost the last plate
he engraved, the famous portrait of Churchill as a Bear,
the " lies," with which the knots of Bruin's club are inscribed, are all " lyes."   This may be passed over, con-
sidering how very lax and vague were our orthographical
canons not more than a century ago, and how many
ministers, divines, poets,—nay princes, and crowned
heads, and nabobs—permitted themselves greater liberties than " lye " for " lie " in the Georgian era.   At this
I have elsewhere hinted, and I think the biographers of
Hogarth are somewhat harsh in accusing him of crass
ignorance, when he only wrote as My Lord Keeper, or
as Lady Betty, or as his grace the Archbishop was wont
to write.   Hogarth, too, was an author.   He published
a book—to say nothing of the manuscript notes of his
life he left.   The whole structure, soul, and strength of
the *Analysis of Beauty* are undoubtedly his ; although
he very probably profited by the assistance—grammatical as well as critical—of some of the clerical dignitaries

who loved the good man. That he did so has been
positively asserted ; but it is forestalling matters to trot
out an old man's hobby, when our beardless lad is not
bound 'prentice yet. I cannot, however, defend him from
the charges of writing " militia," " milicia," " Prussia,"
" Prusia"—why didn't he hazard " Prooshia " at once ? *
—" knuckles," " nuckles "— oh, fie !—" Chalcedonians,"
" Calcidonians ;" " pity, " pitty ; " and " volumes," " vo-
lumns." It is somewhat strange that Hogarth himself
tells us that his first graphic exercise was to " draw the
alphabet with great correctness." I am afraid that he
never succeeded in writing it very correctly. He hated
the French too sincerely to care to learn *their* language ;
and it is not surprising that in the first shop card he
engraved for his master there should be in the French
translation of Mr. Gamble's style and titles a trifling
pleonasm : " bijouxs," instead of " bijoux."

No date of the apprenticeship of Hogarth is anywhere
given. We must fix it by internal evidence. He was
out of his time in the South Sea Bubble year, 1720. On
the 29th of April † in the same year, he started in business for himself. The neatness and dexterity of the
shop card he executed for his master forbid us to assume

---

* This " Prusia" occurred in the dedication of the " March to Finchley "
to Frederick the Great. His friends quizzed him a good deal about the
error, and he undertook to correct it by hand in every proof of the plate
sold. But he soon grew tired of making the mark ~ with a pen over the
single *s*, and at last had the offensive " Prusia " burnished out of the copper
and the orthodox " Prussia " substituted. But even then the quizzers were
not tired, and showed him a Prussian thaler bearing Frederick's effigy, and
the legend of which spoke of him as *Borussiæ Rex*. 'Twas the story of the
old man and his donkey over again.

† Till the legislature deprives the people of their "eleven days," I am
using the old-style calendar.

that he was aught but the most industrious of apprentices. The freedom of handling, the bold sweep of line,
the honest incisive play of the graver manifested in this
performance could have been attained by no Thomas
Idle ; and we must, therefore, in justice grant him his
full seven years of 'prentice servitude. Say then that
William Hogarth was bound apprentice to Mr. Ellis
Gamble,* at the Golden Angel, in Cranbourn Street,
Leicester Fields, in the winter of the year of our Lord,
Seventeen hundred and twelve. He began to engrave
arms and cyphers on tankards, salvers, and spoons, at
just about the time that it occurred to a sapient legislature to cause certain heraldic hieroglyphics surmounted by the Queen's crown, and encircled by the
words " One halfpenny," to be engraven on a metal die,
the which being the first newspaper stamp ever known
to our grateful British nation, was forthwith impressed
on every single half-sheet of printed matter issued as a
newspaper or a periodical. " Have you seen the new
red stamp ?" writes his reverence Doctor Swift. Grub
Street is forthwith laid desolate. Down go *Observators,
Examiners, Medleys, Flying Posts*, and other diurnals,
and the undertakers of the *Spectator* are compelled to
raise the price of their entertaining miscellany.

One of the last head Assay Masters at Goldsmiths'
Hall told one of Hogarth's biographers, when a very—
very old man, that he himself had been 'prentice in

---

* I have seen it somewhere stated that Gamble was a " silversmith of
eminence," residing on or near Snow Hill. " *Cela n'empêche pas*," as the
Hanoverian Queen on her death-bed said to her repentant husband. I see
no reason why Gamble should not have been originally of Snow Hill, and
have emigrated before 1720 to the Court end of the town.

Cranbourn Street, and that he remembered very well
William serving his time to Mr. Gamble. The register
of the boy's indenture should also surely be among the
archives of that sumptuous structure behind the Post
Office, where the worthy goldsmiths have such a side-
board of massy plate, and give such jovial banquets to
ministers and city magnates. And, doubt it not, Ellis
Gamble was a freeman, albeit, ultimately, a dweller at
the West End, and dined with his Company when the
goldsmiths entertained the ministers and magnates of
those days. Yes, gentles; ministers, magnates, kings,
czars, and princes were their guests, and King Charles
the Second did not disdain to get tipsy with Sir Robert
Viner, Lord Mayor and Alderman, at Guildhall. The
monarch's boon companion got so fond of him as to
lend him, *dit-on*, enormous sums of money. More than
that, he set up a brazen statue of the royal toper in the
Stocks flower-market at the meeting of Lombard Street
and the Poultry. Although it must be confessed that
the effigy had originally been cast for John Sobieski
trampling on the Turk. The Polish hero had a Carlovingian periwig given to him, and the prostrate and
miscreant Moslem was "improved" into Oliver Cromwell. [Mem. :—A pair of correctional stocks having
given their name to the flower-market; on the other
hand, may not the market have given *its* name to the
pretty, pale, red flowers, very dear to Cockneys, and
called "stocks ?"]

How was William's premium paid when he was
bound 'prentice ? Be it remembered that silver-plate
engraving, albeit Mr. Walpole of Strawberry Hill calls
it "mean," was a great and cunning art and mystery.

These engravers claimed to descend in right line from the old ciseleurs and workers in niello of the middle ages. Benvenuto, as I have hinted, graved as well as modelled. Marc Antonio flourished many a cardinal's hat and tassels on a *bicchiére* before he began to cut from Rafaelle and Giulio Romano's pictures. The engraver of arms on plate was the same artist who executed delightful arabesques and damascenings on suits of armour of silver and Milan steel. They had cabalistic secrets, these workers of the precious, these producers of the beautiful. With the smiths, " back-hammering " and " boss-beating " were secrets ;—parcel-gilding an especial mystery ; the bluish-black composition for niello a recipe only to be imparted to adepts. With the engravers, the " cross-hatch " and the " double cypher," as I cursorily mentioned at the end of the last chapter, were secrets. A certain kind of cross-hatching went out with Albert Durer, and had since been as undiscoverable as the art of making the *real* ruby tint in glass. No beggar's brat, no parish *protégé*, could be apprenticed to this delicate, artistic, and responsible calling. For in graving deep, tiny spirals of gold and silver curl away from the trenchant tool, and there is precious ullage in chasing and burnishing—spirals and ullage worth money in the market. Ask the Jews in Duke's Place, who sweat the guineas in horsehair bags, and clip the Jacobuses, and rasp the new-milled money with tiny files, if there be not profit to be had from the minutest surplusage of gold and silver.

Goldsmiths and silversmiths were proud folk. They pointed to George Heriot, King James's friend, and the great things he did. They pointed to the peerage. Did

not a Duke of Beaufort, in 1683, marry a daughter of
Sir Josiah Child, goldsmith and banker? Was not Earl
Tylney, his son, half-brother to Dame Elizabeth How-
land, mother of a Duchess of Bedford, one of whose
daughters married the Duke of Bridgewater, another,
the Earl of Essex? Was not Sir William Ward, goldsmith, father to Humble Ward, created Baron Ward by
Charles I.? and from him springs there not the present
Lord Dudley and Ward?* O you grand people who
came over with the Conqueror, where would you be now
without your snug city marriages, your comfortable
alliances with Cornhill and Chepe? Leigh of Stone-
leigh comes from a lord mayor of Queen Bess's time.
Fulke Greville, Lord Brooke, married an alderman's
daughter two years ere Hogarth was apprenticed. The
ancestor to the Lords Clifton was agent to the London
Adventurers in Oliver's time, and acquired his estate in
their service. George the Second's Earl of Rockingham
married the daughter of Sir Henry Furnese, the money-
lender and stock-jobber. The great Duke of Argyll and
Greenwich married a lord mayor's niece. The Earl of
Denbigh's ancestor married the daughter of Basil Fire-
brace, the wine merchant. Brewers, money-scriveners,
Turkey merchants, Burgomasters of Utrecht's daughters,
—all these married blithely into the *haute pairie*. If I
am wrong in my genealogies, 'tis Daniel Defoe who is
to blame, not I; for that immortal drudge of literature
is my informant. Of course such marriages never take
place now. Alliances between the *sacs et parchemins* are
never heard of. Mayfair never meets the Mansion

---

* *The Complete English Tradesman*, i. 234.

House, nor Botolph Lane Belgravia, save at a Ninth of November banquet. I question if I am not inopportune, and impertinent even, in hinting at the dukes and belted earls who married the rich citizens' daughters, were it not that by-and-by 'prentice Hogarth will paint some scenes from a great life drama full of Warton's "ΗΘΟΣ, called *Marriage à la Mode*. Ah! those two perspectives seen through the open windows! In the first, the courtyard of the proud noble's mansion; in the last, busy, mercantile London Bridge: court and city, city and court, and which the saddest picture?

Dominie Hogarth had but a hard time of it, and must have been pinched in a gruesome manner to make both ends meet. That dictionary of his, painfully compiled, and at last with infinite care and labour completed, brought no grist to the mill in Ship Court. The manuscript was placed in the hands of a bookseller, who did what booksellers often do when one places manuscripts in their hands. He let it drop. "The booksellers," writes Hogarth himself, "used my father with great cruelty." In his loving simplicity he tells us that many of the most eminent and learned persons in England, Ireland, and Scotland, wrote encomiastic notices of the erudition and diligence displayed in the work, but all to no purpose. I suppose the bookseller's final answer was similar to that Hogarth has scribbled in the Manager Rich's reply to Tom Rakewell, in the prison scene :— " Sir, I have read your play, and it will not *doo*." A dreadful, heartrending trade was average authorship, .even in the "silver age" of Anna Augusta. A lottery, if you will : the prizeholders secretaries of state, ambassadors, hangers-on to dukes and duchesses, gentlemen

ushers to baby princesses, commissioners of hackney
coaches or plantations; but innumerable possessors of
blanks.   Walla Billa! they were in evil case.   For them
the garret in Grub or Monmouth Street, or in Moorfields; for them the Welshwoman dunning for the milk-
score; for them the dirty bread flung disdainfully by
bookselling wretches like Curll.   For them the shrewish
landlady, the broker's man, the catchpole, the dedication
addressed to my lord, and which seldom got beyond his
lacquey;—hold! let me mind my Hogarth and his silver-
plate engraving.   Only a little may I touch on literary
woes when I come to the picture of the *Distressed Poet*.
For the rest, the calamities of authors have been food
for the commentaries of the wisest and most eloquent of
their more modern brethren, and my bald philosophizings
thereupon can well be spared.

But this premium, this indenture money, this 'prentice
fee for young William : *unde derivatur?*   In the beginning, as you should know, this same 'prentice fee was
but a sort of " sweetener," peace-offering, or *pot de vin* to
the tradesman's wife.   The 'prentice's mother slipped a
few pieces into madam's hand when the boy put his
finger on the blue seal.   The money was given that
mistresses should be kind to the little lads; that they
should see that the trenchers they scraped were not
quite bare, nor the blackjacks they licked quite empty ;
that they should give an eye to the due combing and
soaping of those young heads, and now and then extend
a matronly ægis, lest Tommy or Billy should have somewhat more cuffing and cudgelling than was quite good
for them.   By degrees this gift money grew to be
demanded as a right; and by-and-by comes thrifty

4—2

Master Tradesman, and pops the broad pieces into his till, calling them premium. Poor little shopkeepers in this "silver age" will take a 'prentice from the parish for five pounds, or from an acquaintance who is broken, for nothing perhaps, and will teach him the great arts and mysteries of sweeping out the shop, sleeping under the counter, fetching his master from the tavern or the mughouse when a customer comes in, or waiting at table ; but a rich silversmith or mercer will have as much as a thousand pounds with an apprentice. There is value received on either side. The master is, and generally feels, bound to teach his apprentice *everything* he knows ; else, as worthy Master Defoe puts it, it is "somewhat like Laban's usage to Jacob, viz., keeping back the beloved Rachel, whom he served seven years for, and putting him off with a blear-eyed Leah in her stead ;" and again, it is "sending him into the world like a man out of a ship set ashore among savages, who, instead of feeding him, are indeed more ready to eat him up and devour him." You have little idea of the state, pomp, and circumstance of a rich tradesman, when the eighteenth century was young. Now-a-days, when he becomes affluent, he sells his stock and good-will, emigrates from the shop-world, takes a palace in Tyburnia or a villa at Florence, and denies that he has ever been in trade at all. Retired tailors become country squires, living at "Places" and "Priories." Enriched ironmongers and their families saunter about Pau, and Hombourg, and Nice, passing for British Brahmins, from whose foreheads the yellow streak has never been absent since the earth first stood on the elephant, and the elephant on the tortoise, and the tortoise on nothing

that I am aware of, save the primeval mud from which
you and I, and the Great Mogul, and the legless beggar
trundling himself along in a gocart, and all humanity,
sprang. But in the reign of Anna D. G., it was different.
The tradesman was nothing away from his shop. In it he
was a hundred times more ostentatious. He may have
had his country box at Hampstead, Highgate, Edmonton,
Edgeware; but his home was in the city. Behind the
hovel stuffed with rich merchandise, sheltered by a huge
timber bulk, and heralded to passers by an enormous
sheet of iron and painters' work—his Sign—he built
often a stately mansion, with painted ceilings, with
carved wainscoting or rich tapestry and gilt leather-
work, with cupboards full of rich plate, with wide staircases, and furniture of velvet and brocade. To the
entrance of the noisome *cul-de-sac*, leading to the carved
and panelled door (with its tall flight of steps) of the rich
tradesman's mansion, came his coach—yes, madam, his
coach, with the Flanders mares, to take his wife and
daughters for an airing. In that same mansion, behind
the hovel of merchandise, uncompromising Daniel Defoe
accuses the tradesman of keeping servants in blue liveries
richly laced, like unto the nobility's. In that same
mansion the tradesman holds his Christmas and Shrove-
tide feasts, the anniversaries of his birthday and his
wedding-day, all with much merrymaking and junketing,
and an enormous amount of eating and drinking. In
that same mansion, in the fulness of time and trade, he
dies; and in that same mansion, upon my word, *he lies
in state*,—yes, in state: on a *lit de parade*, under a
plumed tester, with flambeaux and sconces, with blacks
and weepers, with the walls hung with sable cloth, et

cætera, et cætera, et cætera.* 'Tis not only "Vulture Hopkins" whom a "thousand lights attend" to the tomb, but very many wealthy tradesmen are so buried, and with such pomp and ceremony. Not till the mid-reign of George the Third did this custom expire.

[I should properly in a footnote, but prefer in brackets, to qualify the expression "hovel," as applied to London tradesmen's shops at this time, 1712-20. The majority, indeed, merit no better appellation : the windows oft-times are not glazed, albeit the sign may be an elaborate and even artistic performance, framed in curious scroll-work, and costing not unfrequently a hundred pounds. The exceptions to the structural poverty of the shops themselves are to be found in the toymen's —mostly in Fleet Street—and the pastrycooks'—mainly in Leadenhall. There is a mania for toys ; and the toy-shop people realize fortunes. Horace Walpole bought his toy-villa at Strawberry Hill—which he afterwards improved into a Gothic doll's-house—of a retired *Marchand de Joujoux.* The toy-merchants dealt in other

---

* "Let it be interred after the manner of the country, and the laws of the place, and the *dignity of the person.* And Ælian tells us that excellent persons were buried in purple, and men of an ordinary fortune had their graves only trimmed with branches of olive and mourning flowers." So Bishop Taylor in *Holy Dying.* The tide of feeling in this age of ours sets strongly against mortuary pomp ; yet should we remember that with the old pomps and obsequies of our forefathers much real charity was mingled. All the money was not spent in wax-tapers and grim feastings. At the death of a wealthy citizen, hundreds of poor men and women had complete suits of mourning given to them, and the fragments of the "funeral baked meats" furnished forth scores of pauper tables before evensong. Lazarus had his portion when Dives passed away. Now, who profits by a funeral beyond half a dozen lacqueys, and Messrs. Tressel and Hatchment, the undertakers ?

wares besides playthings. They dealt in cogged dice. They dealt in assignations and *billet-doux*. They dealt in masks and dominos. Counsellor Silvertongue may have called at the toyshop coming from the Temple, and have there learnt what hour the countess would be at Heidegger's masquerade. Woe to the wicked city! Thank Heaven we can go and purchase Noah's arks and flexible acrobats for our children now, without rubbing shoulders with Counsellor ·Silvertongue or Lord Fanny Sporus on their bad errands. Frequented as they were by rank and fashion, the toyshops threw themselves into outward decoration. Many of these shops were kept by Frenchmen and Frenchwomen, and it has ever been the custom of that fantastic nation to gild the outside of pills, be the inside ever so nauseous. Next in splendour to the toyshops were the pastrycooks. Such a bill as can be seen of the charges for fresh furnishing one of these establishments about Twelfth Night time! "Sash windows, all of looking-glass plates; the walls of the shop lined up with galley-tiles in panels, finely painted in forest-work and figures; two large branches of candlesticks; three great glass lanterns; twenty-five sconces against the wall; fine large silver salvers to serve sweetmeats; large high stands of rings for jellies; painting the ceiling, and gilding the lanterns, the sashes, and the carved work!" Think of this, Master Brook! What be your *Cafés des Mille Colonnes*, your Véfours, your Vérys, your *Maisons-dorées*, after this magnificence? And at what sum, think you, does the stern censor, crying out against it meanwhile as wicked luxury and extravagance, estimate this Arabian Nights' pastrycookery? At three hundred pounds sterling! Grant that the sum represents six hundred of our money. The Lorenzos the Magnificent, of Cornhill and Regent Street, would think little of as many thousands for the building and ornamentation of their palaces of trade. Not for selling tarts or toys though. The tide has taken a turn; yet some comfortable reminiscences of the old celebrity of the city toy and tart shops linger between Temple Bar and Leadenhall. Farley, you yet delight the young. Holt, Birch, Button, Purssell, at your sober warehouses, the most urbane and beautiful young ladies — how pale the pasty exhalations make them!—yet dispense the most delightful of indigestions.]

So he must have scraped this apprenticeship money together, Dominie Hogarth: laid it by, by cheeseparing from his meagre school fees, borrowed it from some rich scholar who pitied his learning and his poverty, or perhaps become acquainted with Ellis Gamble, who may have frequented the club held at the " Eagle and Child " in the little Old Bailey. " A wonderful turn for limning has my son," I think I hear Dominie Hogarth cry, holding up some precocious cartoon of William's. " I doubt not, sir, that were he to study the humanities of the Italian bustos, and the just rules of Jesuit's perspective, and the anatomies of the learned Albinus, that he would paint as well as Signor Verrio, who hath lately done that noble piece in the new hall Sir Christopher hath built for the blue-coat children in Newgate Street." " Plague on the Jesuits," answers honest (and supposititious) Mr. Ellis Gamble. " Plague on all foreigners and papists, goodman Hogarth. If you will have your lad draw bustos and paint ceilings, forsooth, you must get one of the great court lords to be his patron, and send him to

Italy, where he shall learn not only the cunningness of limning, but to dance, and to dice, and to break all the commandments, and to play on the viol-di-gamby. But if you want to make an honest man and a fair trades- man of him, Master Hogarth, and one who will be a loyal subject to the Queen, and hate the French, you shall e'en bind him 'prentice to me ; and I will be answerable for all his concernments, and send him to church and catechize, and all at small charges to you." Might not such a conversation have taken place ? I think so. Is it not very probable that the lad Hogarth being then some fourteen years old, was forthwith combed his straightest and brushed his neatest, and his bundle or his box of needments being made up by the hands of his loving mother and sisters, despatched west- ward, and with all due solemnity of parchment and blue seal, bound 'prentice to Mr. Ellis Gamble ? I am sure, by the way in which he talks of the poor old Dominie and the dictionary, that he was a loving son. I know he was a tender brother. Good Ellis Gamble—the lad being industrious, quick, and dexterous of hand—must have allowed him to earn some journeyman's wages during his 'prentice-time ; for that probation being out, he set not only himself, but his two sisters, Mary and Ann, up in business. They were in some small hosiery line, and William engraved a shop-card for them, which did not, I am afraid, prosper with these unsubstantial spinsters, any more than did the celebrated lollipop emporium established in *The House with the Seven Gables*. One sister survived him, and to her, by his will, he left an annuity of eighty pounds.

Already have I spoken of the Leicester Square gold

and silversmith's style and titles.   It is meet that you
should peruse them in full :—

So to Cranbourn Street, Leicester Fields, is William
Hogarth bound for seven long years.   Very curious is it
to mark how old trades and old types of inhabitants
linger about localities.   They were obliged to pull old
Cranbourn Street and Cranbourn Alley quite down
before they could get rid of the silversmiths, and even
now I see them sprouting forth again round about the
familiar haunt ; the latest ensample thereof being in the
shop of a pawnbroker—of immense wealth, I presume,
who, gorged and fevered by multitudes of unredeemed

pledges, has suddenly astonished New Cranbourn Street with plate-glass windows, overflowing with plate, jewellery, and trinkets; buhl cabinets, gilt consoles, suits of armour, antique china, Pompadour clocks, bronze monsters, and other articles of *virtù*. But don't you remember Hamlet's in the dear old Dædalean bonnet-building Cranbourn Alley days?—that long low shop whose windows seemed to have no end, and not to have been dusted for centuries; those dim vistas of dish-covers, coffee biggins, and centre-pieces. You must think of Crœsus when you speak of the reputed wealth of Hamlet. His stock was said to be worth millions. Seven watchmen kept guard over it every night. Half the aristocracy were in his debt. Royalty itself had gone credit for plate and jewellery at Hamlet's. Rest his bones, poor old gentleman. He took to building and came to grief. His shop is no more, and his name is but a noise.

In our time, Cranbourn Street and Cranbourn Alley were dingy labyrinths of dish-covers, bonnets, boots, coffee-shops, and cutlers; but what must the place have been like in Hogarth's time? We can have no realizable conception; for late in George the Third's reign, or early in George the Fourth's, the whole *pâté* of lanes and courts between Leicester Square and St. Martin's Lane had become so shamefully rotten and decayed, that they half tumbled and were half pulled down. The labyrinth was rebuilt; but, to the shame of the surveyors and architects of the noble landlord, on the same labyrinthine principle of mean and shabby tenements. You see, rents are rents, little fishes eat sweet, and many a little makes a mickle. Since that period, however, better

ideas of architectural economy have prevailed; and
although part of the labyrinth remains, there has still
been erected a really handsome thoroughfare from
Leicester Square to Long Acre. As a sad and natural
consequence, the shops didn't let, while the little tenements in the alleys that remained were crowded; but let
us hope that the example of the feverish pawnbroker
who has burst out in an eruption of jewellery and art
fabrics, may be speedily followed by other professors of
bric-a-brac.

Gay's *Trivia*, in miniature, must have been manifest
every hour in the day in Hogarth's Cranbourn Alley.
Fights for the wall must have taken place between fops.
Sweeps and small coalmen must have interfered with
the "nice conduct of a clouded cane." The beggars
must have swarmed here: the blind beggar, and the
lame beggar, the stump-in-the-bowl, and the woman
bent double: the beggar who blew a trumpet — the
impudent varlet!—to announce his destitution;— the
beggar with a beard like unto Belisarius, the beggar
who couldn't eat cold meat, the beggar who had been
to Ireland and the Seven United Provinces—was this
"Philip in the tub" that W. H. afterwards drew?—the
beggar in the blue apron, the leathern cap, and the wen
on his forehead, who was supposed to be so like the late
Monsieur de St. Evremonde, Governor of Duck Island;
not forgetting the beggar in the ragged red coat and the
black patch over his eye, who by his own showing had
been one of the army that swore so terribly in Flanders,
and howled Tom D'Urfey's song, "The Queene's old
souldiers, and the ould souldiers of the Queene." Then
there was the day watchman, who cried the hour when

nobody wanted to hear it, and to whose "half-past one," the muddy goose that waddled after him cried "quack." And then there must have been the silent mendicant, of whom Mr. *Spectator* says (1712), "He has nothing to sell, but very gravely receives the bounty of the people for no other merit than the homage due to his manner of signifying to them that he wants a subsidy."* Said I not truly that the old types *will* linger in the old localities? What is this silent mendicant but the "serious poor young man" we have all seen standing mute on the edge of the kerb, his head downcast, his hands meekly folded before him, himself attired in speckless but shabby black, and a spotless though frayed white neckerchief?

---

* I can't resist the opportunity here to tell a story of a Beggar, the more so, that it made me laugh, and was told me by an Austrian officer ; and Austrian officers are not the most laughter-compelling people in the world. My informant happened to alight one day at some post town in Italy, and was at once surrounded by the usual swarm of beggars, who, of course, fought for the honour (and profit) of carrying his baggage. Equally, of course, each beggar took a separate portion of the *impedimenta*—one a hat-box, one an umbrella, and so on—so that each would claim a separate reward. At the expenditure of much patience, and some small change, the traveller had at last paid each extortionate impostor that which was not due to him; when there approached a reverend, but ragged-looking man, with a long white beard, and who, with an indescribable look of dirty dignity, held out his hand like the rest. The traveller had remarked that this patriarch had stood aloof during the squabble for the luggage, and had moved neither hand nor foot in pretending to carry it. Naturally before the traveller disbursed more coin, he briefly desired the man with the white beard to define his claim. The reply was, I think, incomparable for cool and dignified impudence. The patriarch drew himself up to his full height, placed his right hand on his breast, and in slow and solemn accents made answer:—"*Ed anche io sono stato presente.*" " I, too, was present!" Sublime beggar!

Mixed up among the beggars, among the coster-
mongers and hucksters who lounge or brawl on the
pavement, undeterred by fear of barrow-impounding
policemen ; among the varlets who have " young lambs
to sell "—they have sold those sweet cakes since Elizabeth's time ; among the descendants and progenitors of
hundreds of " Tiddy Dolls," and " Colly Molly Puffs ;"
among bailiffs prowling for their prey, and ruffian cheats
and gamesters from the back-waters of Covent Garden ;
among the fellows with hares-and-tabors, the match-
sellers, the masksellers—for in this inconceivable period
ladies and gentlemen wanted vizors at twelve o'clock at
noon—be it admitted,· nevertheless, that the real " quality" ceased to wear them about the end of William's
reign — among the tradesmen, wigs awry, and apron-
girt, darting out from their shops to swallow their matutinal pint of wine, or dram of strong waters ; among all
this *tohu-bohu*, this Galimatias of small industries and
small vices, chairmen come swaggering and jolting
along with the gilded sedans between poles; and lo !
the periwigged, Mechlin-laced, gold-embroidered beau
hands out Belinda, radiant, charming, powdered, patched,
fanned, perfumed, who is come to Cranbourn Alley to
choose new diamonds. And more beaux' shins are
wounded by more whalebone petticoats, and Sir Fopling
Flutter treads on Aramanta's brocaded *queue ;* and the
heavens above are almost shut out by the great projecting, clattering signs. Conspicuous among them is the
" Golden Angel," kept by Ellis Gamble.

Mark, too, that Leicester Fields were then, as now,
the favourite resort of foreigners. Green Street, Bear
Street, Castle Street, Panton Street, formed a district

called, as was a purlieu in Westminster too, by the Sanctuary, "Petty France." Theodore Gardelle, the murderer, lived about Leicester Fields. Legions of high-dried Mounseers, not so criminal as he, but peaceable, honest, industrious folk enough, peered out of the garret windows of Petty France with their blue, bristly gills, red nightcaps, and filthy indoor gear. They were always cooking hideous messes, and made the already unwholesome atmosphere intolerable with garlic. They wrought at water-gilding, clock-making, sign-painting, engraving for book illustrations—although in this department the Germans and Dutch were dangerous rivals. A very few offshoots from the great Huguenot colony in Spitalfields were silk-weavers. There were then as now many savoury-tasting and unsavoury-smelling French ordinaries; and again, then as now, some French washerwomen and clearstarchers. But the dwellers in Leicester Fields slums and in Soho were mainly Catholics frequenting the Sardinian ambassador's chapel in Duke Street, Lincoln's Inn Fields. French hairdressers and perfumers lived mostly under Covent Garden Piazza, in Bow Street and in Long Acre. Very few contrived to pass Temple Bar. The citizens appeared to have as great a horror of them as of the players, and so far as they could, by law, banished them their bounds, rigorously. French dancing, fencing, and posture masters, and quack doctors, lived at the court end of the town, and kept, many of them, their coaches. Not a few of the grinning, fantastic French community were spies of the magnificent King Louis. Sunday was the Frenchmen's great day, and the Mall in St. James's park their favourite resort and fashionable promenade. It answered for them all the purposes which the old colonnade of the Quadrant was wont to serve, and which the flags of Regent Street serve now. On Sunday the blue, bristly gills were clean shaven, the red nightcaps replaced by full-bottomed wigs, superlatively curled and powdered. The filthy indoor gear gave way to embroidered coats of gay colours, with prodigious cuffs, and the skirts stiffened with buckram. Lacquer-hilted swords stuck out behind them. Paste buckles glittered in their shoon. Glass rings bedecked their lean paws. They held their *tricornes* beneath their arms, flourished their canes and inhaled their snuff with the best beaux on town. We are apt to laugh at the popular old caricatures of the French Mounseer, and think those engravings unkind, unnatural, and overdrawn ; but just shave me this bearded, moustached, braided, and be-ringed Jules, Gustave, or Adolphe who comes swaggering to-day from the back of Sherrard Street or Marylebone Street, round by the County Fire Office into Regent Street ; shave me the modern Mounseer quite clean, clap a periwig on his head, a *chapeau bras* beneath his arm, a sword by his side ; clothe his shrunken limbs in eighteenth-century costume ; or better, see the French comedian in some old comedy at the *Français* or the *Odéon*, and you will cry out at once : " There is the Mounseer whom Hogarth, Gilray, Bunbury, and Rowlandson drew." And yet I owe an apology, here, to the Mounseers ; for it was very likely some courteous, albeit grimacing denizen of Petty France who supplied our Hogarth with the necessary French translation of the gold and silversmith's style and titles to engrave on his shop-card.

I am to be pardoned, I hope, for lingering long in Leicester Fields. I shall have to return to the place often, for William Hogarth much affected it. In Leicester Fields he lived years afterwards when he was celebrated and prosperous. Where Sablonière Hotel is now, had he his house, the sign the " Golden Head," and not the " Painter's Head," as I have elsewhere put it. There he died. There his widow lived for many—many years afterwards, always loving and lamenting the great artist and good man, her husband. It was about Leicester Fields too—nay, unless I mistake, in Cranbourn Alley itself, that old nutcracker-faced Nollekens, the sculptor, pointed out William to Northcote the painter. " There," he cried, " see there's Hogarth." He pointed to where stood a little stout-faced sturdy man in a sky-blue coat, who was attentively watching a quarrel between two street boys. It was Mr. Mulready's " Wolf and the Lamb " story a little before its time. The bigger boy oppressed the smaller ; whereupon Hogarth patted the diminutive victim on the head, and gave him a coin, and said with something like a naughty word that he wouldn't stand it, if he was the small boy : no, not he.

Seven years at cross-hatch and double cypher. Seven years turning and re-turning salvers and tankards on the leathern pad, and every month and every year wielding the graver and burnisher with greater strength and dexterity. What legions of alphabets, in double cypher, he must have " drawn with great correctness ; " what dictionary loads of Latin and Norman-French mottoes he must have flourished beneath the coats of arms ! Oh, the scutcheons he must have blazoned in the symbolism of lines ! Blank for argent, dots for or,

horizontal for azure, vertical for gules, close-chequer for
sable. The griffins, the lions, the dragons, rampant,
couchant, regardant, langued, gorged, he must have
drawn! The chevrons, the fesses, the sinoples of the
first! He himself confesses that his just notions of
natural history were for a time vitiated by the constant
contemplation and delineation of these fabulous monsters,
and that when he was out of his time he was compelled
to unlearn all his heraldic zoology. To the end his
dogs were very much in the "supporter" style, and the
horses in the illustrations in Hudibras strongly resemble
hippogriffs.

He must have been studying, and studying hard,
too, at drawing, from the round and plane during his
'prentice years. Sir Godfrey Kneller had a kind of
academy at his own house in 1711; but Sir James
Thornhill did not establish his till long after Hogarth
had left the service of Ellis Gamble. Hogarth tells us
that as a boy he had access to the studio of a neighbouring painter. Who may this have been? Francis
Hoffmann; Hubertz; Hulzberg, the warden of the
Lutheran Church in the Savoy; Samuel Moore of the
Custom House? Perhaps his earliest instructor was
some High Dutch etcher of illustrations, living eastwards
to be near the booksellers in Paternoster Row; or perhaps the "neighbouring painter" was an artist in tavern
and shop signs. Men of no mean proficiency wrought
in that humble but lucrative line of emblematic art in
Anna's "silver age."

That Hogarth possessed considerable graphic powers
when he engraved Ellis Gamble's shop-card, you have
only to glance at the angel holding the palm above the

commercial announcement, to be at once convinced. This figure, however admirably posed and draped, *may* have been copied from some foreign frontispiece. The engraving, however, as an example of pure line, is excellent. We are left to wonder whether it was by accident or by design of quaint conceit that the right hand of the angel has a finger too many.

Of Hogarth's adventures during his apprenticeship, with the single exception of his holiday excursion to Highgate, when there was a battle-royal in a suburban public-house, and when he drew a capital portrait of one of the enraged combatants, the Muse is dumb. He led, very probably, the life of nineteen-twentieths of the London 'prentices of that period: only he must have worked harder and more zealously than the majority of his fellows. Concerning the next epoch of his life the Muse deigns to be far more explicit, and, I trust, will prove more eloquent on your worships' behalf. I have done with the mists and fogs that envelop the early part of my hero's career, and shall be able to trace it now year by year until his death.

III.

A Long Ladder, and Hard to Climb.

WHEN a cathedral chapter have received their *congé d'élire*—so runs the popular and perfectly erroneous tradition—and have made choice of a Bishop, the pastor elect simpers, blushes, and says that really he is much obliged, but that he would rather not accept the proffered dignity : "*Nolo episcopari*," he urges in graceful deprecation. Nobody in or out of the chapter believes in his reluctance, and nobody now-a-days believes in the harmless legend. Thus, too, when the Commons elect a Speaker, a tradition with little more foundation assumes that the right honourable gentleman approaches the foot of the Throne, hints in the most delicate manner that he, the chosen of the Commons, is a blockhead and an impostor, declares that he shall make but an indifferent Speaker, and seeks to be relieved from his onerous charge. At that same moment, perhaps, Messrs. Adams and Ede are embroidering Mr. Speaker's gold robe ; and experienced tonsors near Lincoln's Inn are finishing the last row of curls on the ambrosial horse-hair which to-morrow will be a wig. When you ask a young lady to

take a little more *Mayonnaise de homard,* or entreat her
to oblige the company with " *Entends tu les gondoles ?* "
—that charming Venetian barcarole—does she not ordinarily, and up to a certain degree of pressure, refuse—
say that she would rather not, or that she has a cold ?
Whose health is proposed and drunk amid repeated
cheers, but he rises, and assures the assembled guests
that he is about the last person in the world who should
have been toasted ; that he never felt so embarrassed
in his life—he leads at the common law bar, and on
breaches of promise is immense—and that he wants words
to, &c. &c. ?   At the bar mess he is known as " Talking
Smith," and at school his comrades used to call him
" Captain Jaw."   My friends, we do not place any faith
in these denials ; and forthwith clap the mitre on the
Prelate's head, bow to the Speaker, help the young lady
to arrange the music stool, and intone nine times nine
with one cheer more.

It is strange—it is vexatious ; but I cannot persuade
the ladies and gentlemen who peruse these papers to
believe that I am not writing the Life of William
Hogarth, and that these are merely discursive Essays
on the Man, the Work, and the Time.   People persist
in thinking that it is with him who is now writing a case
of *nolo episcopari.*   Indeed it is no such thing.   I should
dearly wish to write myself Biographer.   " Fain would I
climb, but that I fear to fall."   I told you in the outset
that this Endeavour was no Life.   I disclaimed any
possession of exclusive information.   I claimed a liberal
benefit-of-clergy as to names and dates.   I have had no
access to muniment rooms.   I have explored the contents of no charter chests.   I have disentombed no dusty

records, and rescued no parish registers from the degrading fate of serving to singe a goose. I am timorous,
and seek not to be heard as one speaking with authority.
But the north country won't believe me, and the south
and the midland shake their heads incredulously when I
say this is not Hogarth's Life, but only so much gossip
about him and his pictures and times. I say so again;
and if the public won't be enlightened—*si vult decipi*—
all I can add is *Decipiatur.*

Now as to the exact date of the expiration of Hogarth's apprenticeship—when was it? I have but an
impression. I cannot speak from any certain knowledge,
and assume, therefore, that the expiry was *circa* 1720.
Ireland opines that it was in 1718, William having then
attained his twenty-first year. The registers of the
Goldsmiths' Company might be more explicit, or, better
still, Mr. Scott, the Chamberlain of London, might
enlighten us all, to a month, and to a day. For of old
the chamberlain was the official Nemesis to the ofttimes
unruly 'prentices of London. The idle, or rebellious, or
truant novice, was arraigned before this dread functionary. He had power to relegate the offender to the
carcere duro of Bridewell, there to suffer the penance of
stripes and a bread-and-water diet. For aught I know,
the ministrations of the chamberlain may to this day be
occasionally invoked; but it is in his capacity of a re-
cording official, and as having formerly drawn some fees
from the attestation and registration of indentures, that
his assistance would be useful to me. William Hogarth's
art-and-mystery-parchment may be in the city archives.
What other strange and curiously quaint things those
archives contain we had an inkling the other day, when

the *Liber Albus* was published. But I have not the pleasure of Mr. Scott's acquaintance, and he might say me nay.

Hogarth, I presume, was released from silver servitude in 1718-20. April 29th, 1720, is, as I have elsewhere noted, the date affixed to the shop-card he executed for himself, setting up in business, I hope in friendly rivalry to Ellis Gamble in Little Cranbourn Alley, hard by the " Golden Angel."   I stood and mused in Little Cranbourn Alley lately, and tried to conjure up Hogarthian recollections from that well-nigh blind passage.   But no ghosts rose from a coffee-shop and a French barber's, and a murky little den full of tobacco-pipes and penny valentines ; so, taking nothing by my motion, I sped my slowest to the Sablonière in Leicester Square. Here even my senses became troubled with the odours of French soups, and I could make nothing Hogarthian out of the hostelry, a wing of which was once Hogarth's house.

It is my wish to tell as succinctly as is feasible the story of seven years in Hogarth's progress ; seven years during which he was slowly, painfully, but always steadily and courageously, climbing that precipitous ladder which we have all in some sort or another striven to climb. At the top sits Fame kicking her heels, carrying her trumpet mincingly, making sometimes a feint to put it to her lips and sound it, more frequently looking down superciliously with eyes half closed, and pretending to be unaware of the panting wretch toiling up the weary rungs beneath. Some swarm up this ladder as boys up a pole, hand over hand, a good grip with the knees, a confident, saucy, upward look.   Others stop *in medio*, look round, sigh, or are satisfied, and gravely descend to refresh themselves with bread and cheese for life. Some stagger up, wildly, and tumbling off, are borne, mutilated, to the hospital accident-ward to die. Others there are who indeed obtain the ladder's summit, but are doomed to crawl perpetually up and down the degrees. These are the unfortunates who carry hods to those master bricklayers who have bounded up the ladder with airy strides, or better still, *have been born at the top of the ladder*. Poor hodmen! they make dictionaries, draw acts of parliament, cram the boy-senator for his maiden speech, form Phidias' rough clay-sketch into a shapely, polished marble bust, shade with Indian ink Archimedes' rough draught for the new pump or the tubular bridge, and fill in Sir Joshua's backgrounds. Some there are who go to sleep at the ladder's foot, and some, the few, the felicitous, who reach the summit, breathless but triumphant, boldly bidding Fame blow her loudest blast. Forthwith the venal quean makes the clarion to sound, and all the world is amazed. Lowliness, our Shakspeare says, is "young ambition's ladder:"

> Whereto the climber upward turns his face ;
> But when he once attains the utmost round,
> He then unto the ladder turns his back,
> Looks in the clouds, scorning the base degrees
> By which he did ascend : so Cæsar may.
> Then——

But so did not William Hogarth. He was self-confident and self-conscious enough,* when, after many years of toilsome struggling he turned up the trump-card, and

---

* To me there is something candid, naïve, and often something noble in

his name was bruited about with loud *fanfares* to the crowd. He attained the desired end : this Fame, this renown ; and to vulgarize the allegory, he managed to snatch that comfortable shoulder of mutton which surmounts the greasy pole, and which, although we feign to covet it not, we *must* have. But he never attempted to conceal the smallness of his beginnings, to assert that his ancestors came over with the Conqueror, or to deny that his father came up to London by the waggon. He sets down in his own black and white, how he fought the battle for bread, how he engraved plates, and painted portraits and conversations and assemblies, in order to obtain the necessary bite and sup ; how, with no money,

---

this personal consciousness and confidence, this moderate self-trumpeting. " *Questi sono miei !* " cried Napoleon, when, at the sack of Milan, the MS. treatises of Leonardo da Vinci were discovered ; and he bore them in triumph to his hotel, suffering no meaner hand to touch them. *He* knew —the Conquering Thinker—that he alone was worthy to possess those priceless papers. So too, Honoré de Balzac calmly remarking that there were only three men in France who could speak French correctly : himself, Victor Hugo, and " Théophile " (T. Gautier). So, too, Elliston, when the little ballet-girl complained of having been hissed : " They have hissed *me*," said the awful manager, and the dancing girl was dumb. Who can forget the words that Milton wrote concerning things of his " that posteritie would not willingly let die ? " and that Bacon left, commending his fame to " Foreign nations and to the next age ? " And Turner, simply directing in his will that he should be buried in St. Paul's Cathedral ? That sepulchre, the painter knew, was his of right. And innocent Gainsborough, dying : " We are all going to heaven, and Vandyke is of the company." And Fontenelle, calmly expiring at a hundred years of age : " *Je n'ai jamais dit la moindre chose contre la plus petite vertu.*" 'Tis true, that my specious little argument falls dolefully to the ground when I remember that which the wisest man who ever lived said concerning a child gathering shells and pebbles on the sea-shore, when the great ocean of truth lay all undiscovered before him.

he has often "gone moping into the city," but there
receiving "ten guineas for a plate," has come home,
jubilant, "put on his sword," and swaggered, I doubt it
not, with the most dashing bucks in the coffee-house or
on the Mall. I think they are happy traits in the character of this good fellow and honest man, that he should
have had the courage to accomplish ten guineas' worth
of graver's work, without drawing money on account,
and that he should have had a sword at home for the
red-letter days and sunshiny hours. You, brave young
student and fellow labourer! draw on your corduroys,
shoulder your pick and shovel, be off to the diggings;
do your work, get paid; and then come home, put on
your sword and be a gentleman. One sees Mr. Beverly
or Mr. Telbin slashing away with a large whitewasher's
brush in a scene-painting room, fagging away in canvas
jackets and over-alls, covered with parti-coloured splashes.
Then, the work done, they wash their hands and come
forth spruce and radiant, in peg-tops and kid-gloves.
When our Prime Minister is at Broadlands,* I hear that
he stands up writing at a high desk, not seated like a
clerk, working away bravely at the affairs of the *chose
publique*, as for a wage of five-and-twenty shillings a
week, and afterwards enjoys the relaxation of pruning his
trees, or riding over his estate. Keep then your swords
at home, and don't wear them in working hours; but, the
labour done, come out into the open and claim your rank.

I daresay that for a long time twenty-five shillings a
week would have been a very handsome income to
William the engraver. He covered many silver salvers

---

* This was written in 1860.

and tankards with heraldic devices, but I don't think he
had any "*argenterie, bagues et bijouxs*," or other precious
stock of his own on sale.   Most probable is it, that his
old master gave him work to do after he had left his
service.   I wonder if Mr. Gamble, in after days, when
his apprentice had become a great man, would ever hold
forth to tavern coteries on the share he had had in
guiding the early efforts of that facile hand !   I hope
and think so ; and seem to hear him saying over his
tankard : " Yes, sir, I taught the lad.   He was bound to
me, sir, by his worthy father, who was as full of book
learning as the Cockpit is of Hanover rats.   He could
not draw a stroke when he came to me, sir.   He was
good at his graving work, but too quick, too quick, and
somewhat rough.   Never could manage the delicate
tintos or the proper reticulations of scroll-foliage.   But
he was always drawing.   He drew the dog.   He drew
the cat.   He drew Dick, his fellow 'prentice, and Molly
the maid, and Robin Barelegs the shoeblack at the
corner of Cranbourn Street.   He drew a pretty con-
figurement of Mistress Gamble, my wife deceased, in her
Oudenarde tire, and lapels of Mechlin point, and Sunday
sack.   But there was ever a leaning towards the carica-
tura in him, sir.   Sure never mortal since Jacques Callot
the Frenchman (whose ' Habits and Beggars' he was
much given to study) ever drew such hideous, leering
satyrs.   And he had a way, too, of making the griffins
laugh and the lions dance gambadoes, so to speak, on
their hind legs in the escocheons he graved, which would
never have passed the College of Arms.   Sir, the tankard
is out : what ! drawer, there."

Thus Ellis Gamble mythically seen and heard.   But to

the realities. In 1720 or '21, Hogarth's father, the poor old dominie, was removed to a land where no grammar disputations are heard, and where one dictionary is as good as another. Hogarth's sisters had previously kept a " frock shop" in the city ; they removed westward after the old man's death, and probably occupied their brother's place of business in Little Cranbourn Alley, when, giving up a perhaps momentary essay in the vocation of a working tradesman, he elected to be, instead, a working artist. For Mary and Ann Hogarth he engraved a shop-card, representing the interior of a somewhat spacious warehouse with sellers and customers, and surmounted by the king's arms. The sisters could not have possessed much capital ; and there have not been wanting malevolent spirits—chiefly of the Wilkite way of thinking—to hint that the Misses Hogarths' " old frock-shop" was indeed but a very old slop-, not to say rag-shop, and that the proper insignia for their warehouse would have been not the royal arms, but a certain image, sable, pendent, clad in a brief white garment : a black doll of the genuine Aunt Sally proportions.

William Hogarth out of his apprenticeship is, I take it, a sturdy, ruddy-complexioned, clear-eyed, rather round-shouldered young fellow, who as yet wears his own hair, but has that sword at home—a silver-hilted or a prince's metal one—and is not averse to giving his hat a smart cock, ay, and bordering it with a narrow rim of orrice when Fortune smiles on him. Not yet was the ῎ΗΘΟΣ developed in him. It was there, yet latent. But, instead, that quality with which he was also so abundantly gifted, and which combined so well with his

sterner faculties—I mean the quality of humorous observation—must have begun to assert itself. " Engraving
on copper was at twenty years of age my utmost ambition," he writes himself. Yes, William, and naturally so.
The monsters and chimeras of heraldry and Mr. Gamble's
back-shop had by that time probably thoroughly
palled on him. Fortunate if a landscape, or building,
or portrait had sometimes to be engraved on a silver
snuff-box or a golden fan-mount. The rest was a
wilderness of apocryphal natural history, a bewildering
phantasmagoria of strange devices from St. Benet's Hill,
expressed in crambo, in jargon, and in heraldic romany :
compony, gobony, and chequy ; lions erased and tigers
couped ; bucks trippant and bucks vulnèd ; eagles se-
greiant, and dogs sciant ; bezants, plates, torteaux, pomeis,
golps, sanguiny-guzes, tawny and saltire.* The revulsion
was but to be expected—was indeed inevitable, from the
disgust caused by the seven years' transcription of these
catalogues of lying wonders, to the contemplation of the
real life that surged about Cranbourn Alley and its
infinite variety of humours, comic and tragic. " Engraving on copper" at twenty might be the utmost ambition
to a young man mortally sick of silver salvers ; but how
was it at twenty-one and twenty-two ?

" As a child," writes William, " shows of all kind gave

---

* The bezant (from Byzantium) was a round knob on the scutcheon,
blazoned yellow. " Golp " was purple, *the colour of an old black eye*, so
defined by the heralds. "Sanguine" or "guzes" were to be congested
red, like bloodshot eyes ; "torteaux" were of another kind of red, like
" Simnel cakes." " Pomeis " were to be green like apples. " Tawny "
was orange. There were also "hurts" to be blazoned blue, as bruises are.
—*New View of London*, 1712.

me pleasure." To a lad of his keen eye and swift perception, all London must have been full of shows. Not
only was there Bartlemy, opened by solemn procession
and proclamation of Lord Mayor—Bartlemy with its
black-puddings, pantomimes, motions of puppets, rope-
dancers emulating the achievements of Jacob Hall,
sword-swallowing women, fire-eating salamanders, High
Dutch conjurors, Alsatian and Savoyard-Dulcamara
quacks selling eye-waters, worm-powders, love-philters,
specifics against chincough, tympany, tissick, chrisoms,
head-mould-shot, horse-shoe-head, and other strange ail-
ments, of which the Register-General makes no mention
in his Returns, now-a-days ;* not only did Southwark,
Tottenham and May Fair flourish, but likewise Horn Fair
by Charlton, in Kent, easy of access by Gravesend tilt-
boat, which brought to at Deptford Yard, and Hospital
Stairs at Greenwich. There were two patent playhouses,
Lincoln's Inn and Drury Lane; and there were Mr.
Powell's puppets at the old Tennis-court, in James
Street, Haymarket—mysterious edifice, it lingers yet!
looking older than ever, inexplicable, obsolete, elbowed
by casinos, poses plastiques, cafés, and American bowl-
ing-alleys, yet refusing to budge an inch before the
encroachments of Time, who destroys all things, even
tennis-courts. It was "old," we hear, in 1720; I have

---

* I believe Pope's sneer against poor Elkanah Settle (who died very comfortably in the Charterhouse, 1724, ætat. 76 : he was alive in 1720, and
succeeded Rowe as laureate), that he was reduced in his latter days to
compass a motion of St. George and the Dragon at Bartholomew fair, and
himself enacted the dragon in a peculiar suit of green leather, his own
invention, to have been a purely malicious and mendacious bit of spite.
Moreover, Settle died years after Pope assumed him to have expired.

been told that tennis is still played there.   Gramercy!
by whom?   Surely at night, when the wicked neighbourhood is snatching a short feverish sleep, the "old
tennis-courts" must be haunted by sallow, periwigged
phantoms of Charles's time, cadaverous beaux in laced
bands, puffed sleeves, and flapped, plumed hats.   Bats
of spectral wire strike the cobweb-balls; the moonlight
can make them cast no shadows on the old brick-wall.
And in the gallery sits the harsh-visaged, cynic king,
Portsmouth at his side, his little spaniels mumbling the
rosettes in his royal shoes.

In a kind of copartnership with Mr. Powell's puppets
—formerly of the Piazza, Covent Garden, was the famous
Faux, the legerdemain, or sleight-of-hand conjuror—the
Wiljalba Frikell of his day, and whom Hogarth mentions in one of his earliest pictorial satires.   But Faux
did that which the Russian magician, to his credit, does
not do : he puffed himself perpetually, and was at
immense pains to assure the public through the newspapers that he was *not* robbed returning from the
Duchess of Buckingham's at Chelsea.   From Faux's
show at the "Long-room," Hogarth might have stepped
to Heidegger's—hideous Heidegger's masquerades at the
King's Theatre in the Haymarket, where also were held
"*ridotti*," and "*veglioni*"—junketings of an ultra Italian
character, and all presented in 1722 by the Middlesex
grand jury as intolerable nuisances.   Many times, also,
did the stern Sir John Gonson (*the Harlot's Progress*
Gonson), justice of peace, much feared by the Phrynes
of the hundreds of Drury, inveigh in his sessions-charges
against the sinful *ridotti* and the disorderly *veglioni*.
Other performances took place at the King's Theatre.

There was struggling for its first grasp on the English
taste and the English pocket—a grasp which it has never
since lost—that anomalous, inconsistent, delightful entertainment, the Italian Opera. Hogarth, as a true-born
Briton, hated the harmonious exotic; and from his
earliest plates to the grand series of the *Rake's Progress*,
indulges in frequent flings at Handel (in his *Ptolomeo*,
and before his immortal Oratorio stage), Farinelli,
Cuzzoni, Senesino, Faustina, Barrenstadt, and other
"soft simpering whiblins." Yet the sturdiest hater of
this "new taste of the town" could not refrain from
admiring and applauding to the echo that which was
called the "miraculously dignified exit of Senesino."
This celebrated *sortita* must have resembled in the
almost electrical effect it produced, the elder Kean's
"Villain, be sure thou prove," &c. in *Othello;* John
Kemble's "Mother of the world—" in *Coriolanus;*
Madame Pasta's "Io," in *Medea;* and Ristori's world-
known "*Tu*," in the Italian version of the same dread
trilogy. One of the pleasantest accusations brought
against the Italian Opera was preferred some years
before 1720, in the *Spectator*, when it was pointed out
that the principal man or woman singer sang in Italian,
while the responses were given, and the choruses chanted
by Britons. *Judices*, in these latter days, I have "assisted" at the performance of the *Barber of Seville* at
one of our large theatres, when *Figaro* warbled in Italian
with a strong Spanish accent, when Susanna was a
Frenchwoman, Doctor Bartolo an Irishman, and the
chorus sang in English, and without any H's.

More shows remain for Hogarth to take delight in.
The quacks, out of Bartlemy time, set up their standings

in Moorfields by the madhouse (illustrated by Hogarth
in the *Rake's Progress*), and in Covent Garden Market
(W. H. in the plate of *Morning*), by Inigo Jones's rustic
church, which he built for the Earl of Bedford : " Build
me a barn," quoth the earl. " You shall have the bravest
barn in England," returned Inigo, and his lordship had
it.   There were quacks too, though the loud-voiced
beggars interferred with them, in Lincoln's Inn Fields,
and on Tower Hill, where the sailors and river-side
Bohemians were wont to indulge in their favourite diver-
sion of "whipping the snake."   There were grand shows
when a commoner was raised to the peerage or promoted
in grade therein—a common occurrence in the midst of
all the corruption entailed by the Scottish union and
Walpole's wholesale bribery.   On these occasions, depu-
tations of the heralds came from their dusty old college
in Doctor's Commons, and in full costume, to congratu-
late the new peer, the viscount made an earl, or the
marquis elevated to a dukedom, and to claim by the way
a snug amount of fees from the newly-blown dignitary.
Strange figures they must have cut, those old kings-at-
arms, heralds, and pursuivants !   Everybody remembers
the anecdote, since twisted into an allusion to Lord
Thurlow's grotesque appearance, of a servant on such an
occasion as I have alluded to, saying to his master,
" Please, my lord, there's a gentleman in a coach at the
door would speak with your lordship ; and, saving your
presence, *I think he's the knave of spades.*"   I burst out
in unseemly cachinnation the other day at the opening
of Parliament, when I saw Rougecroix trotting along the
royal gallery of the peers, with those table-napkins stiff
with gold embroidery pendent back and front of him like

6

heraldic advertisements. The astonishing equipment
was terminated by the black dress pantaloons and patent-
leather boots of ordinary life. *Je crevais de rire:* the
Lord Chamberlain walking backwards was nothing to it ;
yet I daresay Rougecroix looked not a whit more absurd
than did Bluemantle and Portcullis in 1720 with red
heels and paste buckles to their Cordovan shoon, and
curly periwigs flowing from beneath their cocked hats.

Shows, more shows, and William Hogarth walking
London streets to take stock of them all, to lay them up
in his memory's ample store-house. He will turn all he
has seen to good account some day. There is a show
at the museum of the Royal Society, then sitting at
Gresham College. The queer, almost silly things, exhibited there! queer and silly, at least to us, with our
magnificent museums in Great Russell Street, Lincoln's
Inn Fields and Brompton. I am turning over the Royal
Society catalogue as I write : the rarities all set down
with a ponderous, simple-minded solemnity. "Dr.
Grews" is the conscientious editor. Here shall you find
the "sceptre of an Indian king, a dog without a mouth ;
a Pegue hat and organ ; a bird of paradise ; a Jewish
phylactery ; a model of the Temple of Jerusalem ;
a burning-glass contrived by that excellent philosopher
and mathematician Sir Isaac Newton" (hats off) ; "three
landskips and a catcoptrick paint given by Bishop Wil-
kins ; a gun which discharges seven times one after the
other presently" (was this a revolver ?) ; "a perspective
instrument by the ingenious Sir Christopher Wren"
(hats off again) ; "a pair of Iceland gloves, a pot of
Macassar poison" (oh ! Rowland) ; "the tail of an
Indian cow worshipped on the banks of the river Ganges ;

a tuft of coralline ; the cramp fish which by some humour
or vapour benumbs the fisherman's arms," and so forth.
Hogarth will make use of these "curios" in the fourth
scene of the *Marriage à la Mode*, and presently, for the
studio of Sidrophel in his illustrations to *Hudibras.*

And there are shows of a sterner and crueler order.
Now a pickpocket yelling under a pump ; now a half-
naked wretch coming along Whitehall at the tail of a
slow-plodding cart, howling under the hangman's lash
(that functionary has ceased to be called "Gregory,"
from the great executioner G. Brandon, and is now, but
I have not been able to discover for what reason, "Jack
Ketch").* Now it is a libeller or a perjurer in the
pillory at Charing in Eastcheap or at the Royal Exchange. According to his political opinions do the mob
—the mob are chiefly of the Jacobite persuasion—pelt
the sufferer with eggs and ordure, or cheer him, and fill
the hat which lies at his foot on the scaffold with half-
pence and even silver. And the sheriffs' men, if duly
fee'd, do not object to a mug of purl or mum, or even
punch, being held by kind hands to the sufferer's lips.
So, in Hugo's deathless romance, does Esmeralda give
Quasimodo on the *carcan* to drink from her flask. Mercy
is as old as the hills, and will never die. Sometimes in
front of "England's Burse," or in Old Palace Yard, an
odd, futile, much-laughed-at ceremony takes place : and
after solemn proclamation, the common hangman makes
a bonfire of such proscribed books as *Pretenders no Pre-*

---

* 1720. The horrible room in Newgate Prison where in cauldrons of
boiling pitch the hangman seethed the dissevered limbs of those executed
for high treason, and whose quarters were to be exposed, was called "Jack
Ketch's kitchen."

tence, A sober Reply to Mr. Higgs's Tri-theistical Doctrine.
Well would it be if the vindictiveness of the government
stopped here ; but alas ! king's messengers are in hot
pursuit of the unhappy authors, trace them to the tripe-
shop in Hanging Sword Alley, or the cock-loft in Honey
Lane Market, where they lie three in a bed ; and the
poor scribbling wretches are cast into jail, and delivered over to the tormentors, losing sometimes their
unlucky ears. There is the great sport and show every
market morning, known as " bull banking," a sweet suc-
cursal to his Majesty's bear-garden and Hockley in the
Hole. The game is of the simplest ; take your bull in a
narrow thoroughfare, say, Cock Hill, by Smithfield ;
have a crowd of *hommes de bonne volonté ;* overturn a
couple of hackney coaches at one end of the street, a
brewer's dray at the other : then harry your bull up and
down, goad him, pelt him, twist his tail, till he roar and
is rabid. This is " bull-banking," and oh ! for the sports
of merry England ! William Hogarth looks on sternly
and wrathfully. He will remember the brutal amuse-
ments of the populace when he comes to engrave the
Four Stages of Cruelty. But I lead him away now to
other scenes and shows. There are the wooden horses
before Sadler's Hall ; and westward there stands an uncomfortable " wooden horse " for the punishment of soldiers who are picketed thereon for one and two hours.
This wooden horse is on St. James's Mall, over against
the gun-house. The torture is one of Dutch William's
legacies to the subjects, and has been retained and improved on by the slothfully cruel Hanoverian kings.
Years afterwards (1745-6), when Hogarth shall send his
picture of the *March to Finchley* to St. James's for

inspection of his sacred Majesty King George the Second, that potentate will fly into a guard-room rage at the truthful humour of the scene, and will express an opinion that the audacious painter who has caricatured his Foot Guards, should properly suffer the punishment of the picket on the "wooden horse" of the Mall.

Further afield. There are literally thousands of shop-signs to be read or stared at. There are prize-fights—predecessors of Fig and Broughton contests—gladiatorial exhibitions, in which decayed Life-guardsmen and Irish captains trade-fallen, hack and hew one another with broadsword and backsword on public platforms. Then the "French prophets," whom John Wesley knew, are working sham miracles in Soho, emulating—the impostors!—the marvels done at the tomb of the Abbé Diacre or Chanoine, Paris, and positively holding exhibitions in which fanatics suffer themselves to be trampled, jumped upon, and beaten with clubs, for the greater glory of Molinism ;* even holding academies, where the youth of both sexes are instructed in the arts of foaming at the mouth, falling into convulsions, discoursing in unknown tongues, revealing stigmata produced by the aid of lunar caustic, and other moon-struck madnesses and cheats. Such is revivalism in 1720. William Hogarth is there, observant. He will not forget the French prophets when he executes almost the last and noblest of his plates—albeit, it is directed against English revivalists, *Credulity, Superstition and Fanaticism*. He leaves Soho, and

---

* Compare these voluntary torments with the description of the *Doseh*, or horse-trampling ceremonial of the Sheik El Bekree, over the bodies of the faithful, in Lane's *Modern Egyptians*.

wanders eastward and westward. He reads Madam
Godfrey's six hundred challenges to the female sex in
the newspapers; sitting, perhaps, at the " Rose," without
Temple Bar; at the "Diapente," whither the beaux,
feeble as Lord Fanny, who could not " eat beef, or horse,
or any of those things," come to recruit their exhausted
digestions with jelly-broth. He may look in at mug-
houses, where stum, 'quest ales, Protestant masch-beer,
and Derby stingo are sold. He may drop in at Owen
Swan's, at the "Black Swan" Tavern in Saint Martin's
Lane, and listen to the hack-writers girding at Mr. Pope,
and at the enormous amount of eating and drinking in
Harry Higden's comedies. He may see the virtuosi at
Childs's, and dozens of other auctions (Edward Melling-
ton was the George Robins of the preceding age; the
famous Cobb was his successor in auction-room eloquence and pomposity), buying china monsters. He
may refect himself with hot furmity at the " Rainbow "
or at " Nando's," mingle (keeping his surtout well but-
toned) with the pickpockets in Paul's, avoid the Scotch
walk on 'Change, watch the garish damsels alight from
their coaches at the chocolate-houses, mark the gamesters rushing in, at as early an hour as eleven in the
morning, to shake their elbows at the " Young Man's ;"
gaze at the barristers as they bargain for wherries at the
Temple Stairs to take water for Westminster—a pair of
sculls being much cheaper than a hackney coach—meet
the half-pay officers at Whitehall, garrulously discussing
the King of Spain's last treaty, as the shoeblacks polish
their footgear with oil and soot—Day and Martin are yet
in embryo; stand by, on Holborn Hill, about half-past
eleven, as Jack Hall, the chimney sweep, winds his sad

way in Newgate cart, his coffin before him, and the
ordinary with his book and nosegay by his side, towards
St. Giles's Pound, and the ultimate bourne, Tyburn. Jack
Hall has a nosegay, too, and wears a white ribbon in his
hat to announce his innocence. The fellow has committed a hundred robberies. And Jack Hall is very far
gone in burnt brandy. Hogarth marks—does not forget
him. Jack Hall—who seems to have been a kind of
mediocre Jack Sheppard, although his escape from Newgate was well-nigh as dexterous, and quite as bold as
the prison-breaking feat of the arch rascal, Blueskin's
friend—will soon reappear in one of the first of the
Hogarthian squibs ; and the dismal procession to Tyburn
will form the *dénoûment* to the lamentable career of
Tom Idle.

Hogarth must have become *poco a poco* saturated with
such impressions of street life. From 1730 the tide of
reproduction sets in without cessation ; but I strive to
catch and to retain the fleeting image of this dead
London, and it baulks and mocks me :—the sham bail,
" duffers" and " mounters," skulking with straws in their
shoes about Westminster Hall ; the law offices in Chancery Lane and the " devil's gap" between Great Queen
Street and Lincoln's Inn Fields ; the Templars, the
mootmen, and those who are keeping their terms in
Lincoln's and Gray's Inn, dining in their halls at noon,
eating off wooden trenchers, drinking from green earth-
enware jugs, and summoned to commons by horn-blow ;
—the furious stockjobbers at Jonathan's and Garraway's,
at the sign of the " Fifteen Shillings," and in Thread-
needle Row ; the fine ladies buying perfumery at the
" Civet Cat," in Shire Lane, by Temple Bar—perfumery,

now-a-days, is much wanted in that unsavoury *locale ;*
the Jacobite ballad-singers growling sedition in Seven
Dials ; the Hanoverian troubadours crooning, on their
side, worn-out scandal touching " Italian Molly " (James
the Second's Mary of Modena) and " St. James's warn-
ing-pan " in the most frequented streets ; riots and tu-
mults, spy-hunting, foreigner mobbing, of not unfrequent
occurrence, all over the town ; gangs of riotous soldiers
crowding about Marlborough House, and casting shirts
into the great duke's garden, that his grace may see of
what rascally stuff—filthy dowlas instead of good calico,
the contractors have made them. Alas ! a wheezing,
drivelling, almost idiotic dotard is all that remains of the
great duke, all that is left of John Churchill. He had
just strength enough at the Bath the season before to
crawl. home in the dark night, in order to avoid the
expense of a chair. There are fights in the streets, and
skirmishes on the river, where revenue cutters, custom-
house jerkers, and the " Tartar pink," make retributive
raids on the fresh-water pirates : light and heavy horse-
men, cope-men, scuffle-hunters, lumpers, and game-
watermen. There are salt-water as well as fresh-water
thieves ; and a notable show of the period is the execution of a pirate, and his hanging in chains at Execution
dock. All which notwithstanding, it is a consolation to
learn that " Captain Hunt, of the *Delight,*" is tried at
Justice Hall for piracy, and " honourably acquitted."
I know not why, but I rejoice at the captain's escape.
He seems a bold, dashing spirit ; and, when captured,
was " drinking orvietan with a horse-officer." But when
I come to reperuse the evidence adduced on the trial, I
confess that the weight of testimony bears strongly

against Captain Hunt, and that in reality it would seem that he *did* scuttle the "*Protestant Betsey*," cause the boatswain and "one Skeggs, a chaplain, transporting himself to the plantations"—at the request of a judge and jury, I wonder?—to walk the plank, and did also carbonado the captain with lighted matches and Burgundy pitch prior to blowing his (the captain's) brains out. Hunt goes free; but pirates are cast, and sometimes swing. Hogarth notes, comments on, remembers them. The gibbeted corsairs by the river's side shall find a place in the third chapter of the history of Thomas Idle.

So wags the world in 1720. Hogarth practising on copper in the intervals of arms and crest engraving, and hearing of Thornhill and Laguerre's staircase-and-ceiling-painting renown, inwardly longing to be a Painter. Sir George Thorold is lord mayor. Comet Halley is astronomer royal. *vice* Flamsteed, deceased the preceding year. Clement XI. is dying, and the Jews of Ferrara deny that they have sacrificed a child at Easter, *à la* Hugh of Lincoln. The great King Louis is dead, and a child reigns in his stead. The Regent and the Abbé Dubois are making history one long scandal in Paris. Bernard Lens is miniature painter to the king, in lieu of Benjamin Acland, dead. Mr. Colley Cibber's works are printed on royal paper. Sheffield, Duke of Bucks, erects a plain tablet to the memory of John Dryden in Westminster Abbey: his own name in very large letters, Dryden's in more moderately-sized capitals. Madam Crisp sets a lieutenant to kill a black man, who has stolen her lapdog. Captain Dawson bullies half the world, and half the world bullies Captain Dawson: and bullies or is so bullied still to this day.

In disjointed language, but with a very earnest purpose, I have endeavoured to trace our painter's Prelude, —the growth of his artistic mind, the ripening of his perceptive faculties under the influence of the life he saw. Now, for the operation of observation, distilled in the retort of his quaint humour. I record the work he did ; and first, in 1720, mention "four drawings in Indian ink " of the characters at Button's coffee-house.*
In these were sketches of Arbuthnot, Addison, Pope (as it is conjectured), and a certain Count Viviani, identified years afterwards by Horace Walpole, when the drawings came under his notice. They subsequently came into Ireland's possession. Next Hogarth executed an etching, whose subject was of more national importance. In 1720-21, as all men know, England went mad, and was drawn, jumping for joy, into the Maëlstrom of the South Sea Bubble. France had been already desperately insane, in 1719, and Philip, the Regent, with John Law of Lauriston, the Edinburgh silversmith's son, who had been rake, bully, and soldier, and had stood his trial for killing Beau Wilson in a duel, had between them gotten up a remarkable mammon-saturnalia in the Palais Royal

---

* Daniel Button's well-known coffee-house was on the south side of Russell Street, Covent Garden, nearly opposite Tom's. Button had been a servant of the Countess of Warwick, and so was patronized by her spouse, the Right Hon. Joseph Addison. Sir Robert Walpole's creature, Giles Earl, a trading justice of the peace (compare Fielding and " 300*l.* a year of the dirtiest money in the world,") used to examine criminals, for the amusement of the company, in the public room at Button's. Here, too, was a lion's head letter-box, into which communications for the *Guardian* were dropped. At Button's, Pope is reported to have said of Patrick, the lexicographer, who made pretensions to criticism, that "a dictionary-maker might know the meaning of one word, but not of two put together."

and the Rue Quincampoix. Law lived *en prince* in the
Place Vendôme. They show the window now whence
he used to look down upon his dupes. He died, a few
years after the bursting of his bubble, a miserable bankrupt adventurer at Venice. And yet there really was
something tangible in his schemes, wild as they were.
The credit of the Royal Bank averted a national bankruptcy in France, and some substantial advantage might
have been derived from the Mississippi trade. At all
events, there actually was such a place as Louisiana. In
this country, the geographical actualities were very little
consulted. The English South Sea scheme was a
swindle, *pur et simple*. Almost everybody in the country
caught this cholera-morbus of avarice. Pope dabbled
in S. S. S. (South Sea Stock): Lady Mary Wortley
Montagu was accused of cheating Ruremonde, the
French wit, out of 500*l*. worth of stock. Ladies laid
aside ombre and basset to haunt 'Change Alley. Gay
" stood to win " enormous sums—at one time imagined
himself, as did Pope also, to be the " lord of thousands,"
but characteristically refused to follow a friend's advice to
realize at least sufficient to secure himself a " clean shirt
and a shoulder of mutton every day for life." He persisted in holding, and lost all. Mr. Aislabie, the Chancellor of the Exchequer, was deeply implicated in S. S. S.
transactions, as were also many peers and members of
parliament. The amiable and accomplished Craggs, the
postmaster-general, the friend of all the wits, and for
whose tomb Pope wrote so touching an epitaph, tar-
nished his reputation indelibly by unscrupulous jobbery.
He died of the small-pox, just in time to avoid disgrace
and ruin ; but his poor old father was sold up, and was

borne to the grave shortly afterward, broken-hearted.
Lord Stanhope ruptured a blood-vessel in replying to
a furious speech of the Duke of Wharton (who lived a
profligate and died a monk) against S. S., and did not
long survive. Samuel Chandler, the eminent Noncon-
formist divine, was ruined, and had to keep a book-stall
for bread. Hudson, known as "Tom of Ten Thousand,"
went stark mad, and moved about 'Change just as the
"Woman in Black" and the "Woman in White" (the
son of the one, and the brother of the other were hanged
for forgery,) used to haunt the avenues of the Bank of
England. The South Sea Company bribed the Government, bribed the two Houses, and bribed the Court
ladies, both of fair and of light fame. Erengard Melu-
sina Schuylenberg, Princess von Eberstein, Duchess of
Munster (1715), and Duchess of Kendal (1729)— Hogarth engraved the High Dutch hussey's arms—the
Countess of Platen, and her two nieces, and Lady Sun-
derland, with Craggs and Aislabie, got the major part
of the fictitious stock of 574,000*l.* created by the company. The stock rose to thirteen hundred and fifty
pounds premium ! Beggars on horseback tore through
the streets. There were S. S. coaches with *Auri sacra
fames* painted on the panels. Hundreds of companies
were projected, and "took the town" immensely.
Steele's (Sir Richard's) Fishpool Company, for bringing
the finny denizens of the deep by sea to London—
Puckle's Defence Gun — the Bottomree, the Coral-
fishery, the Wreck-fishing companies, were highly spoken
of. Stogden's remittances created great excitement in
the market. There were companies for insurance against
bad servants, against thefts and robberies, against fire

and shipwreck.   There were companies for importing
jack-asses from Spain (coals to Newcastle !) ; for trading
in human hair (started by a clergyman) ; for fattening
pigs ; for making pantiles, Joppa and Castile soap ; for
manufacturing lutestring ; " for the wheel of a perpetual
motion ;" and for extracting stearine from sun-flower-
seed.   There were Dutch bubbles, and oil bubbles, and
water bubbles—bubbles of timber, and bubbles of glass.
There were the " sail cloth," or " Globe permits "—mere
cards with the seal of the " Globe " tavern impressed on
them, and " permitting " the fortunate holders to acquire
shares at some indefinite period in some misty sailcloth
factory.   These sold for sixty guineas a piece.   There
was Jezreel Jones's trade to Barbary, too, for which the
permits could not be sold fast enough.   Welsh copper
and York Buildings' shares rose to cent. per cent. premium.   Sir John Blunt, the scrivener, rose from a mean
estate to prodigious wealth, prospered, and " whale
directors ate up all."   There was an S. S. literature, an
S. S. anthology.

> Meantime, secure on Garrway's cliffs,
>   A savage race, by shipwreck fed,
> Lie waiting for the founder'd skiffs,
>   And strip the bodies of the dead.

Pshaw! have we not Mr. Ward's capital picture in
the Vernon collection, and hundreds of pamphlets on
S. S. in the British Museum ?   The end came, and was,
of course, irrevocable and immortal smash.   Ithuriel's
spear, in the shape of a *scire facias* in the *London Gazette*,
pierced this foully iridescent bubble through and through,
producing precisely the same effect as the publication of
Mr. Spackman's inexorable railway statistics in a supple-

ment to *The Times* newspaper, A.D. 1845. The city
woke up one morning and found itself ruined. The
Sword-blade company went bankrupt. Knight, the S. S.
cashier, fled, but was captured at Tirlemont in Flanders,
at the instance of the British resident in Brussels, and
thrown into the citadel of Antwerp, from which he presently managed to escape. In an age when almost
every one had committed more or less heinous acts of
roguery, great sympathy was evinced for rogues. At
home, however, there were some thoughts of vengeance.
Honest men began, for the first time these many months,
to show their heads, and talked of Nemesis and Newgate.
Aislabie resigned. The end of the Craggses you have
heard. Parliament-men were impeached and expelled
the House. Patriots inveighed against the injuries which
corrupt ministers may inflict on the sovereigns they serve,
and quoted the history of Claudian and Sejanus. The
directors—such as had not vanished—were examined by
secret committees, and what effects of theirs could be
laid hold of were confiscated for the benefit of the thousands of innocent sufferers. I have waded through many
hundred pages of the parliamentary reports of the period,
and have remarked, with a grim chuckle, the similarities
of swindling between this fraud and later ones. Cooked
accounts, torn-out leaves, erasures, *and a small green
ledger with a brass lock*—these are among the flowers of
evidence strewn on the heads of the secret committees.
Knight took the key away with him, forgetting the
ledger, I presume. The lock was forced, and there came
floating out a bubble of fictitious stock. The old story,
gentles and simples. " *Comme Charles Dix, comme
Charles Dix,*" muttered wretched, wigless, Smithified old

Louis Philippe, as he fled in a *fiacre* from the Tuileries in '48 ; and this S. S. swindle of 1720 was only " *Comme Charles Dix*,"—the elder brother of 1825 and 1845 manias, of Milk Companies, Washing Companies, Poyais Loans, Ball's Pond Railways, Great Diddlesex Junctions, Borough, British, and Eastern Banks, and other thieveries which this age has seen.

Did William Hogarth hold any stock ? Did he ever bid for a " Globe permit ?" Did he hanker after human hair ? Did he cast covetous eyes towards the gigantic jack-asses of Iberia ? *Ignoramus :* but we know at least that he made a dash at the bubble with his sharp pencil. In 1721 appeared an etching of *The South Sea, an Allegory*. It was sold at the price of one shilling by Mrs. Chilcot, in Westminster Hall, and B. Caldwell, in Newgate Street. The allegory is laboured, but there is a humorous element diffused throughout the work. The comparatively mechanical nature of the pursuits from which Hogarth was but just emancipated shows itself in the careful drawing of the architecture and the comparative insignificance of the figures. The Enemy of mankind is cutting Fortune into collops before a craving audience of rich and poor speculators. There is a huge " roundabout," with "who'll ride ?" as a legend, and a throng of people of all degrees revolving on their wooden hobbies. In the foreground a wretch is being broken on the wheel—perhaps a reminiscence of the terrible fate of Count Horn, in Paris. L. H., a ruffian, is scourging a poor fellow who is turning his great toes up in agony. These are to represent Honour and Honesty punished by Interest and Villany. In the background widows and spinsters are crowding up a

staircase to a "raffle for husbands," and in the right-hand
corner a Jewish high-priest, a Catholic priest, and a
Dissenting minister, are gambling with frenzied avidity.
Near them a poor, miserable starveling lies a-dying, and
to the left there looms a huge pillar, with this inscription
on the base—"This monument was erected in memory
of the destruction of the city by South Sea, 1720." It
is to be observed that the figure of the demon hacking
at Fortune, and the lame swash buckler, half baboon,
half imp, that keeps guard over the flagellated man, are
copied, pretty literally, from Callot.

You know that I incline towards coincidences. It is
surely a not unremarkable one that Callot, a Hogarthian
man in many aspects, but more inclined towards the
grotesque-terrible than to the humorous observant, should
have been also in his youth a martyr to heraldry. His
father was a grave, dusty old king-at-arms, in the service
of the Duke of Lorraine, at Nancy. He believed
heraldry, next to alchemy, to be the most glorious
science in the world, and would fain have had his son
devote himself to tabard and escocheon work ; but the
boy, after many unavailing efforts to wrestle with these
Ephesian wild beasts, with their impossible attitudes and
preposterous proportions, fairly ran away and turned
gipsy, stroller, beggar, picaroon—all kinds of wild Bohemian things. Had Hogarth been a French boy, he, too,
might have run away from Ellis Gamble's griffins and
gargoyles. He must have been a great admirer of
Callot, and have studied his works attentively, as one
can see, not only from this South Sea plate, but from
many of the earlier Hogarthian performances, in which,
not quite trusting himself yet to run alone, he has had

recourse to the Lorraine's strong arm. Many other sym-
pathetic traits are to be found in the worthy pair.   In
both a little too much swagger and proneness to denounce
things that might have had some little sincerity in them.
The one a thorough foreigner, the other as thorough an
Englishman.   The herald's son of Nancy was always " the
noble Jacques Callot ; " the heraldic engraver's apprentice
of Cranbourn Alley was, I wince to learn, sometimes
called " Bill Hogarth."

One of Hogarth's earliest employers was a Mr. Bowles,
at the " Black Horse in Cornhill," who is stated to have
bought his etched works by weight—at the munificent
rate of half-a-crown a pound.   This is the same Mr. Bowles
who, when Major the engraver was going to France to
study, and wished to dispose of some landscapes he had
engraved that he might raise something in aid of his
travelling expenses, offered him a bright, new, burnished,
untouched copper-plate for every engraved one he had
by him.   This Black Horse Bowles, if the story be true,
must have been ancestor to the theatrical manager who
asked the author *how much he would give him* if he produced his five-act tragedy ; but I am inclined to think
the anecdote a bit of gossip *tant soit peu* spiteful of the
eldest Nicholls.   Moreover, the offer is stated to have
been made " over a bottle."   'Twas under the same
incentive to liberality that an early patron of the present
writer once pressed him to write " a good poem, in the
Byron style—you know," and offered him a guinea for
it, down.   Copper, fit for engraving purposes, was at
least two shillings a pound in Bowles's time.   The half-
crown legend, then, may be apocryphal ; although we
have some odd records of the mode of payment for art

7

and letters in those days, and in the preceding time :—
Thornhill painting Greenwich Hall for forty shillings
the Flemish ell ; Dryden contracting with Left-legged
Jacob to write so many thousand lines for so· many
unclipped pieces of money ; and Milton selling the
manuscript of *Paradise Lost* to Samuel Simmons for
five pounds.

Mr. Philip Overton at the Golden Buck, over against
St. Dunstan's Church, in Fleet Street, also published
Hogarth's early plates. He was the purchaser, too, but
not yet, of the eighteen illustrations to *Hudibras*. Ere
these appeared, W. H. etched the *Taste of the Town*, the
Small Masquerade Ticket, the *Lottery*—a very confused
and obscure allegory, perhaps a sly parody on one of
Laguerre or Thornhill's floundering pictorial parables.
Fortune and Wantonness are drawing lucky numbers,
Fraud tempts Despair, Sloth hides his head behind a
curtain ; all very interesting probably at the time, from
the number of contemporary portraits the plate may
have contained, but almost inexplicable and thoroughly
uninteresting to us now. The *Taste of the Town*, which
is otherwise the *first* Burlington Gate satire (not the
Pope and Chandos one) created a sensation, and its
author paid the first per-centage on notoriety, by seeing
his work pirated by the varlets who did for art that
which Edmund Curll, bookseller and scoundrel, did for
literature.

Burlington Gate, No. 1, was published in 1723. Hogarth seems to have admired Lord Burlington's love for
art, though he might have paid him a better compliment
than to have placarded the gate of his palace with
an orthographical blunder. There is in the engraving

"THE TASTE OF THE TOWN."

"accademy" for academy. The execution is far superior
to that of the *South Sea*, and the figures are drawn with
much *verve* and decision. In the centre stand three
little figures, said to represent Lord Burlington, Campbell the architect, and his lordship's "postilion." This is
evidently a blunder on the part of the first commentator.
The figure is in cocked hat, wide cuffs, and buckled
shoes, and is no more like a postilion than I to Hercules.
Is it the earl's "poet," and not his "postilion," that is
meant? To the right (using showman's language),
sentinels in the peaked shakoes of the time, and with
oh! such clumsy, big-stocked brown-besses in their
hands, guard the entrance to the fane where the pantomime of *Doctor Faustus* is being performed. From the
balcony above Harlequin looks out. *Faustus* was first
brought out at the theatre, Lincoln's Inn Fields, in '23. It
had so prodigious a run, and came into such vogue, that
after much grumbling about the "legitimate" and invo-
cations of "Ben Jonson's ghost" (Hogarth calls him
Ben Johnson), the riva Covent Garden managers were
compelled to follow suit, and in '25 came out with their
Doctor Faustus—a kind of saraband of infernal persons
contrived by Thurmond the dancing-master. He, too,
was the deviser of "*Harleykin Sheppard*" (or Shepherd),
in which the dauntless thief who escaped from the Middle
Stone-room at Newgate in so remarkable a manner received a pantomimic apotheosis. Quick-witted Hogarth
satirized this felony-mania in the caricature of Wilks,
Booth, and Cibber, conjuring up "Scaramouch Jack Hall."
To return to Burlington Gate. In the centre, Shakspeare's
and Jonson's works are being carted away for waste
paper. To the left you see a huge projecting sign or

show-cloth, containing portraits of his sacred Majesty George the Second in the act of presenting the management of the Italian Opera with one thousand pounds; also of the famous Mordaunt Earl of Peterborough and sometime general of the armies in Spain. He kneels, and in the handsomest manner, to Signora Cuzzoni the singer, saying (in a long apothecary's label), "Please accept eight thousand pounds!" but the Cuzzoni spurns at him. Beneath is the entrance to the Opera. Infernal persons with very long tails are entering thereto with joyful countenances. The infernal persons are unmistakable reminiscences of Callot's demons in the *Tentation de St. Antoine.* There is likewise a placard relating to "Faux's Long-room," and his "dexterity of hand."

In 1724, Hogarth produced another allegory called the *Inhabitants of the Moon,* in which there are some covert and not very complimentary allusions to the "dummy" character of royalty, and a whimsical fancy of inanimate objects, songs, hammers, pieces of money, and the like, being built up into imitation of human beings, all very ingeniously worked out. By this time, Hogarth, too, had begun to work, not only for the ephemeral pictorial squib-vendors of Westminster Hall —(those squibs came in with him, culminated in Gillray, and went out with H. B.; or were rather absorbed and amalgamated into the admirable *Punch* cartoons of Mr. Leech)—but also for the regular booksellers. For Aubry de la Mottraye's *Travels* (a dull, pretentious book) he executed some engravings, among which I note *A woman of Smyrna in the habit of the country*—the woman's face very graceful, and the *Dance*, the Pyrrhic dance of the Greek islands, and the oddest fandango that ever was

seen.   One commentator says that the term "as merry
as a grig" came from the fondness of the inhabitants of
those isles of eternal summer for dancing, and that it
should be properly " as merry as a Greek."   *Quien sabe?*
I know that lately in the Sessions papers I stumbled
over the examination of one Levi Solomon, *alias* Cockle-
put, who stated that he lived in Sweet Apple Court, and
that he "went a-grigging for his living."   I have no
Lexicon Balatronicum at hand ; but from early researches
into the vocabulary of the " High Mung " I have an
indistinct impression that " griggers " were agile vagabonds, who danced and went through elementary feats
of posture-mastery in taverns.

In '24, Hogarth illustrated a translation of the *Golden
Ass of Apuleius.*   The plates are coarse and clumsy ;
show no humour ; were mere pot-boilers, *gagne-pains*,
thrusts with the burin at the wolf looking in at the
Hogarthian door, I imagine.   Then came five frontispieces for a translation of *Cassandra.*   These I have not
seen.   Then fifteen head-pieces for Beaver's *Military
Punishments of the Ancients*, narrow little slips full of
figures in chiaroscuro, many drawn from Callot's curious
martyrology, *Les Saincts et Sainctes de l'Année*, about
three hundred graphic illustrations of human torture !
There was also a frontispiece to the *Happy Ascetic*, and
one to the Oxford squib of *Terræ Filius*, in 1724, but of
the joyous recluse in question I have no cognizance.

In 1722 (you see I am wandering up and down the
years as well as the streets), London saw a show—and
Hogarth doubtless was there to see—which merits some
lines of mention.   The drivelling, avaricious dotard, who,
crossing a room and looking at himself in a mirror,

sighed and mumbled, "That was once a man:"—this poor wreck of mortality died, and became in an instant, and once more, John the great Duke of Marlborough. On the 9th of August, 1722, he was buried with extraordinary pomp in Westminster Abbey. The saloons of Marlborough House, where the corpse lay in state, were hung with fine black cloth, and garnished with bays and cypress. In the death-chamber was a chair of state surmounted by a "majesty scutcheon." The coffin was on a bed of state, covered with a "fine holland sheet," over that a complete suit of armour, gilt, *but empty*. Twenty years before, there would have been a waxen image in the dead man's likeness within the armour, but this hideous fantasy of Tussaud-tombstone effigies had in 1722 fallen into desuetude.* The garter was buckled round the steel leg of this suit of war-harness ; one listless gauntlet held a general's truncheon ; above the vacuous helmet with its unstirred plumes was the cap of a Prince of the Empire. The procession, lengthy and splendid, passed from Marlborough House through St. James's Park to Hyde Park Corner, then through Piccadilly, down St. James's Street, along Pall Mall, and by King Street, Westminster, to the Abbey. Fifteen pieces of cannon rumbled in this show. Chelsea pensioners, to the number of the years of the age of the deceased, preceded the car. The colours were wreathed in crape and cypress. Guidon was there, and the great standard, and many bannerols and achievements of arms. "The

---

* Not, however, to forget that another Duchess, Marlborough's daughter, who loved Congreve so, had after his death a waxen image made in his effigy, and used to weep over it, and anoint the gouty feet.

mourning horse with trophies and plumades " was gorgeous. There was a horse of state and a mourning horse, sadly led by the dead duke's equerries. And pray note : the minutest details of the procession were copied from the programme of the Duke of Albemarle's funeral (Monk) ; which, again, was a copy of Oliver Cromwell's —which, again, was a reproduction, on a more splendid scale, of the obsequies of Sir Philip Sidney, killed at Zutphen. Who among us saw not the great scarlet and black show of 1852, the funeral of the Duke of Wellington ? Don't you remember the eighty-four tottering old Pensioners, corresponding in number with the years of our heroic brother departed ? When gentle Philip Sidney was borne to the tomb, *thirty-one* poor men followed the hearse. The brave soldier, the gallant gentleman, the ripe scholar, the accomplished writer was so young. Arthur and Philip ! And so century shakes hand with century, and the new is ever old, and the last novelty is the earliest fashion, and old Egypt leers from a glass-case, or a four thousand year old fresco, and whispers to Sir Plume, " I, too, wore a curled periwig, and used tweezers to remove superfluous hairs."

In 1726, Hogarth executed a series of plates for *Blackwell's Military Figures*, representing the drill and manœuvres of the Honourable Artillery Company. The pike and half-pike exercise are very carefully and curiously illustrated ; the figures evidently drawn from life ; the attitudes very easy. The young man was improving in his drawing ; for in 1724, Thornhill had started an academy for studying from the round and from life at his own house, in Covent Garden Piazza ; and Hogarth —who himself tells us that his head was filled with the

paintings at Greenwich and St. Paul's, and to whose
utmost ambition of scratching copper, there was now probably added the secret longing to be a historico-allegorico-
scriptural painter I have hinted at, and who hoped some
day to make Angels sprawl on coved ceilings, and
Fames blast their trumpets on grand staircases—was
one of the earliest students at the academy of the
king's sergeant painter, and member of parliament
for Weymouth. Already William had ventured an
opinion, *bien tranchée*, on high art. In those days there
flourished—yes, flourished is the word—a now forgotten
celebrity, Kent the architect, gardener, painter, deco-
rater, upholsterer, friend of the great, and a hundred
things besides. This artistic jack-of-all-trades became
so outrageously popular, and gained such a reputation
for taste—if a man have strong lungs, and persist in
crying out that he is a genius, the public are sure to
believe him at last—that he was consulted on almost every
tasteful topic, and was teased to furnish designs for the
most incongruous objects. He was consulted for picture-
frames, drinking-glasses, barges, dining-room tables,
garden-chairs, cradles, and birthday gowns. One lady he
dressed in a petticoat ornamented with columns of the
five orders ; to another he prescribed a copper-coloured
skirt, with gold ornaments. The man was at best but a
wretched sciolist ; but he for a long period directed the
"taste of the town." He had at last the presumption to
paint an altar-piece for the church of St. Clement Danes.
The worthy parishioners, men of no taste at all, burst
into a yell of derision and horror at this astounding
croûte. Forthwith, irreverent young Mr. Hogarth lunged
full butt with his graver at the daub. He produced an

engraving of *Kent's Masterpiece*, which was generally
considered to be an unmerciful caricature ; but which he
himself declared to be an accurate representation of the
picture. 'Twas the first declaration of his *guerra al
cuchillo* against the connoisseurs.   The caricature, or
copy, whichever it was, made a noise ; the tasteless
parishioners grew more vehement, and, at last, Gibson,
Bishop of London (whose brother, by the way, had
paid his first visit to London in the company of Dominie
Hogarth), interfered, and ordered the removal of the
obnoxious canvas.   " Kent's masterpiece" subsided into
an ornament for a tavern-room.   For many years it was
to be seen (together with the landlord's portrait, I
presume) at the " Crown and Anchor," in the Strand.
Then it disappeared, and faded away from the visible
things extant.

With another bookseller's commission, I arrive at
another halting-place in the career of William Hogarth.
In 1726-7 appeared his eighteen illustrations to Butler's
Hudibras.   They are of considerable size, broadly and
vigorously executed, and display a liberal instalment of
the *vis comica*, of which William was subsequently to be
so lavish.   Ralpho is smug and sanctified to a nicety.
Hudibras is a marvellously droll-looking figure, but he
is not human, is generally execrably drawn, and has a
head preternaturally small, and so pressed down between
the clavicles, that you might imagine him to be of the
family of the anthropophagi, whose heads do grow
beneath their shoulders.   There is a rare constable, the
perfection of Dogberryism-*cum*-Bumbledom, in the
tableau of Hudibras in the stocks.   The widow is graceful and beautiful to look at.   Unlike Wilkie, Hogarth

could draw pretty women :* the rogue ·who chucks the widow's attendant under the chin is incomparable, and Trulla is a most truculent brimstone. The "committee" is a character-full study of sour faces. The procession of the "Skimmington" is full of life and animation ; and the concluding tableau, " Burning rumps at Temple Bar," is a wondrous street-scene, worthy of the ripe Hogarthian epoch of *The Progresses, The Election, Beer Street and Gin Lane.* This edition of Butler's immortal satire had a great run ; and the artist often regretted that he had parted absolutely, and at once, with his property in the plates.

So now then, William Hogarth, next shall the moderns know thee—student at Thornhill's Academy —as a painter as well as an engraver. A philosopher —*quoique tu n'en doutais guère*—thou hast been all along.

---

* "They said he could not colour," said old Mrs. Hogarth one day to John Thomas Smith, showing him a sketch of a girl's head. "It's a lie ; look there : there's flesh and blood for you, my man."

IV.

The Painter's Progress.

ABOUT the year of grace 1727 the world began to hear of William Hogarth, not only as a designer and engraver of pasquinades and book-plates, but as a painter in oils. He had even begun to know what patronage was ; and it was, doubtless, not without a reason that his *Hudibras* series was dedicated to "William Ward, Esquire, of Great Houghton, Northamptonshire." In his early heraldic days, I find that he was once called upon to engrave an "Apollo in all his glory, azure." He probably copied the figure from some French print ; but in 1724 he was hard at work copying Apollo, and Marsyas to boot, at Thornhill's Academy. Although he was sensible enough not to neglect the cultivation of the main chance, and with all convenient speed betook himself to the profitable vocation of portraiture or " face painting ; " obtaining almost immediately from his connection with the king's sergeant painter, some aristocratic commissions—it is curious to observe that the young man's bent lay in the direction of the historico-allegorical, then running neck-and-neck with the upholstery style of adornment. He had the epic-fever. Who among us has not suffered from that *fièvre brulante*—that generous malady of youth? How many contented sub-editors and quiet booksellers' readers do we not know, who, in their hot adolescence, came to town, their portmanteaus bursting with the "Something-iad," in twenty-four cantos, or with blank-verse tragedies running to the orthodox five acts? Stipple, the charming domestic painter; Jonquil, who limns flowers and fruits so exquisitely, commenced with their enormous cartoons and show-cloth oil-pictures : "Orestes pursued by the Eumenides," "Departure of Regulus,"— *la vieille patraque*, in short—the old, heroic, impossible undertakings. And did not Liston imagine that he was born to play *Macbeth?* and did not Douglas Jerrold project a treatise on Natural Philosophy? and where is the little boarding-school miss that has not dreamt of riding in a carriage with a coronet on the panels, and being called her ladyship? Amina thinks the grandiloquent music of *Norma* would suit her; the maiden speech of young Quintus Briscus is a tremendous outburst against ministers. Quintus is going to shake the country, and cut the Gordian knot of red-tape. The session after next he will be a junior Lord of the Treasury, the demurest and most complacent of placemen. Peers, politicians, pamphleteers, and players : we all find our level. Rolling about the board is not to be tolerated for any length of time : we *must* peg in somewhere, and happy the man who finds himself in the right hole, and is satisfied with that state of life into which it has pleased heaven to call him!

Hogarth has his *fièvre brulante;* and, although he painted portraits, "conversations," and "assemblies," to eke out that livelihood of which the chief source was the

employment given him by Philip Overton, Black-Horse
Bowles, and the booksellers, he continued to hanker
after torsos, and flying trumpets, and wide-waving wings,
and flaunting drapery, and the other paraphernalia that
went to furnish forth the apotheoses of monarchs and
warriors in full-bottomed wigs. This prosperous school
of art has long been in hopeless decay. You see the
phantom caricature of it, only, in hair-dressers' "toilette
saloons" and provincial music-halls. Timon's villa—the
futile, costly caprice—has vanished. Old Montagu
House is no more. Doctor Misaubin's house, in St.
Martin's Lane, the staircase painted by Clermont (the
Frenchman asked a thousand, and actually received
five hundred guineas for his work), is not within my ken.
Examples of this florid, truculent style, are becoming
rarer and rarer every day. Painted ceilings and staircases yet linger in some grand old half-deserted country
mansions, and in a few erst gorgeous merchants' houses
in Fenchurch and Leadenhall, now let out in flats as
offices and chambers. If you have no objection to
hazard a crick in your neck, you may crane it, and stare
upwards at the ceil-paintings at Marlborough House, in
Greenwich Hall, and on Hampton Court Palace staircase. The rest has ceded before stucco and stencilled
paper-hangings; and even the French, who never neglect
an opportunity or an excuse for ornamentation, and who
still occasionally paint the ceilings of their palaces, seem
to have quite lost the old Lebrun and Coypel traditions
of perspective and fore-shortening—overcharged and
unnatural as they were (P. P. Rubens, in the Banqueting
House, Whitehall, inventor)—and merely give you a
picture stuck upon a rooftree, in which the figures are

attenuated vertically, instead of sprawling down upon
you, isometrically upside down.

Hogarth became useful to Sir James Thornhill.
This last, a worthy, somewhat pompous, but industrious
magnifico of the moment, a Covent Garden Caravaggio
and cross between Raphael Mengs and the Groom-
porter, had wit enough to discern the young designer and
graver's capacity, and condescended to patronize him.
There is reason to believe that he employed William to
assist in the production of his roomy works. When
ceilings and domes were to be painted at two guineas
the Flemish ell, it is not likely that Royal Sergeant-
painters and knights of the shire for Melcombe Regis
could afford or would vouchsafe to cover with pigments
and with their own courtly hands the whole of the
required area. The vulgar, of course, imagined that the
painter did all ; that Thornhill lay for ever stretched on
a mattress, swinging in a basket three hundred feet
high in the empyrean of Wren's dome, daubing away
at his immense Peters and Pauls, or else stepping
backwards to the edge of a crazy platform to contemplate
the work he had done, and being within an ace of
toppling over to inevitable crash of death beneath, when
an astute colour-grinder saved his beloved master by
flinging a brush at Paul's great toe—cruel to be kind,
and so causing the artist, in indignant apprehension of
injury to his beloved saint, to rush forward, saving his own
life and the toe likewise. A pretty parallel to this story is
in that of the little boy in the Greek epigram who has
crawled to the very edge of a precipice, and is attracted
from his danger by the sight of his mother's breast. A
neat little anecdote, but—it is somewhat musty. It is a

myth, I fear. The vulgar love such terse traditions.
Zeuxis refusing to sell his pictures, because no sum of
money was sufficient to buy them, and imitating fruit
so nicely that the birds came and pecked at it ; Parrha-
sius cozening Zeuxis into the belief that his simulated
curtain was real, and crucifying a bondman (the wretch !)
that he might transfer his contortions to canvas ; Apelles
inducing a horse to neigh in recognition of the steed he
had drawn ; Amurath teaching a French ¦painter how
properly to design the contracted muscles of the neck
when the head is severed from the body by causing a
slave to be decapitated in his presence ; Correggio
receiving the price of his master-work in farthings, or
some vile copper Italian coinage, and dying under the
weight of the sack in which he was carrying the sordid
wage home ; Cimabue ruddling the fleeces of his lambs
with saintly triptychs, and the late Mr. Fuseli eating raw
pork-chops for supper in order to design the " Night-
mare," more to the life : all these are *ben trovati,—ma
non son veri,* I suspect.

Thornhill had not all his domes and ceilings and
staircases to himself. When Augustus found Rome of
brick and left it of marble, he did not execute all the
quarrying and chiselling with his own imperial hands.
In 1727, the painter M.P. for Melcombe Regis was at
the high tide of celebrity. Many of the Flemish ells
were covered by assistants. Here, I fancy, Van Shacka-
back of Little Britain, and sometime of Ghent in the Low
Countries, was dexterous at war and art trophies, lyres,
kettle-drums, laurel wreaths, bass-viols, and S. P. Q. R.s,
charmingly heaped up on a solid basis of cloud. Then
little Vanderscamp, who had even been employed about

the great king's alcoves at Versailles, was wondrous
cunning at the confection of those same purple and
cream-coloured vapours.   Lean Monsieur Carogne from
Paris excelled in drapery ; Gianbattista Ravioli, ex-
history painter to the Seigniory of Venice, but vehemently
suspected of having been a galley-slave in the Venetian
arsenal, was unrivalled in flying Cupids.   All these
foreign aides-de-camp sprawled on their mattresses and
made their fancy's children to sprawl ; goodman Thornhill
superintending, touching up now and then, blaming,
praising, pooh-poohing, talking of the gusto, taking
snuff, then putting on his majestic wig and his grand
laced hat, and departing in a serene manner in his
coach to St. James's or the House, thinking perhaps
of one Rafaelle who painted the *loggie* and *stanze*
of the Vatican, and of what a clever fellow he, James
Thornhill, was.

To him presently entered young Hogarth.   The
indulgence of William's own caustic whim had served
an end he may not have recked of.   He had contrived
to pay Thornhill the most acceptable compliment that
can be paid to a vain, shallow, pompous man.   He had
lampooned and degraded his rival.   He had pilloried
Kent in the parody of the wretched St. Clement Danes'
altar-piece, and had had a fling at him, besides, in
Burlington Gate, where, in sly ridicule of the earl's
infatuation for this Figaro of art, Kent's effigy is placed
on a pinnacle above the statues of Rafaelle and Michael
Angelo.   It is a capital thing to have a friend in court
with a sharp tongue, or better still, with a sharp pen or
pencil, who will defend you, and satirize your enemies.
The watch-dog Tearem at home, to defend the treasure-

chest, is all very well in his way; but the wealthy worldling should also entertain Snarler, the bull-terrier, to bite and snap at people's heels. Not that for one moment I would insinuate that Hogarth strove at all unworthily to toady or to curry favour with Sir James Thornhill. The sturdiness and independence of the former are visible in his very first etching. The acorn does not grow up to be a parasite. But Hogarth's poignant humour happened to tally with the knight's little malices. Hogarth, there is reason to assume, believed in Thornhill more than he believed in Kent. The first, at least, could work, was a fair draughtsman, and a not contemptible painter, albeit his colour was garish, his conception preposterous, his execution loaded and heavy. He showed at all events a genuine interest in, and love for that art, in which he might not himself have excelled. Kent was a sheer meretricious impostor and art-manufacturing quack, and Hogarth was aware of him at once, and so scarified him. Moreover, a young man can scarcely—till his wisdom-teeth be cut —avoid drifting temporarily into some clique or another. Cibber must have had his admirers, who mauled Pope prettily among themselves; and moreover, Sir James Thornhill, knight, sergeant painter, and M.P., had a DAUGHTER—one mistress Jane :—but I am forestalling matters again.

Although it is difficult to imagine anything more confused, misunderstood, and hampered with rags and tatters of ignorance, or—worse than ignorance—false taste, than was English Art in 1727, Cimmerian darkness did not wholly reign. There were men alive who had heard their fathers tell of the glories of Charles the

First's gallery at Whitehall; there were some princely English nobles, then as now, patrons and collectors; there were treasures of art in England, although no Waagen, no Jameson, had arisen to describe them, and there were amateurs to appreciate those treasures. The young peer who went the grand tour took something else abroad with him besides a negro-boy, a tipsy chaplain, and a pug-dog. He brought other things home beyond a broken-nosed busto, a rusted medal, a receipt for cooking *risotto* and the portrait of a Roman beggar and a Venetian *corteggiana*. He frequently acquired exquisite gems of painting and statuary abroad, and on his return formed a noble gallery of art. It is unfortunately true that his lordship sometimes played deep at "White's" or the "Young Man's," and, losing all, was compelled to send his pictures to the auction room; but even then his treasures were disseminated, and wise and tasteful men were the purchasers. To their credit, the few celebrated artists then possessed by our country were assiduous gatherers in this field. Sir Godfrey Kneller collected Vandykes. Richardson the elder, a pleasing painter, whose daughter married Hudson, Sir Joshua Reynolds's master, left Rafaelle and Andrea del Sarto drawings, worth a large sum.* Jervas, Pope's

---

* Richardson, senior, was a pupil of Charles the Second's Riley. He was born in 1666, was apprenticed to a scrivener, and at twenty turned painter. In 1734, he edited an edition of *Paradise Lost*, with notes. He was not a highly educated man, but had given his son a university training; and, once letting fall the unfortunate expression, that "he looked at classical literature through his son," remorseless Hogarth drew Richardson, junior, impaled with a telescope, the sire peeping through at a copy of Virgil. But Richardson seems to have been an honest, kindly-hearted man; and William Hogarth, as in every case where he had not a downright rogue to deal with,

friend, and by that polished, partial man artistically much overrated, being at the best but a weak, diaphanous, grimacing enlarger of fans and firescreens, became rich enough to form a handsome cabinet of paintings, drawings, and engravings. We are apt to bear much too hardly on. the patron-lords and gentlemen of the eighteenth century. Many were munificent, enlightened, and accomplished ; but we devour the piquant satires on Timon and Curio and Bubo, and have patron and insolence, patron and ignorance, patron and neglect, patron and gaol, too glibly at our tongue's end. Is it not to be wished that thinking people should bear *this* in mind : that not only were there strong men who lived *before* Agamemnon, but that there were strong men who lived *besides* Agamemnon—his contemporaries, in fine, to whom posterity has not been generous, not even just, and whose strength has been forgotten ?

.The earliest known picture of William Hogarth is one called the *Wanstead Assembly*, long, and by a ridiculous blunder, corrupted into " Wandsworth." The

---

repented of his severity, cancelled the copies of his squib, and destroyed the plate. Richardson was quite a Don in the Art world. * He died in 1745, and two years afterwards his collections were sold. The sale lasted eighteen days. The drawings fetched 2,060*l.* ; the pictures, 700*l.* Richardson's son, to all appearances, might have served very well as a sample of those monstrous jackasses that the South Sea Bubbler proposed to import from Spain. He declared himself " a connoisseur, and nothing but a connoisseur," and babbled and scribbled much balderdash in Italianized English. He was not alone. Pope even proposed to found a science of "picture tasting," and to call it "connoissance." In our days the science has been christened "fudge." I have seen the portrait of Richardson the elder, in whose features some one has said that " the good sense of the nation is characterized ;" but if this dictum be true, the most sensible-looking man in England must have been a foolish fat scullion.

term "Assembly" was a little bit of art-slang. A
portrait being a portrait, and a "conversation" a group
of persons, generally belonging to one family; by an
"assembly" was understood a kind of pictorial rent-roll,
or domestic "achievement," representing the lord, or the
squire, the ladies and children, the secretaries, chaplains,
pensioned poets, led-captains, body-flatterers, hangers-
on, needy clients, lick-trenchers, and scrape-plates, the
governesses and tutors, the tenants, the lacqueys, the
black-boys, the monkeys, and the lapdogs: *tutta la
baracca* in fact. In the *Wanstead Assembly* was a
portrait of the first Earl Tylney, and many of his vassals
and dependants; and shortly after the completion of the
picture, Mitchell, for whose opera of *The Highland Clans*
Hogarth designed a frontispiece, complimented the
artist on his performance in smooth couplets :—

> Large families obey your hand,
> Assemblies rise at your command.

It was William's frequent fortune during life to be much
celebrated in verse. Swift, you know, apostrophized him
as "hum'rous Hogart;" Mitchell, as we have seen, lauds
his "families" and "assemblies." Shortly afterwards,
the tender and graceful Vincent Bourne, who wrote the
Jackdaw, and whose innocent memory, as "Vinny
Bourne," is yet cherished in Westminster School, where
he was junior master, addressed the painter in Latin
"hendecasyllables." Hoadley, chancellor and bishop,
spurred a clumsy Pegasus to paraphrase his pictures in
verse. Churchill, when he was old, tried to stab him
with an epistle; David Garrick and Samuel Johnson
competed for the honour of writing his epitaph.

Between 1727 and 1730, Hogarth appears to have

painted dozens of single portraits, "conversations," and "assemblies." In the list he himself scheduled are to be noticed "four figures for Mr. Wood" (1728); "six figures for Mr. Cock" (1728); "an assembly of twenty-five figures for my Lord Castlemaine" (1729); "five for the Duke of Montagu;" nine for Mr. Vernon, four for Mr. Wood, and so forth. The prices paid for "assemblies" appear to have fluctuated between ten and thirty guineas. The oddest, and nearly the earliest commission he received for a portrait was in 1726, when several of the eminent surgeons of the day subscribed their guinea a-piece for him to compose a burlesque "conversation" of Mary Tofts, the infamous rabbit-breeding impostor of Godalming, and St. André, chirurgeon to the king's household, a highly successful and most impudent quack, who had made himself very busy in the scandalous hoax, and pretended to believe in Tofts. For the story that Hogarth made a drawing of Jack Sheppard in Newgate (1724), at the time when Sir James painted the robber's half-length in oils—the imaginary scene is admirably etched by George Cruikshank, in one of his illustrations to Mr. Ainsworth's strange novel—there does not seem any foundation. W. H. certainly painted Sarah Malcolm, the murderess, in her cell, in 1733; and from that well-known and authenticated fact some persons may have jumped at the conclusion that he was limner in ordinary to the Old Bailey.

I dwelt persistently in the preceding section of these essays upon the scenes and characters, the vices and follies, the humours and eccentricities, the beauties and uglinesses, that Hogarth must have seen in his young manhood, and asked and thought about, and which

must have sunk into his mind and taken root there.
Satirists can owe but little to inspiration. They can
move the world with the lever of wit, but they must have
a fulcrum of fact. Their philosophy is properly of the
inductive order. Without facts, facts to reason upon,
their arguments would be tedious and pointless. Wherein
lies the force or direction of satirizing that Chinese
mandarin whom you never saw—that Zulu Kaffir who
never came out of his kraal but once, and then to steal
a cow? It was Hogarth's faculty to catch the manners
living as they rose: it was his province to watch their
rising, and to walk abroad, an early bird, to pick up the
worms of knavery and vice, to range the ample field, and
see what the open and what the covert yielded. From
twenty to thirty the social philosopher must OBSERVE.
If he grovel in the mud even, he must observe and take
stock of the humane passer-by who stoops to pick him
up. After thirty he had better go into his study, turn
on his lamp, and turn out the contents of his mind's
commonplace book upon paper. This is the only valid
excuse for what is termed, after a Frenchman's Quartier-
Latin-argot phrase, "Bohemianism:" the only excuse for
Fielding's Govent Garden escapades, for Callot's gipsy
flights, for Shakspeare's deer-stealing. Young Diogenes
the cynic is offensive and reprehensible, but he is no
monstrosity. He is going to the deuce, but he may
come back again. I will pardon him his tub, his dingy
body-linen, his nails bordered sable; but the tub-career
should have its term, and Diogenes should go and wash,
and if he can afford it, wear fine linen with a purple
hem thereunto, as Plato did. It is pleasanter to walk in
the groves of Academe, than to skulk about the purlieus

of the Mint. Besides, Bohemianism has its pains as well
as its pleasures, and Fortune delights in disciplining with
a scourge of scorpions those whom she destines to be
great men : *Alla gioventù molto si perdona.* Cæsar was
snatched from the stews of Rome to conquer the world.
But for the middle-aged Bohemian—the old, ragged,
uncleanly, shameful Diogenes—there is no hope and no
excuse.

In that which I daresay you thought a mere digres-
sion, I strove my best to guide you through the labyrinthine London, which Hogarth must have threaded time
after time before he could sit down, pencil or graver in
hand, and say, " This is ' Tom King's coffee-house,' this
is a ' modern midnight conversation,' this is the ' progress
of a rake,' and this the ' career of a courtesan.' I have
seen these things, and I know them to be true."* Nor in
the least do I wish to convey that in ranging the streets
and beating the town, Hogarth had any fixed notions of
collecting materials for future melodramas and satires.
Eminently to be distrusted are those persons who,
when they should be better employed, prowl about
the tents of Kedar, and pry into the cave of Adullam,
pleading their desire to " see life," and to "pick up
character." They are generally blind as bats to all
living, breathing life ; and the only character they pick
up is a bad one for themselves. I apprehend that
Hogarth just took life as it came ; only the Light was
in him to see and to comprehend. A right moral feeling,
an intuitive hatred of wicked and cruel things, guided

* " *J'ai vu les mœurs de mon temps, et j'ai publié ces lettres.*"—J. J. ROUS-
SEAU : *La Nouvelle Héloise.*

and strengthened him. Amid the loose life of a loose age, the orgies at Moll King's and Mother Douglass's might have been frolics *at the time* to him, and only frolics. A fight in a night-cellar was to him precisely as the yellow primrose was to Peter Bell: a yellow primrose, and nothing more. He was to be afterwards empowered and commanded to turn his youthful follies to wise ends, and to lash the vices which he had once tolerated by his presence.

The philosophic prelude to his work was undoubtedly his town wanderings, 1720-30. The great manipulative skill, the grace of drawing visible, when taken in comparison with the comic excrescences in the *Hudibras*— the brilliance and harmony of colour he manifested in the *Progresses* and the *Marriage à la Mode*—have yet to be accounted for. A lad does not step at once from the engraving bench to the easel, and handle the hog's-hair brush with the same skill as he wields the burin and the etching point. The Hogarthian transition from the first to the second of these stages is the more remarkable when it is remembered that, although bred an engraver, and although always quick, dexterous, and vigorous with the sharp needle and the trenchant blade, he could never thoroughly master that clear, harmonious, full-bodied stroke in which the French engravers excelled, in which Hogarth's own assistants in after life (Ravenet, Scotin, and Grignion) surpassed him, but which was afterwards, to the pride and glory of English chalcography, to be brought to perfection by Woollett and Strange. Yet Hogarth the engraver seemed in 1730 to change with pantomimic rapidity into Hogarth the painter. The matter of his pictures may often be questionable; the manner leaves scarcely anything for exceptional criticism. His colour is deliciously pure and fresh; he never loads, never spatters paint about with his palette knife; never lays tint over tint till a figure has as many vests as the gravedigger in *Hamlet*. Whites, grays, carnations *stand* in his pictures and defy time; no uncertain glazings have changed his foregrounds into smears and streaks and stains. He was great at Manchester in 1857; great at the British Institution in 1814, when not less than fifty of his works were exhibited, great in body, richness, transparency; he is great, nay prodigious, in the English section of the National Gallery, where gorgeous Sir Joshua, alas! runs and welters and turns into adipocere; and Gainsborough (in his portraits —his landscapes are as rich as ever)—grows pallid and threadbare, and Turner's suns are grimed, and even Wilkie cracks and tesselates. I think Hogarth came fresh, assured and decided, to his picture-painting work, from a kind of second apprenticeship under Thornhill, and from compassing the "conversations" and "assemblies." The historico-allegorico-mural decorations were a species of scene-painting; they involved broad and decisive treatment. The hand learnt perforce to strike lines and mark-in muscles at once. The maul-stick could seldom be used; the fluttering wrist, the nerveless grasp were fatal: the eye could not be performing a perpetual goose-step between canvas and model. Look at Salvator, at Loutherbourg, at Stanfield, and Roberts, to show what good a scene-painting noviciate can do in teaching an artist to paint in one handling, *à la brochette* as it were. Who can fancy a Madonna when one fancies half-a-dozen other Madonnas simpering beneath the built-up tints? Next, Hogarth went to his portraits. They were a course of physiognomy invaluable to him —of fair faces, stern faces, sensual, stupid, hideous and pretty little baby faces. From the exigencies of the "conversations" and "assemblies" he learnt composition, and the treatment of accessories; learnt to paint four-and-twenty fiddlers, not "all of a row," but disposed in ellipse or in pyramid-form. The perception of female beauty, and the power of expressing it, were his by birthright, by heaven's kindness; I am despondent only at his animals, which are almost invariably impossible deformities.*

The Duke of Montagu and my Lord Castlemaine having ordered "conversations" from Hogarth, there was of course but one thing necessary to put the seal to his artistic reputation. That thing, so at least the patron may have thought, was the patronage of the eminent Morris. Morris is quite snuffed out now—evaporated even as the carbonic acid gas from yesterday's flask of champagne; but in 1727 he was a somewhat notable person. He was a fashionable upholsterer in Pall Mall,

---

* Beautiful female faces in Hogarth's plates and pictures.—Among others, the bride-elect with handkerchief passed through her wedding-ring; the countess kneeling to her dying lord (in the *Marriage*); the charming wife mending the galligaskins in the *Distressed Poet;* the poor wretch whom the taskmaster is about to strike with a cane, in the Bridewell scene of the *Rake's Progress;* the milkmaid, in the *Enraged Musician;* the blooming English girl (for she is no more an Egyptian than you or I) in "*Pharaoh's Daughter;*" the pure soul who sympathises with the mad spendthrift, in the Bedlam scene of the *Rake's Progress;* the hooped belle who is chucking the little black boy under the chin, in the *Taste in High Life*—a priceless performance, and one that should be re-engraved in this age, as a satire against exaggerated crinoline. Lord Charlemont's famous picture, *Virtue in Danger*, I have not seen.

and not only sold, but manufactured, those tapestry arras hangings which, paper-staining being in embryo, were still conspicuous ornaments of the walls of palaces, the nobility's saloons. Morris kept a shop much frequented by the noble tribes, at the sign of the "Golden Ball" in Pall Mall. There seems to have been a plethora of Golden Balls in London about this time, just as though all the Lombards had quarrelled among themselves, and set up in business each man for himself, with no connection with the golden ball over the way. In 1727, and for a century and a half before, the best and most celebrated painters were employed to execute designs for tapestry. You know who drew for the Flemish weavers that immortal dozen of cartoons, seven of which are at Hampton Court, and which have been recently so wonderfully photographed. Rubens and Vandyke, the stately Lebrun, and the meek Lesueur, made designs also for these woven pictures. There are penitent thieves and jesting Pilates from Hans Holbein's inspiration in many faded hangings. Thornhill had been himself commissioned by Queen Anne to make sketches for a set of tapestry hangings emblematic of the union between England and Scotland. And does not the fabric of the Gobelins yet flourish? Did not Napoleon the Third vouchsafe the gift of a magnificent piece of tapisserie to one of our West-End clubs? Morris, the upholsterer, had many of the "first foreign hands" in his employ; but, being a Briton, bethought himself magnanimously to encourage real native British talent. My lord duke had employed Hogarth; Morris likewise determined on giving a commission to the rising artist. He sought out William, conferred with him, explained his wishes, and

a solemn contract was entered between William Hogarth
for the first part, and Joshua Morris for the second, in
which the former covenanted to furnish the latter with
a design on canvas of the *Element of Earth*, to be afterwards worked in tapestry.   The painter squared his
canvas and set to work ; but when the design was completed Morris flatly refused to pay the thirty pounds
agreed upon as remuneration. It seems that the timorous
tradesman, who must clearly have possessed a large
admixture of the "element of earth" in his composition,
had been informed by some good-natured friend of
Hogarth that the tapestry-designer was no painter, but
a "low engraver." Horror ! To think of a mean wretch
who had earned his livelihood by flourishing initials on
flagons and cutting plates in *taille douce* for the booksellers, presuming to compete with the flourishing
foreigners employed by the eminent and ineffable Morris !
'Twas as though some destitute index-maker of the Hop
Gardens, some starved ballad-monger of Lewkner's
Lane, had seduced Mr. Jacob Tonson into giving him
an order for a translation of the *Æneid* into heroic verse.
Amazed and terrified, the deceived Joshua Morris rushed
to Hogarth's painting-room and accused him of mis-
representation, fraud, covin, and other crimes.   How
would ever my lord duke and her ladyship—perhaps
Madam Schuylenburg-Kendal herself—tolerate tapestry
in their apartments designed by a base churl, the quondam apprentice of a silversmith in Cranbourn Alley, the
brother of two misguided young women who kept a
slop-shop ?   Hogarth coolly stated that he should hold
the upholsterer to his bargain.   He admitted that the
Element of Earth was a "bold undertaking," but

expressed an opinion that he should "get through it well enough." He brought the thing to a termination ; and it was, I daresay, sufficiently of the earth earthy. Joshua resolutely withheld payment. No copper-scratcher should defraud him of thirty pounds. The young man, formerly of Little Cranbourn Alley, was not to be trifled with. If Morris had been a lord and had refused (as one of Hogarth's sitters absolutely did) to pay for his portrait, on the ground that it wasn't like him, the artist might have taken a satirical revenge, and threatened to add tails to all the figures in the *Element of Earth*, and send the canvas to Mr. Hare, the wild-beast-man, as a showcloth. But the Pall Mall uphol-sterer was a tradesman, and Hogarth, all artist as he knew himself to be, was a tradesman too. So he went to his lawyer's, and sued Morris for the thirty pounds, " painter's work done." Bail was given and justified, and on the 28th of May, 1728, the great cause of Hogarth against Morris came on *in communi banco*, before the chief justice in Eyre. The defendant pleaded *non assumpsit*. Issue was joined, and the gentlemen of the long-robe went to work. For the defendant, the alleged fraudulent substitution of an engraver for a painter was urged. The eminence of Morris's tapestry and uphol-stery was adduced. It was sworn to that he employed " some of the finest hands in Europe." Bernard Dorridor, De Friend, Phillips, Danten, and Pajou, " some of the finest hands," appeared in the witness-box and deposed to what first-rate fellows they all were, and to William Hogarth being a mere mechanic, the last of the lowest, so to speak. But the ready painter was not without friends. He subpœnaed more of the " finest hands."

Up came King, Vanderbank, the opera scene-painter, Laguerre, son and successor to Charles the Second's Laguerre, and Verrio's partner, and the serene Thornhill himself: who, I doubt it not, was bidden by my lord to sit on the bench, was oracular in his evidence as to the young man's competency, smiled on the chief justice, and revolved in his majestic mind the possibility of the Lords of the Treasury giving him a commission (had they the power) to paint the walls and ceilings of all the courts of justice with allegories of Themis, Draco, Solon, Justinian, and Coke upon Lyttleton, to be paid for out of the suitors' fee fund. We know now how tawdry and trashy these painted allegories were ; but Thornhill and Laguerre were really the most reliable authorities to be consulted as to the standard of excellence then accepted in such performances. The verdict very righteously went against the defendant, whose plea was manifestly bad, and Joshua Morris was cast in thirty pounds. I delight to fancy that the successful party straightway adjourned to the Philazers' Coffee-house, in Old Palace Yard, and there, after a slight refection of hung beef and Burton ale, betook themselves to steady potations of Lisbon wine in magnums — there were prohibitive duties on claret—until each man began to see allegories of his own, in which Bacchus was the capital figure. I delight to fancy that the Anglo-Frenchman Laguerre clapped Hogarth on the back, and told him that he was " von clevare fellow," and that Sir James shook his young friend by the hand, enjoined him to cultivate a true and proper gusto, and bade him Godspeed. Majestic man ! he little thought that when his own celebrity had vanished, or was but as the shadow of the shadow of smoke, his young friend was to be famous to the nations and the glory of his countrymen.*

---

* The damages and costs must have amounted to a round sum ; but it is to me marvellous that in those days of legal chicanery the action should have been so brief, and so conclusively decided. Those were the days when, if you owed any one forty shillings, you were served with writs charging you with having committed a certain trespass, to wit at Brentford, being in the company of Job Doe (not always *John* Doe) ; with "that having no settled abode, you had been lurking and wandering about as a vagabond ;" with that (this was in the Exchequer) "out of deep hatred and malice to the body politic, you had kept our sovereign lord the king from being seised of a certain sum, to wit, two millions of money, for which it was desirable to escheat the sum of forty shillings towards the use of our sovereign and suffer- ing lord aforesaid." In the declaration, it was set forth, that you had gone with sticks and staves, and assaulted and wounded divers people ; and the damages were laid at 10,000*l.*, of which the plaintiff was reasonable enough to claim only the moderate sum of forty shillings. The capias took you at once for any sum exceeding 2*l.*, and you had to find and justify bail, if you did not wish to pine in a spunging-house, or rot in the Fleet. These were the days, not quite five thousand, and some of them not quite one hundred and fifty years ago, when criminal indictments were drawn in Latin, and Norman-French was an important part of legal education (see Pope and Swift's *Miscellanies*, "Stradling *versus* Styles"), and prisoners were brought up on habeas laden with chains. See Layer's case in the *State Trials*, Lord Campbell's agreeable condensation in the *Lives of the Chief Justices*. Layer was a barrister, a man of birth and education, but was implicated in an abortive Jacobite plot. His chains were of such dreadful weight, that he could sleep only on his back. He was suffering from an internal complaint, and pathetically appealed to Pratt, C.J., who was suffering from a similar ailment, to order his irons to be taken off, were it only on the ground of common sympathy. The gentleman gaoler of the Tower, who stood by him on the floor of the court while he made this application, was humanely employed in holding up the captive's fetters to ease him, partially, of his dreadful burden. Prisoner's counsel urged that the indignity of chains was unknown to his "Majesty's prisoners in the Tower ;" that the gentleman gaoler and the warders did not know how to set about the hangman's office of shackling captives ; that there were no fetters in the Tower beyond the "Scavenger's Daughter," and the Spanish Armada relics, and that they had been obliged to procure fetters from Newgate. But Pratt, C.J., was inexorable. He was a stanch Whig ; and so, civilly but sternly, remanded

For all the handshakings and libations of Lisbon,
Sir James was to live to be very angry with his young
friend, although the quarrel was to last but a little
while. Hogarth had looked upon Thornhill's daughter
Jane, and she was fair, and regarded him, too, with not
unfavourable eyes. He who has gained a lawsuit should
surely be successful in love. Meanwhile—I don't think
he was much given to sighing or dying—he went on
painting, in spite of all the Morrises in upholsterydom.
Poor Joshua himself came to grief. He seems to have
been bankrupt ; and on the 15th of May, 1729, the
auctioneer knocked down to the highest bidder all the
choice stock of tapestry in Pall Mall. Hogarth's *Element of Earth* may have been " Lot 90 ;" but one rather
inclines to surmise that Morris slashed the fatal canvas
with vindictive scissors to shreds and mippets the day
his lawyer's bill came in.

To record the tremendous success of that *Newgate
Pastoral*, the suggestion of the first idea of which lies
between Swift, Pope, Arbuthnot, and Gay, does not
come within my province. The history of the *Beggar's
Opera*, that made " Rich Gay and Gay Rich," is too well
known to bear repetition. Hogarth, however, has left

---

the prisoner, all ironed as he was, to the Tower.   Christopher Layer was
soon afterwards put out of his misery by being hanged, drawn, and quar-
tered ; but he was much loved by the people, and his head had not been
long on Temple Bar when it was carried off as a relic.   It is almost impossible to realize this cool, civil, legal savagery, in the era so closely following
Anna Augusta's silver age.   Sir Walter Scott was in evidently an analogous
bewilderment of horror when he described the execution of Feargus McIvor :
a fiction certainly, but with its dreadful parallels of reality in the doom of
Colonel Towneley, Jemmy Dawson, Dr. Cameron, and scores more unfortunate and misguided gentlemen who suffered the horrible sentence of the
law of high treason at Carlisle, at Tyburn, or on Kennington Common.

his mark on the famous operatic score. For Rich, the Covent Garden manager, he painted (1729) a picture of the prison scene in which Lucy and Polly are wrangling over Macheath, of which several replicas in oil, some slightly varied, as well as engravings, were afterwards executed. Portraits of many of the great personages of the day are introduced in open boxes *on* the stage. Macheath was a portrait of the comedian Walker ; and the Polly was the beauteous Lavinia Fenton, the handsome, kindly, true-hearted actress with whom the Duke of Bolton, to the amusement and amazement of the town, fell in love, and fairly ran away. The Duchess of Bolton was then still alive, and lived for many years afterwards ; and poor Polly had to suffer some part of the penalty which falls on those with whom dukes elope ; but at the duchess's death, her lord showed that he was not of Mrs. Peachum's opinion, that "'tis marriage makes the blemish," and right nobly elevated Polly to the peerage. She lived long and happily with him, survived him, and died late in the last century, very old, and beloved, and honoured for her modesty, charity, and piety. "The lovely young Lavinia once had friends," writes Thomson in the *Seasons ;* but our Lavinia lost not her friends to her dying day. If Tenison, and Atterbury, and Sherlock had nothing to say against Eleanor Gwyn, let us trust that the severest moralist could find charitable words wherewith to speak of Lavinia, Duchess of Bolton.*

A sterner subject, the prologue to a dismal drama of human life, was now to engross the pencil of this painter,

---

* Hogarth painted a beautiful separate portrait of her—a loving, trustful face, and *such* lips—which has been engraved in mezzotint. I should properly have added it to my catalogue of the Hogarthian Beauties.

who was now making his presence known and felt among
his contemporaries. I speak of the strange solemn
picture of the *Committee of the House of Commons* taking
evidence of the enormities wreaked on the wretched
prisoners in the Fleet by Huggins and Bambridge. Let
us drag these mouldering scoundrels from their dis-
honoured graves, and hang them up here on Cornhill,
for all the world to gaze at, even as the government of
the Restoration (but with less reason) hung the carcases
of Cromwell and Bradshaw on Tyburn gibbet. Huggins
—save the mark !—was of gentle birth, and wrote himself
" Armiger." He had bought the patent of the warden-
ship of the Fleet from a great court lord, and when the
trade of torturing began, through usance, to tend towards
satiety, he sold his right to one Bambridge, a twin demon.
The atrocities committed by the pair may very rapidly
be glanced at. Huggins's chief delight was to starve
his prisoners, unless they were rich enough to bribe him.
Bambridge's genius lay more towards confining his
victims, charged with fetters, in underground dungeons,
with the occasional recreation of attempting to pistol
and stab them. The moneyed debtors both rascals
smiled upon. Smugglers were let out through a yard
in which dogs were kept ; ran their cargoes ; defrauded
the revenue, and came back to " college." One, who
owed 10,000*l.* to the crown, was permitted to make his
escape altogether. A certain T. Dumay went several
times to France, being all the time in the " custody," as
the sham was facetiously termed, of the Warden of the
Fleet. What was such a fraud in an age when the
highest legal authorities (who would not take the fetters
off Christopher Layer) gravely doubted whether the rules

of the King's Bench might not extend to Bombay, in the East Indies?* These surreptitiously enlarged prisoners were called "pigeons." They had bill transactions with the tipstaves; they drew on Huggins, and then pleaded their insolvency. On the other hand, the poor debtors were very differently treated. A broken-down baronet, Sir William Rich, on refusing to pay the "baronet's fee," or "garnish," of five pounds, was heavily fettered, kept for months in a species of subterranean dog-kennel; the vivacious Bambridge sometimes enlivening his captivity by threatening to run a red-hot poker through his body. This cheerful philanthropist, who was wont to range about the prison with a select gang of turnkeys, armed with halberts and firelocks, ordered one of his myrmidons to fire on "Captain Mackpheadris"—(what a name for a captain in difficulties! Lieutenant Lismahago is nothing to it). As, however, even these callous bravoes hesitated to obey so savage a behest, and as there was absolutely nothing to be squeezed in the way of garnish out of this lackpenny Captain Mackpheadris, Bambridge locked the poor wretch out of his room, and turned him out to starve in an open yard called the "Bare." Here Mack, who was seemingly an old campaigner, built himself, out of broken tiles and other rubbish, a little hovel in an angle of the wall, just as the evicted Irish peasantry in famine and fever times were wont to build little kraals of turf-sods and wattles over dying men in ditches; but Bambridge soon heard of the bivouac, and ordered it to be pulled down. J. Mendez Sola, a Portuguese, was by

---

* A similar doubt—was it not by Lord Ellenborough?—has been expressed within our own times.

the same kind guardian fettered with a hundredweight of iron, and incarcerated in a deadhouse, *with dead people in it*, moreover ! Others languished in dens called " Julius Cæsar's chapel," the upper and lower "Ease," and the " Lyon's Den," where they were stapled to the floor. Attached to the prison itself was an auxiliary inferno in the shape of a spunging-house kept by Corbett, a creature of Bambridge. The orthodox process seemed to be, first to fleece you in the spunging-house and then to flay you alive in the gaol. Of course, Mr. Bambridge went snacks with Mr. Corbett. Very few scruples were felt in getting fish for this net. In one flagrant instance, a total stranger was seized as he was giving charity at the grate for poor prisoners, dragged into Corbett's, and only released on paying "garnish," and undertaking not to institute any proceedings against his kidnappers. When a prisoner had money to pay the debt for which he had been arrested, he often lay months longer in hold for his "fees." The caption fee was 5*l.* 16*s.* 4*d.* ; the " Philazer "—whoever that functionary may have been, but his was a patent place in the Exchequer—the judge's clerk, the tipstaves, the warden, all claimed their fees. Fees had to be paid for the favour of lighter irons, and every fresh bird in the spunging-house cage paid his "footing," in the shape of a six-shilling bowl of punch. When—as from time to time, and to the credit of human nature, occurred—a person visited the gaol, " on behalf of an unknown lady," to discharge all claims against persons who lay in prison for their fees only, Bambridge often sequestered his prisoners till the messenger of mercy had departed. But he was always open to pecuniary conviction, and from the wife of one prisoner he took, as a bribe, forty guineas and a "toy," being the model of a "Chinese Jonque in amber set with silver," for which the poor woman had been offered eighty broadpieces. In these our days, Bambridge would have discounted bills, and given one-fourth cash, one-fourth wine, one-fourth camels' bridles, and one-fourth ivory frigates. When an Insolvent Act was passed, Bambridge demanded three guineas a piece from those desirous of availing themselves of the relief extended by the law; else he would not allow them to be "listed," or inserted in the schedule of insolvents. And by a stroke of perfectly infernal cunning this gaoler-devil hit upon a plan of preventing his victims from taking proceedings against him by taking proceedings against *them*. After some outrage of more than usual enormity, he would slip round to the Old Bailey and prefer a bill of indictment against the prisoners he had maltreated, for riot, or an attempt to break prison. He had always plenty of understrappers ready to swear for him; and the poor, penniless, friendless gaol-bird was glad to compromise with his tormentor by uncomplaining silence.*

---

* These horrors were not confined to the Fleet. The King's Bench and the Marshalsea were nearly as bad; and, in the former prison, gangs of drunken soldiers—what could the officers have been about?—were frequently introduced to coerce the unhappy inmates. The Bench and Marshalsea were excellent properties. The patent rights were purchased from the Earl of Radnor for 5,000*l.*, and there were some sixteen shareholders in the profits accruing from the gaol. Of the Marshalsea, evidence is given of the turnkeys holding a drinking bout in the lodge, and calling in a poor prisoner to "divert" them. On this miserable wretch they put an iron scull-cap and a pair of thumbscrews, and so tortured him for upwards of half-an-hour. Then, somewhat frightened, they gave him his discharge, as a *douceur;* but the miserable man fainted in the Borough High Street, and being carried into St. Thomas's Hospital, presently died there.

Already had these things been censured by highest
legal authorities ; at least the judges had occasionally
shaken their wise heads and declared the abuses in the
Fleet to be highly improper : " You may raise your walls
higher," quoth Lord King ; " but there must be no prison
within a prison." An excellent dictum if only acted
upon.   At last, the prisoners began to die of ill-usage,
of starvation and disease ; or rather, *it began to be known*
that they were so dying, and died every year of our
Lord.   A great public outcry arose.   Humane men
bestirred themselves.   The legislature was besieged with
petitions.   Parliamentary commissioners visited the gaol,
and a committee of the House of Commons sat to hear
those harrowing details of evidence of which I have
given you a summary.   Bambridge was removed from
his post ; but the *vindicte publique* was not appeased.
First, Huggins, the retired esquire, and Barnes, his
assistant, were tried at the Old Bailey for the murder
of Edward Arne, a prisoner.   Page, the hanging judge,
presided ; but from that stern fount there flowed waters
of mercy for the monster of the Fleet.   Owing chiefly
to his summing up, a special verdict was returned, and
Huggins and the minor villain were acquitted.   Huggins's
son was a well-to-do gentleman of Headley Park, Hants,
had a taste for the fine arts, translated *Ariosto*, and collected Hogarthian drawings !   It was as though Samson
should have collected miniatures of Louis the Sixteenth,
or Simon the cobbler statuettes of the poor little captive
Capet of the Temple.

Next, the coarser scoundrels, Bambridge and Corbett,
were tried for the murder of a Mr. Castell, who had been
thrust into Corbett's spunging-house while the small-pox

was raging there, and died.   Bambridge, too, was
acquitted through some legal quibble ; but the widow of
the murdered man had another quibble, by which she
hoped to obtain redress.   She retained the famous
casuist Lee, the sage who in a single action once pleaded
seventy-seven pleas.   She sued out an appeal of murder
against the warden and his man.   This involved the
"wager of battle," which you remember in the strange
Yorkshire case some forty years ago, and which was at
last put an end to by statute.   The appellee could either
fight the appellant *à la* dog of Montargis, or throw
himself on his country, *i. e.* submit to be tried again.
Bambridge and Corbett chose the latter course, were
again tried, and again escaped.   They were, however,
very near being torn to pieces by the populace.   Lord
Campbell says, I venture to think unjustly, that
Mrs. Castell was incited to the appeal by a "mobbish
confederation."*   Good heaven ! was anything but a
confederation of the feelings of common humanity necessary to incite all honest men to bring these wretches
to justice ?   I suppose that it was by a "mobbish confederation" that the villanous Austin, of Birmingham
gaol, was tried, and that after all his atrocities of gag-

---

* Did the poet Thomson, the kind-hearted, tender, pure-minded man,
belong to the "mobbish confederation ?"   Hear him in the *Seasons*, in
compliment to the commissioners for inquiring into the state of the gaols :—

> " Where sickness pines, where thirst and hunger burn,
> Ye sons of mercy, yet resume the search ;
> *Drag forth the legal monsters into light !*
> Wrench from their hands Oppression's iron rod,
> And make the cruel feel the pains they give."

It is slightly consolatory to be told by antiquary Oldys that Bambridge cut his
throat in 1749 ; but the ruffian should properly have swung as high as Haman.

ging, "jacketing," and cramming salt down his prisoners' throats, he, too, escaped with an almost nominal punishment. Lee, the casuist (he was afterwards Chief Justice), was so disgusted with the result of the trial, that he vowed he would never have aught to do with facts again, but henceforth would stick to law alone. I am not lawyer enough to know why the case against Bambridge and Corbett broke down ; I only know that these men were guilty of murder most foul and most unnatural, and that one of our most ancient legal maxims is explicit as to their culpability.*

A committee of gentlemen in large wigs, sitting round a table in a gloomy apartment, and examining witnesses likewise in wigs, is not a very inspiring theme for a painter ; but I have always considered Hogarth's rendering of the proceedings to be one of the most masterly of Hogarth's tableaux. The plate was a great favourite with Horace Walpole, who described with much discrimination the various emotions of pity, horror, and indignation on the countenances of the spectators ; the mutely eloquent testimony of the shackles and manacles on the table ; the pitiable appearance of the half-starved prisoner who is giving evidence ; and, especially, the Judas-like appearance of Bambridge (who was present), his yellow cheeks and livid lips, his fingers clutching at the button-holes in his coat, and his face advanced, "as if eager to lie." There was a large sale for the engraving taken from this picture, and Hogarth gained greatly in reputation from its production.

---

* "If a prisoner die through duresse of the gaoler, it is *murder in the gaoler*."—St. German's *Doctor and Student*. Why was this not quoted at Birmingham ?

He had need of reputation, and of money too. A very serious crisis in his life was approaching. He had found more favour in the eyes of Jane Thornhill. *"On n'épouse pas les filles de grande maison avec des coquilles de noix,"* writes a wise Frenchman, and William Hogarth's fortune might decidedly at this time have been comfortably " put into a wine-glass and covered over with a gooseberry leaf," as was suggested of the immortal Mr. Bob Sawyer's profits from his druggist's shop. Sir James Thornhill was a greater don in art than Sir Godfrey, or than Richardson, or Jervas. He hated Sir Godfrey, and strove to outshine him. If extent of area is to be taken as a test of ability, Thornhill certainly beat Kneller hollow. To a Lombard Street of allegory and fable in halls and on staircases the German could only show a china orange of portraiture. Thornhill was a gentleman. His father was poor enough ; but he was clearly descended from Ralph de Thornhill (12 Henry III. 1228).* When he became prosperous, he bought back the paternal acres, and built a grand house at Thornhill, hard by Weymouth. He had been a favourite with Queen Anne. He had succeeded Sir Christopher Wren in the representation of Melcombe Regis, his native place. His gains were enormous. Though he received but two guineas a yard for St. Paul's, and twenty-five shillings a yard for painting the

---

* Rev. James Dallaway, whose notes to Walpole's *Anecdotes* are very excellent. Mr. Wornum, the last editor of Walpole, annotated by Dallaway, puzzles me. He must be an accomplished art-scholar : is he not the Wornum of the Marlborough House School ? but he calls Swift's Legion Club the "Congenial Club," utterly ignoring Swift's ferocious text, an excerpt from which he quotes.

staircase of the South Sea House (with bubbles, or with an allegory of Mercury putting the world in his pocket ?), instead of 1,500*l.* which he demanded, he had a magnificent wage for painting the hall at Blenheim, and from the noted Styles, who is said to have spent 150,000*l.* in the embellishments of Moor Park, he received, after a law-suit and an arbitration, 4,000*l.* To be sure Lafosse got nearly 3,000*l.* for the staircase and saloons of Montagu House (the old British Museum). Look at the etching of Sir James Thornhill, by Worlidge. He is painting in an elaborately-laced coat with brocaded sleeves ; and his wig is as so many curds in a whey of horsehair : no one but a Don could have such a double chin.

With the daughter of this grandee of easeldom, this favourite of monarchs, this Greenwich and Hampton Court Velasquez, William Hogarth, painter, engraver, and philosopher, but as yet penniless, had the inconceivable impudence, not only to fall in love, but to run away. I rather think that Lady Thornhill connived at the surreptitious courtship, and was not inexorably angry when the stolen match took place ; but as for the knight, he would very probably just as soon have thought of Mars, Bacchus, Apollo and Virorum coming down from an allegorical staircase, and dancing a saraband to the tune of " Green Sleeves " on the north side of Covent Garden Piazza, as of his young *protégé* and humble friend Willy Hogarth presuming to court or to marry his daughter. Oh ! it is terrible to think of this rich man, this father of a disobedient Dinah, walking his studio all round, vowing vengeance against that rascally Villikins, and declaring that of his large fortune she shan't reap the benefit of one single pin !

Oh! cruel "parient," outraged papa, Lear of genteel life! He frets, he fumes, he dashes his wig to the ground. He remembers him, perchance, of sundry small moneys he has lent to Hogarth, and vows he will have him laid by the heels in a spunging-house ere the day be out. Send for a capias, send for a mittimus! Send for the foot-guards, the tipstaves, and the train-bands, for Jane Thornhill has levanted with William Hogarth!

They were married at old Paddington Church on the 23rd of March, 1729. Thus runs the parish register: "William Hogarth, Esq. and Jane Thornhill, of St. Paul's, Covent Garden." Marriage and hanging go together they say, and William and Jane went by Tyburn to have *their* noose adjusted. In the *Historical Chronicle* for 1729, the bridegroom is described as "an eminent designer and engraver;" but in Hogarth's own family Bible, a worn, squat, red-inked, interlined little volume, printed early in the reign of Charles the First, and now reverentially preserved by Mr. Graves, the eminent print-publisher of Pall Mall, there is a certain flyleaf, which I have seen, and which to me is of infinitely greater value than Historical Chronicle or Paddington Parish Register, for there, in the painter's own hand-writing, I read — " W. Hogarth married Sir James Thornhill's daughter, March 23rd, 1729."

Papa-in-law was in a fury, set his face and wig against the young couple, would not see them, would not give them any money, cast them out of the grand piazza mansion to starve, if they so chose, among the cabbage-stumps of the adjacent market. It behoved William to work hard. I don't think he ever resided with his wife in Cranbourn Alley. He had given that messuage up to his sisters. What agonies the member for Melcombe Regis, the scion of Henry the Third's Thornhills, must have endured at the thought of that abhorred "old frock-shop!" There is reason to believe that for some time previous to his marriage Hogarth had resided in Thornhill's own house, and had so found opportunities for his courtship of the knight's daughter. Of young Thornhill, Sir James's son, he was the intimate friend and comrade. Where he spent his honeymoon is doubtful; but it was either in 1729 or 1730 that he began to take lodgings at South Lambeth, and to form the acquaintance of Mr. Jonathan Tyers, the lessee of Vauxhall Gardens.

In the tranquillity and sobriety of a happy married life, Hogarth began for the first time deeply to philoso-phize. He had eaten his cake. He had sown his wild oats. He was to beat the town no more in mere indif-ference of carousal; he was to pluck the moralist's flower from the strange wild nettles he had handled. In this age have been found critics stupid and malevolent enough to accuse every author who writes with a purpose, and who endeavours to draw attention to social vices, of imposture and of hypocrisy. He should be content, these critics hold, to describe the things he sees; he is a humbug if he moralize upon them. It is not unlikely that the vicious Fribbles of Hogarth's time held similar opinions, and took Hogarth to be a reckless painter of riotous scenes, and who just infused sufficient morality into them " to make the thing go off." It was otherwise with him, I hope and believe. I am firmly convinced that the sin and shame of the evils he depicted were as deeply as they were vividly impressed on Hogarth's mind—that he was as zealous as any subscriber to a Refuge, a Reformatory, or a Home can be now, to abate a dreadful social evil ; that his hatred for the wickedness of dissolute men, his sympathy for women fallen and betrayed, his utter loathing for those wretched scandals to their sex, the women whose trade it is to decoy women, was intense and sincere. I do *not* believe in the sincerity of Fielding, who could grin and chuckle over the orgies of the Hundreds of Drury and the humours of the bagnio. I find even the gentle and pure-minded Addison simpering in the *Freeholder* about certain frequenters of Somerset House masquerades. But Hogarth's satire in the *Harlot's Progress* never makes you laugh. It makes you rather shudder and stagger, and turn pale. The six pictures which form this tragedy were painted immediately after his marriage. They were painted in the presence of a young, beautiful, and virtuous woman, who read her Bible, and loved her husband with unceasing tenderness ; and casting to the winds the mock morality and lip-virtue that fear to speak of the things depicted in this *Progress*, I say that no right-minded man or woman will be the worse for studying its phases.

Some time before Hogarth painted the *Harlot's Progress*, a hundred and thirty years ago, Edward Ward and Tom Brown had described in coarse, untranscribable, but yet graphic terms, the career of these unfortunates. The former, although a low-lived pottlepot at the best of times, makes some honest remarks concerning the barbarous treatment of the women in Bridewell.* "It's

---

* The clumsy police of the time seem to have entirely ignored the existence of unchaste women till they became riotous, were mixed up in

not the way to reform 'em," he says plainly. But Hogarth first told the whole truth, and nothing but the truth. He first told the story of a courtesan without either ribald jesting or sickly sentimentality; and he, much more than if he had been a royal duke mincingly handling trowel and mallet, laid the first stone of the Magdalen Hospital.

"*Ora,*" writes an appreciative Venetian biographer of Hogarth, "*conduce una bella dalla barca in cui nacque ad un albergo di Londra, da un magnifico palazzo in un lupanare, dal lupanare in prigione, dalla prigione all' ospitale,*

---

tavern brawls, had given offence to the rich rakes, or, especially, were discovered to be the mistresses of thieves and highwaymen. Then they were suddenly caught up, taken before a justice, and committed to Bridewell—either the *ergastolo* in Bridge Street, or the *presidio* in Tothill Fields—I take the former. Arrived there, they were kept till noon on board-day, Wednesday. Then they were arraigned before the honourable Board of Governors, the president with his hammer in his high-backed chair. The wretched Kate stands among the beadles clad in blue, at the lower end of the room, which is divided into two by folding doors. Then, the accusation being stated, the president cries, "How say you, gentlemen, shall Katherine Hackabout receive present punishment?" The suffrages are collected; they are generally against Kate, who is forthwith seized by the beadles, half unrobed, and receives the "civility of the house," *i. e.* the correction of stripes, which torture is continued (the junior beadle wielding the lash) till the president strikes his hammer on the table as a signal for execution to stop. "Knock! Sir Robert; oh, good Sir Robert, knock!" was a frequent entreaty of the women under punishment; and "Knock, knock!" was shouted after them in derision by the boys in the street, to intimate that they had been scourged in Bridewell. Being sufficiently whealed, Kate was handed over to the taskmaster, to be set to beat hemp, and to be herself caned, or scourged, or fettered with a log like a stray donkey, according to his fancy and the interests of the hemp manufacture. Many women went through these ordeals dozens of times. "It's not the way to reform 'em," observes Ned Ward; and for once, I think, the satirical publican, who travelled in "ape and monkey climes," is right.—*Vide* Smollett: *Roderick Random;* Cunningham: *Handbook of London;* and, *Bridewell Hospital Reports,* 1720—1799.

dall' ospitale alla fossa." This is the tersest summary
I know. The Venetian loses not a word. From the
cottage where she was born to an inn ; from an inn to a
palace ; thence to a bagnio, thence to prison, thence to
a sick-room, thence to the grave. This is the history of
Kate Hackabout.

Each tableau in the *Harlot's Progress* is complete
in itself; but there is a "solution of continuity"—the
progression is not consecutive : more than once a hiatus
occurs. Thus, it is Mother Needham, the horrible pro-
curess, who first accosts the innocent country girl in the
inn-yard ; and it is the infamous Colonel Charteris who
is leering at her. The magnificent "palazzo" belongs,
however, to a Jew financier ; and after the disturbance
of the table kicked over, and the gallant behind the
door, we can understand how she sinks into the mistress
of James Dalton, the highwayman. But how comes she
to be dressed in brocade and silver when she is beating
hemp in Bridewell ? The *Grub Street Journal* tells us
that the *real* Hackabout was so attired when by the fiat
of nine justices she was committed to penitential fibre-
thumping ; but the pictorial Kate in the preceding
tableau, sitting under the bed-tester with the stolen
watch in her hand, is in very mean and shabby attire.
Do people put on their best clothes to go to the House
of Correction ? or, again, when being captured—Sir John
Gonson allowed her to dress herself, discreetly waiting
outside the door meanwhile — did she don her last
unpawned brocaded kirtle and her showiest lappets, in
order to captivate the nine stern justices withal ? The fall
to the garret, after her release from prison, I can well
understand. Some years have elapsed. She has a ragged

10

little wretch of a boy, who toasts a scrap of bacon before the fire, while the quacks squabble about the symptoms of her malady, and the attendant harridan rifles her trunk—it is the same old trunk with her initials in brass nails on it that we see in the yard of the Bell Inn, Wood Street, in Scene the First!—of its vestiges of finery. The ragged boy is, perchance, James Dalton, the high-wayman's son, long since translated to Tyburnia. The real Hackabout's brother was indeed hanged with much completeness. But I can't at all understand how in the next tableau this poor creature, when her woes are all ended, has a handsome and even pretentious funeral, moribund, as we saw her, in her dismal garret but just before. Had Fortune cast one fitful ray on her as she sank into the cold dark house? Had a bag of guineas been cast to jingle on her hearse? She was a clergy-man's daughter, it seems. Had the broken-hearted old curate in the country sent up sufficient money to bury his daughter with decency? Had the sisterhood of the Hundreds of Drury themselves subscribed for the enlargement of obsequies which might excuse an orgy? There is plenty of money from somewhere in this death-scene, to a certainty. The boy who sits at the coffin foot, winding the string round his top, has a new suit of mourning, and a laced hat. That glowering undertaker has been liberally paid to provide gloves and scarves; the clergyman—I hope he's only a Fleet chaplain—has evidently been well entertained; there is a whole Jordan of gin flowing : gin on the coffin-lid ; gin on the floor ; and on the wall there is even an " achievement of arms," the dead woman's scutcheon.

On every scene in the *Harlot's Progress* a lengthy

essay might be written. Well, is not every stone in this city full of sermons? Are there no essays to be written on the Kate Hackabouts who are living, and who die around us every day? Better for the nonce to close that dreary coffin, wish that we were that unconscious child who is sitting at the feet of Death, and preparing to spin his pegtop amid the shadows of all this wretchedness and all this vice.

V.

Between London and Sheerness.

As one, Reader, who concludes haply, through hearsay, that his uncle William has left him a ten pound legacy ; but, going afterwards to Doctors' Commons, paying his shilling, and reading that said uncle's will,—receiving letters from stately lawyers, full of congratulations, at seventy-pence a piece,—being bowed and kotoued to by people who were wont to cut him, and overwhelmed with offers of unlimited credit by tradesfolk who yesterday would not trust to the extent of a pair of woollen hose—discovers that he has inherited a fine fortune ; so may an author scarcely help feeling who has commenced a modest little series of papers in the hope that they would fill a gap and serve a turn, and who finds himself now, roaming through a vast country, inexhaustible in fertility, undermined with treasure, and overstocked with game : of all which he is expected to give a faithful and accurate report. Yes, the world Hogarthian is all before me, where to choose. Facilities for " opening up " the teeming territory present themselves on every side. Authorities accumulate ; microscopes and retrospective spy-glasses are obligingly lent. The Chamberlain of London politely throws open his archives. I am permitted to inspect a Hogarth-engraved silver-plate, forming part of the paraphernalia of the famous past-Overseers' box of St. Margaret's, Westminster. Father Prout sends me from Paris an old Hogarth etching he has picked up on the Quai Voltaire, and, withal, more humour and learning in a sheet of letter-paper than ever I shall have in my head in a lifetime. A large-minded correspondent in Cheshire insists on tearing a portrait and biography of W. H. from an old book in his possession, and sending the fragments to me. From the blue shadows of the Westmoreland Fells comes, by book-post, a copy of "Ald Hoggart's" poems. A friend promises to make interest with the authorities of the Painters' Company for any Hogarthian memorabilia their records may contain. Another friend advises that I should straightway memorialize the Benchers of the Honourable Society of Lincoln's Inn, for information relative to W. H.'s entertainment by the "Sages de la Ley," A.D. 1750. I am bidden to remember that I should visit the Foundling Hospital, to see the *March to Finchley ;* that there are original Hogarths in Sir John Soane's Museum, and in the church of St. Mary Redclyffe, Bristol.* And, upon my word, I have a collection of correspondence about Hogarth that reads like an excerpt from the *Clergy List.* Their reverences could not be more prolific of pen and ink were I a heterodox Bampton Lecturer. How many times I have been clerically reminded of a blunder I committed (in No. I.) in assigning a wrong county as the locality of St. Bee's

---

* I was at Bristol in the summer of 1858 ; but the fine old church was then in process of restoration, and the Hogarths, I heard, had been temporarily removed. Have those curious altar-pieces been since restored ?

College. How many times I have been enlightened as to the derivation of the hangman's appellation of Jack Ketch. From rectories, parsonages, endowed grammar-schools, such corrections, such explanations, have flowed in amain. Not to satiety, not to nausea, on the part of their recipient. To him it is very good and pleasant to think that some familiar words on an old English theme can interest cultivated and thoughtful men. It is doubly pleasant to be convinced that he was not in error when, in the first section of these essays, he alluded to the favour with which William Hogarth had ever been held by the clergy of the Church of England.

Yes, I have come into a fine fortune, and the balance at the banker's is prodigious. But how if the cheque-book be lost? if the pen sputter, if the ink turn pale and washy, or thick and muddy? Alnaschar! it is possible to kick over that basketful of vitreous ware. Rash youth of Siamese extraction, it may have pleased your imperial master to present you with a white elephant. Woe! for the tons of rice and sugar that the huge creature consumes, the sweet and fresh young greenstuff for which he unceasingly craves;—and you but a poor day labourer? You must have elephants, must you? Better to have gone about with a white mouse and a hurdigurdy : the charitable might have flung you coppers. Shallow, inept, and pretentious, to what a task have you not committed yourself! Thus to me have many sincere friends—mostly anonymous—hinted. These are the wholesome raps on the knuckles a man gets who attempts without being able to accomplish; who inherits, and lacks the capacity to administer. Many a fine fortune is accompanied by as fine a lawsuit—

remember the legatee cobbler in *Pickwick*—and dire is
the case of the imprudent wight who finds himself some
fine morning in contempt, with Aristarchus for a Lord
Chancellor! But I have begun a journey. The descent
of Avernus is as facile as sliding down a *Montagné Russe;*
—*sed revocare gradum :*—no, one mustn't revoke, nor in
the game of. life, nor in the game of whist. We will go
on, if you please ; and I am your very humble servant
to command.

The stir made by the publication of the set of
engravings from the six pictures of the *Harlot's Progress*
was tremendous. Twelve hundred copies of the first
impression were sold. Miniature copies of some of the
scenes were engraved on fan-mounts. Even, as occurred
with George Cruikshank's *Bottle*, the story was drama-
tized, and an interlude called *The Jew Decoyed ; or a
Harlot's Progress*, had a must successful " run." It is
worthy of observation that the perverse and depraved
taste of the town took it as rather a humorous thing
that the courtesan, splendidly kept by a Hebrew money-
lender, should decoy and betray her keeper. *The Jew
Decoyed.* Ho! ho! it was a thing to laugh at. Who
sympathizes with M. Géronte in the farce—the poor
feeble old dotard — when Arlechino runs off with his
daughter, and Pierrot the *gracioso* half cuts his nose
off while he is shaving him, picking his pocket and
treading on his tenderest corns, meanwhile ? The tradesmen and lodging-house keepers who are swindled and
robbed by clown and pantaloon in the pantomime ; the
image boys, fishmongers, and greengrocers whose stock
in trade is flung about the stage ; the peaceable watch-
maker, who tumbles over on the slide artfully prepared

in front of his own door with fresh butter, by the miscreant clown; the grenadier bonneted with his own
busby; the young lady bereft of her bustle; the mother
of the baby that is sate upon, swung round by the legs,
and crammed into a letter-box: is any pity evoked for
those innocent and ill-used persons? I am afraid there
is none. I have seen a policeman in the pit roaring with
laughter at the pummelling and jostling his simulated
brother receives on the stage. It is remarkable to watch
the keen delight with which exhibitions of petty cruelty
and petty dishonesty, of a gay, lively description, are
often regarded. I can understand the pickpocket
detected by Charles the Second's keen eye in annexing
a snuff-box at court, laying his finger by the side of his
nose, and taking the monarch into his confidence. I
can understand cynic Charles keeping the rogue's secret
for the humour of the thing. And, verily, when I see
children torturing animals, and senseless louts grinning and jeering, and yelling "Who shot the dog!"
after a gentleman in the street, because he happens to
wear the honourable uniform of a volunteer, and persons
who are utter strangers to one belated runaway joining
in the enlivening shout and chase of "Stop thief!" I can
begin to understand the wicked wisdom of the American
Diogenes who coolly indited this maxim: "If you see a
drowning man, throw a rail at him."

Hogarth's engravings of the adventures of Kate
Hackabout were extensively and grossly pirated. In
those days, as in these, there were pictorial Curlls in the
land. The author of the foregoing has had the honour
to see some early and trifling pictorial performances of his
own pirated upon pocket-handkerchiefs and shirt-fronts;

but, dear me, what a legal pother would have arisen at
Manchester if any one had pirated those beautiful patent
cylinders on which the piracies must have been so neatly
engraved! Some vile imitations of Hackabout were
even cut on wood; and I should dearly like to know if
any impressions of those blocks are extant. Mr. Ottley
has none in his *History of Chalcography;* but a series of
woodcuts so long after Albert Durer and Maso Fine-
guerra, so long before Bewick the revivalist's time,
would be deeply interesting.* Hogarth smarted under
this injury, as well he might. The artist had always a
strong admixture of the British tradesman in his composition, and, as was his wont when injured, he bellowed
lustily. He moved the Lords of the Treasury. He
moved the Houses of Lords and Commons; and, at
last (1735), he obtained an Act of Parliament, specially
protecting his copyrights in his prints. As usual, too,
he celebrated the victory with a loud and jubilant cock-
crow, and complimented Parliament on their recognition
of the principles of truth and right, in an allegorical
etching, with a flowery inscription. It is good to learn·
that the Legislature were tender to this artist even after
his death, and that his widow, Jane Hogarth, obtained,
by another special Act, a renewal of his copyrights for
her sole use and benefit. In this age of photography

---

* There is a mania just now for giving excessive prices for steel and
copper engravings. There is a millennium for artists' proofs. The auctioneers only know what a genuine Marc Antonio Raimondi is worth; but
I am told that a "Sunday" proof of the *March to Finchley*—the original
plate was dated on a Sunday, but the *dies non* was subsequently erased by
Hogarth—will fetch thirty guineas in the market. The price seems as
exorbitant as those sometimes given for a "breeches" or a "vinegar"
Bible.

and electro-printing, do we not need a law of artistic
copyright somewhat more definite and more stringent
than the loose statutes that lawyers quibble about and
interpret different ways?

Ere I quit the subject of the *Harlot's Progress*, it is
meet to advert to a little dictum of good Mr. Fuseli, the
ambidextrous Anglo-Swiss, who painted the *Lazar-house*
and other horrifying subjects, who used to swear so
dreadfully at the clerks in Coutts' banking-house, and
who called for his umbrella when he went to see Mr.
Constable's showery pictures. " The characteristic discrimination and humorous exuberance," says Fuseli, in a
lecture, " which we admire in Hogarth, but which, like
the fleeting passion of a day, every hour contributes
something to obliterate, will soon be unintelligible by
time or degenerate into caricature : the chronicle of
scandal, and the history-book of the vulgar." I have the
highest respect for the learning and acumen of Fuseli ;
but I think he is wholly wrong in assuming that
Hogarth's humour or discrimination will *ever* become
" unintelligible by time," or will " degenerate into caricature." Look at this *Harlot's Progress*. Who cares to
know, now, that Charteris continues to rot ; that he was
guilty of every vice but prodigality and hypocrisy—
being a monster of avarice and a paragon of impudence ;
that he was condemned to death for a dreadful crime,
and only escaped the halter by the interest of aristocratic friends ; that he was a liar, a cheat, a gambler,
a usurer, and a profligate ; that he amassed an estate of
ten thousand a year ; that he was accursed while living,
and that the populace almost tore his body from his
remote grave in Scotland ? Who cares to know how

many times Mother Needham was carted — although you may be sure they were not half so frequent as she deserved. Is it important to know exactly whether the Caucasian financier was intended for Sir Henry Furnese, or for Rafael Mendez, or Israel Vanderplank. The quack Misaubin * and his opponent are forgotten. Stern Sir John Gonson † and his anti-Cyprian crusades are forgotten. For aught we can tell, the Bridewell gaoler, the Irish servant, the thievish harridan, the Fleet parson, the glowering undertaker, may all be faithful portraits of real personages long since gone to dust. It boots little even to know if Kate were really Kate or Mary Hack-about, or Laïs, or Phryne, or Doll Common. She is

---

* Dr. Misaubin lived at 96, St. Martin's Lane. Of his staircase, painted by Clermont, the Frenchman, I have already spoken. Those were the days when "Mrs. Powell, the colourman's mother, used to make a pipe of wine every year from the vines that grew in the garden in St. Martin's Lane." Traces of its old rurality may also be found in the name of one of its noisomest offshoots—the "Hop Gardens." Dr. Misaubin "flourished" in 1732. He was not a Frenchman born, but of French Huguenot extraction. He was an arrant and impudent quack, but a good-natured man, and dispensed the huge fortune he amassed liberally enough. More anent him when he grows older and more wrinkled in the *Marriage à la Mode*. All this man's gold, however, turned in the end to dry leaves. His grandson, Angiband, dissipated the pill and nostrum fortune, and died of Geneva-on-the-brain in St. Martin's Workhouse. Engraver Smith (J. T.) says that Misaubin's father was a Protestant clergyman, and mentions a "family picture" representing the Doctor in all his glory, with his son on his knees, and his reverend papa at a table behind, and arrayed in full canonicals.

† Everybody seems to have had Latin verses, eulogistic or abusive, addressed to him in those days. Thus the "Sapphics" of Mr. Loveling, a young gentleman of the university, to the rigorous Middlesex Justice :—

"Pellicum, Gonsone, animosus hostis,
Per minus castas Druriæ tabernas
Lenis incedens, abeas Diones
    Æquus Alumnis ! "

And so forth.

dead, and will sin and suffer stripes no more. But the
humour and discrimination of the painter yet live, the
types he pourtrayed endure to this hour. I saw Charteris
the day before yesterday, tottering about in shiny boots
beneath the Haymarket Colonnade. The quacks live
and prosper, drive mail-phaetons, and enter horses for
the Derby. The Jew financier calls himself Mr. Mont-
morenci de Levyson, and lends money at sixty per cent.,
or as Julius McHabeas, Gent., one of her Majesty's
attorneys-at-law, issues a writ at the suit of his friend
and father-in-law Levyson. And Kate decoys and
cozens the financier every day in a cottage *ornée* at
Brompton or St. John's Wood. Kate! there is her
"miniature brougham" gliding through Albert Gate.
There is her barouche on the hill at Epsom. There she
is at the play, or in the garden, flaunting among the
coloured lamps. There she is in the Haymarket, in the
Strand, in the New Cut, in the workhouse, in the police
cell, in the hospital. There she is on Waterloo Bridge,
and there—God help her!—in the cold, black river,
having accomplished her "progress." Take away the
whipping-post from Bridewell; and for the boudoir paid
for by the Jew, substitute the garish little sitting-room
that Mr. Holman Hunt painted in his wonderful picture
of the *Awakened Conscience*, and one can realize the
"humour" and "discrimination" of Hogarth in a tale as
sad that progresses around us every day.

Every one who has the most superficial acquaintance
with a Hogarthian biography has heard the story of how
Mrs. Hogarth, or her mamma, Dame Alice Thornhill,
placed the six pictures of the *Harlot's Progress* in Sir
James's breakfast parlour one morning, ready for the

knight on his coming down. "Very well, very well," cried the king's sergeant painter, rubbing his hands, and well nigh pacified : "the man who can paint like this wants no dowry with my daughter." I am glad to believe the story ; but I don't believe, as some malevolent commentators have insinuated, that Sir James Thornhill made his son-in-law's talent an excuse for behaving parsimoniously to the young couple after he had forgiven them. There is nothing to prove that Sir James Thornhill was a stingy man. He had a son who was a great crony of Hogarth, accompanied him on the famous journey to Rochester and Sheerness, and afterwards became sergeant-painter to the navy. I fancy that he was a wild young man, and cost his father large sums. It is certain, however, that Sir James frequently and generously assisted his daughter and son-in-law. He set them up in their house in Leicester Fields ; and he appears to have left Hogarth a considerable interest in his house at 104, St. Martin's Lane, whither he had removed from Covent Garden, and the staircase of which he had painted, according to his incorrigible custom, with "allegories." The great artists of those days used to employ one another to paint the walls and ceilings of each other's rooms. Thus Kneller gave commissions to the elder Laguerre, and Thornhill himself employed Robert Brown, the painter who was so famous for "crimson curtains," and who justified having painted two signs for the Paul's Head Tavern in Cateaton Street, on the ground that Correggio had painted the sign of the "Muleteer." Be it mentioned likewise, to Thornhill's honour, that he fruitlessly endeavoured to persuade Lord Halifax to found a Royal Academy in the King's Mews, Charing Cross. It would be better, perhaps, in this place to make an end of goodman Thornhill. Besides Worlidge's portrait, there is one by Hogarth in oil, of which a vigorous etching was executed by Samuel Ireland. The portrait was purchased of Mrs. Hogarth, in 1781, and was deemed by her an excellent likeness. Thornhill died at his seat, " Thornhill," near Weymouth, in 1734.* He had transferred his academy or drawing-school, call it what you will, from Covent Garden to St. Martin's Lane; and to Hogarth he bequeathed all his casts and bustos, all his easels and drawing-stools, all the paraphernalia of his studio. These William ultimately presented to the academy held in St. Peter's Court, St. Martin's Lane, in premises that had formerly been the studio of Roubiliac the sculptor.

I told you that at about the time of his marriage our artist took summer lodgings at Vauxhall, and first made

---

* He sat for Melcombe Regis in the two last parliaments of George the First. The borough was then a mere pocket one, in the gift of the back-stairs. Thornhill's "employments" were continued to him for some time by George the Second ; but, like his predecessor, Sir Christopher Wren, he was removed to make way for place-men who, without any very high attainments, could be useful to the ministry. Thenceforth, the "goodman" amused himself by painting easel-pictures. He was taken for death in an access of gout, and died in his chair on the 4th of May, and was buried at Stalbridge on the 13th. He had greatly beautified the ancestral mansion and estate, and had erected, on an adjacent hill, an obelisk to the memory of George the First, which was visible to all the country side. Hogarth himself records the death of his father-in-law, in Sylvanus Urban's obituary in the *Gentleman's Magazine*—then a very young publication, indeed. He says that he was "the greatest history painter this age has seen;" and states that, as king's sergeant painter, he had to decorate all his majesty's coaches, barges, and "the royal navy." Are we to understand from this that Thornhill was expected to carve and gild the figure-heads of three-deckers !

the acquaintance of Mr. Jonathan Tyers, the "enter-prizing" lessee of the once famous "Royal Property." With Tyers he ever maintained a fast friendship, and he materially and generously assisted him in the decoration of the gardens ; for, frugal tradesman as Hogarth was, and sturdily determined to have the rights he had bargained for, he was continually giving away something. We have noticed his donation to the Petro-Roubiliac Academy ; to St. Bartholomew's Hospital, of which he was a governor, he gave the picture of the *Pool of Bethesda ;* and the governors of the Foundling Hospital know how nobly munificent was this honest Christian man to the nascent charity. He gave them handsome pictures ; he gave them a large proportion in the shares of other picture auctions—shares as good as money : he painted a splendid portrait of Thomas Coram, the grand old sea-captain, who spent his fortune in cherishing deserted children, and in his old age was not ashamed to confess that he had spent his all in doing good ; that his fortune was funded in Heaven—let us trust he is drawing his dividends now,—and that here below he was destitute.* His example incited many more notable

---

* Thomas Coram was born in 1668. He had amassed a competence in following the sea, and lived at Rotherhithe, like Captain Lemuel Gulliver, and that greater mariner, Captain Cuttle. In his way to and from the maritime districts of the town, his honest heart was frequently afflicted by the sight of destitute and abandoned children. Probably he had never heard of St. Vincent de Paul—this rough tarry-breeks of the Benbow and Cloudesley Shovel era—but he set about doing the selfsame work as that for which the foreign philanthropist was canonized. Coram had already effected much good by procuring an Act granting a bounty on naval stores imported to Georgia—where the colonists were frequently left destitute— and by devising an admirable scheme for the education of Indian girls.

artists to contribute pictures to the charity : and the halls of the Foundling became the chief art-lounge in London. The Royal Academy Exhibition, even, with its annual revenue of infinite shillings, sprang from this odd germ. The Foundling Hospital, I have heard, has wandered from its original purpose ; and few of its first attributes are now recognizable in its constitution ; but I hope they still teach every little boy and girl foundling to murmur a prayer for Thomas Coram and William Hogarth.

For the embellishment of the supper-boxes at Vauxhall, William made several designs ; but there is not much evidence to prove that he *painted* any of them with his own hand. The paintings were mostly executed by Hogarth's fast friend, Frank Hayman, and perhaps by Lanscroon, singer and scene-painter, son of old Lanscroon, Riario's condisciple with Laguerre's son-in-law Tijou, and the author of a meritorious set of prints illustrating *Hob at the Well.* For Vauxhall, Hogarth made the designs of the *Four Parts of the Day,* which he afterwards himself engraved, and which had great success.

Most of us have seen a very ugly, tasteless mezzo-tinto engraving representing Henry VIII. in an im-

---

The Foundling hospital was, however, his great work. He obtained the charter of incorporation for it, A.D. 1739. These were the words, of which I have given the sense above :—"I have not wasted the little wealth of which I was formerly possessed in self-indulgence or vain expense ; and am not ashamed to confess, that in this, my old age, I am poor." They raised a pension of a hundred a year for the benevolent veteran ; Sir Samson Gideon and Dr. Brocklesby being chief managers of the fund. Captain Coram did not live long to enjoy the pension ; and at his death, it was continued to poor old Leveridge, to whose volume of songs William Hogarth contributed a frontispiece.

possible attitude, leering at a coarse Anne Boleyn.
I am always sorry to see the words " *Hogarth pinxit*,"
in the left-hand corner of this inelegant performance,
and sorrier to know that he did indeed achieve that daub ;
and that the picture was hung in the "old great room
at the right hand of entry into the gardens." Indeed it
is a barbarous thing. The background is, I suppose,
intended to represent an apartment in Cardinal Wolsey's
sumptous mansion at York Place ; but it would do better
for a chamber at the " Rose," or at the " Three Tuns,"
in Chandos Street. I can speak of it no more with
patience. Why paint it, William ? Yet it had all the
honours of the mezzotint scraper ; it is engraved likewise in line ; and Allan Ramsay—" Gentle Shepherd "
Ramsay—who should have known better, wrote some
eulogistic verses by way of epigraph. Nor did Jonathan
Tyers of Vauxhall look the gift horse in the mouth.
He was glad to hang the sorry canvas in his old great
room ; and in testimony of many kindnesses received
from the painter, who had " summer lodgings at South
Lambeth," presented him with a perpetual ticket of
admission to the gardens for himself and friends. Fancy
being on the free-list of Vauxhall for ever ! The ticket
was of gold, and bore this inscription :—

In perpetuam beneficii memoriam.

Hogarth was a frequent visitor at the " Spring Gardens,"
Vauxhall. There, I will be bound, he and his pretty
young wife frequently indulged in that cool summer
evening's stroll which the French call *prendre le frais*.
There he may have had many a bowl of arrack punch
with Harry Fielding—he was to live to be firm friends

11

with the tremendous author of " *Tom Jones ;* " there I think he may have met a certain Ferdinand Count Fathom, and a Somersetshire gentleman of a good estate but an indifferent temper and conversation, by name Western, together with my Lady. Bellaston (in a mask and a cramoisy grogram sack, laced with silver), and, once in a way, perhaps Mr. Abraham Adams, clerk.   There is an authentic anecdote, too, of Hogarth standing one evening at Vauxhall listening to the band, and of a countryman pointing to the roll of paper with which the conductor was beating time, and asking what musical instrument " that white thing was ? " " Friend," answered William, "*it is a single handed drum !*"—not a very bright joke, certainly ; but then, as has been pertinently observed, a quibble can be excused to Hogarth, if a conundrum can be pardoned to Swift.

We would paint our pictures and our progresses in 1730-1-2-3.   We were gaining fame.   The Lords of the Treasury, as related by old under-Secretary Christopher Tilson, could examine and laugh over our plates even at the august Council Board, in the Cockpit, and, adjourning, forthwith proceed to purchase impressions at Bakewell's shop, near Johnson's Court, in Fleet Street.   " Frances Lady Byron "—more of her lord hereafter—was sitting to us for her portrait.   Theophilus Cibber had pantomimized us.   " Joseph Gay " — the wretched pseudonym of some Grub Street, gutter-blood rag-galloper—had parodied in " creaking couplets " the picture-poem of *Kate Hackabout.** Vinny Bourne had

---

* One moment ere I leave the male and female naughtinesses in this drama for good.   Charteris, Hackabout, brother and sister, James Dalton,

headed his "hendecasyllables," *Ad Gulielmum Hogarth*
Παραινέτικον. Somerville, author of the *Chase,* had dedicated his *Hobbinol* to us : we were son-in-law to a knight
and M.P., but we were not yet quite emancipated from

the highwayman, whose "wig-box" you see in plate iii. of the *H. P.*, and
Mother Needham, who continued the traditions of Dryden's *Mother Dulake*
("Wild Gallant,") to Foote's *Mother Cole*, all faded into space before
1733. The colonel "Don Francisco"—as people with a snigger called
Charteris—was very nearly being hanged. He was cast for death ; but
being immensely rich, and having, moreover, and luckily, a lord of the
land, the Earl of Wemyss, for his son-in-law, he managed to escape. Not,
indeed, Scot-free. He was compelled to make a handsome settlement on
his victim, one Ann Bond, prosecutrix in the case for which Don Francisco
had so close a riddance of "*sus. per coll.*" being written against his name.
The sheriffs of London, and the high bailiff of Westminster, had, moreover,
made a seizure of his rich goods and chattels, immediately after his conviction.
He had to compound with them for the restitution of his effects, and this
cost him nearly nine thousand pounds. The profligate old miser had to sell
his South Sea stock, to raise the amount ; a fact which the newspapers of
the day record with much exultation. But Nemesis was not yet satisfied.
The colonel's wife came back from Scotland on purpose to reproach her
lord. The wretched man on his part fled *to* Scotland, and died in Edinburgh
soon afterwards. Dalton, of the "wig-box," having been "boned,"
"habbled," or "snabbled," and confined for some time in the "Rumbo,"
or "Whid," finished his career at the "nubbing cheat," at the top of the
Edgeware Road. In other words—the first are the elegant terms used by
the City marshal in his controversial pamphlet the *Regulator*, written in
disparagement of Mr. Jonathan Wild the great—Mr. James Dalton was
arrested, and after lying some time in Newgate, was duly tried, sentenced
and hanged. "He was a thief from his cradle, and imbibed the principles
of his art with his mother's milk." He went between his father's legs in the
cart to his fatal exit at Tyburn. *Sic itur ad astra ;* and thus Plutarch in the
shape of the ordinary of Newgate. As for Mother Needham, she was
sentenced to stand twice in the pillory. The first ordeal she underwent
close to her own house, in Park Place, St. James'. She was very ill, and
lay "all along" under these Caudine forks, "thus evading the law, which
required that her face should be exposed." Two days afterwards, "com-
plaining of the ingratitude of the publick"—the mob had pelted her
pitilessly—"and dreading the second pillorying to which, in Old Palace
Yard, she was doomed, she gave up the ghost."

struggles, and hardship, and poverty. As yet we were very badly paid, and our small earnings were gnawed away by the villanous pirates soon to succumb to the protective Act of Parliament which Huggins was to draw —how strangely and frequently that detested name turns up—and draw not too efficiently on the model of the old literary copyright statute of Queen Anne. Morris had paid us the thirty pounds adjudged for the *Element of Earth:* but no munificent, eccentric old maid had as yet arisen to gratify us with sixty guineas for a single comic design: *Taste in High Life.* We were poor, albeit not lowly. The wolf was not exactly at the door. He didn't howl from morning to night; but, half-tamed, he built himself a kennel in the porch, and snarled sometimes over the threshold. Let it be told again that we, William, were "a punctual pay-master." So it behoved us to paint as many portraits and conversations as we could get commissions for, and do an occasional stroke of work on copper-plate for the booksellers. Coypel and Vandergucht, both approved High Dutch draughtsmen of the time, shared the patronage of the better class of booksellers with us; but none of us worked for the polecat Edmund Curll.

One of us, however, made a smart onslaught about this time on Edmund Curll's most rancorous foe, Alexander Pope. Many pages ago I hinted at this attack, as almost the only one that could be traced directly to Hogarth; although many claim to discern little portraits in disparagement of Pope Alexander in the print of the *Lottery*, in *Rich's Triumphal Entry to Covent Garden* (in which a suppositious Pope beneath the piazza is maltreating a copy of the *Beggars' Opera*

—why ? had he not a hand in it ?), and in the *Characters
at Button's Coffee-house*. There can be no mistake,
however, about the Pope in the print known as *False
Taste*, or the second *Burlington Gate*. There is no need
that I should trench on the province of Mr. Carruthers,
who, in his edition of Pope, has so admirably narrated the ins and outs of the quarrel between the poet
and the magnificent Duke of Chandos, further than
to express an opinion that the duke had treated the
little man of Twickenham with, at least, courtesy ; and
that Pope's description of "Timon's villa" was at best
somewhat lacking in courtesy. Hogarth took the
Chandos side in the squabble—the malevolent still hint
in deference to Sir James Thornhill and his old grudge
against Kent, the Corinthian petticoat man, and *protégé*
of Lord Burlington. In the print you see Pope perched
on a scaffolding, and as he whitewashes Burlington
Gate, bespattering the passing coach of the Duke of
Chandos. It would have been well for William to have
avoided these partisan personalities. They never brought
him anything but grief. He should have remembered
Vinny Bourne's allocution—

> Qui mores hominum improbos, ineptos,
> Incidis . . . .

Rogues, and rakes, and misers, and fanatics, and quacks,
were his quarry. It was his to scourge the vices of the
great ; ay, and to laugh at their foibles. He has, indeed,
well generalized the mansion and villa building mania
in the courtyard perspective of the *Marriage à la Mode*,
but he should have had nothing directly to do with
Burlington Gate or with Canons.

The real scope and bent of his genius were to be

triumphantly manifested at this very period by his
wonderful composition *The Modern Midnight Conversation.* I don't think there is a single artistic design
extant which exemplifies to the spectator so forcibly
and so rapidly the vices of a coarse and sensual epoch.
Most of us have seen that grand picture in the Luxembourg at Paris, the *Décadence des Romains* of Coutuse,
with those stern citizens of the old Brutus stamp gazing
in moody sorrow on the enervated patricians, crowned
with flowers, golden-sandalled, purple-robed, rouged, and
perfumed, lapped in feasting and luxury, and the false
smiles of meretricious women ; listening to dulcet music ;
sipping the Chian and Falernian, babbling the scandal of
the bath to their freedmen, or lisping sophisms in
emasculated Greek to their hireling philosophers.   One
has but to glance at that picture to know that the
empire is in a bad way ; that certain Germanic barbarians
are sharpening short swords or whittling clubs into
shape far away, and that the Roman greatness is in the
Valley of the Shadow of Death.   I remember once
seeing in an old curiosity shop of the Rue Lafitte a
water-colour drawing, probably limned by some *rapin*
for some Sophie Arnould of the quarter, and sold at one
of her periodical boudoir-and-alcove auctions—a drawing
almost as eloquent and as suggestive as the *Décadence.*
A group of ragged little boys, in the peasant costume of
Louis the Well-Beloved's time, have lifted up a heavy
curtain.   You see, beyond, the interior of a *petite maison.*
Farmers general, marquises, abbés, are junketing with
the Sophie Arnoulds of the epoch.   The uplifted table-
cloth shows the keys of a harpsichord beneath, on which
one of the fair dames is tinkling.   There are no

servants to disturb the company ; the dainty dishes rise through noiseless traps.   Artificial flowers, champagne, wax candles, Sèvres china and *vermeil* plate, diamonds, and embroidery : of all these there is an abundance. Outside, where the little ragged hungry boys are, you see snow and naked trees, and a little dead baby in a dead mother's arms.   A fanciful performance, and too violently strained, perhaps ; yet òne that tells, undeniably, that the age is going *wrong ;* that this champagne will one day turn red as blood ; that these wax candles will light a flame not to be put out, but that will burn the *petite maison* about the ears of Farmers general, Sophie Arnoulds, and company ; that the strumming of yonder harpsichord will be inaudible when the dreadful tocsin begins to boom.   I need but allude to the Dutch Kermesses of Teniers, and Ostade, and Jan Steen, and the camp-life pictures of Wouvermans and Dick Stoop, for those acquainted with those masters to understand the marvellous and instantaneous concentration of all the low, sordid, brutal passions and pastimes of the epoch ; the daily life and sports and duties of the boor who swigs the beer and smokes the pipe ; of the vrau, who peels the carrots, swaddles the child, and beats the servant-maid with a broomstick ; of the ruffian soldier, rubbing down his eternal white horse, braying away with his trumpet, gambling under the tilt of his tent, or brabbling with the baggage-waggon woman, who reclines yonder among her pots and kettles.   These things come upon us at once ; and we are seised and possessed with the life of the time ; but the force and suggestiveness of the works I have named become weak and ambiguous when compared with this *Modern Midnight Conversation*, this picture paraphrase of the immortal "*Propos des Buveurs*" of Francois Rabelais. You see an epoch of dull, brutish, besotted revelry : an epoch when my lord duke was taken home drunk in his sedan from the Rose to his mansion in Great Queen Street, Lincoln's Inn Fields ; his chair-men and flambeau-men very probably as drunk as he ; and his chaplain and groom of the chambers receiving him with bloodshot eyes and hiccuping speech ; —when Jemmy Twitcher lay in the kennel as drunk as my lord duke ; only, there was nobody to take him home ; when there were four thousand ginshops in London ; and a grave publicist issued a broadsheet, giving "two hundred and sixty plain and practical reasons" for the legislative suppression of the trade in "the dreadful liquor called Geneva." I wish I could persuade the temperance societies that this is in comparison a sober age ; and that 130 years ago, not only did wine and punch slay their thousands among the upper classes, but gin and brandy—both of which were horribly cheap—slew their tens of thousands among the populace. Wait till we come to the Hogarthian tableaux of Beer Street and Gin Lane. In this *Modern Midnight Conversation*, everybody is tipsy. The parson, the doctor, the soldier, the gambler, and the bully—the very drawer himself—are all intoxicated. Few of the company can see out of more than one eye. Pipes are lighted, and go out again for want of sober puffing. Songs are commenced, and the second couplet forgotten. Wigs are pushed awry, or quite fall off. The furniture is overturned ; rivulets of punch flow over the table, and on to the puddled ground. Men, losing the reins of reason, not only see, but think double ; take

their own cracked voices for those of interlocutors;
quarrel with themselves; give each other the lie, and
vow they will draw upon themselves if they, themselves,
say something—they know not what—again. This is
the state of drunkenness that cankered, and bloated, and
corrupted Church and State, in the debased reigns of
the two first Brunswickers; that sent the king fuddled
to Heidegger's masquerade, and the minister reeling in
his blue ribbon to the House, and made tavern roysterers
of the young nobles of Britain. When one has had to
wade through the minor chronicles of this time, it
becomes distressingly easy to recognize the terrible
truth of the *Modern Midnight Conversation.**

Now although William Hogarth, now in his thirty-
fifth year, was passably virtuous, and I have heard no
instance of his indulging in any modern conversation at
midnight or other times, to the extent of becoming overtaken in strong drinks—there was plenty of cakes and
ale in the Hogarthian philosophy. He was a brisk man,
liberal and hospitable in his own house, and not averse

---

* The *Modern Midnight Conversation* had a great vogue abroad, and is
still, perhaps, one of the best known of Hogarth's works. Copies, adapta-
tions, paraphrases of it have been multiplied to a vast extent in Germany.
There is a well-known French version, *Société nocturne, nommée communé-
ment Cotterie de Débauche en Punch ;* and a collection of heads from the
Conversation, catalogued as *Têtes des onze membres, gravées par M. Riepen-
hausen.* One ingenious artist even formed a gallery of small wax models
of the principal figures. And finally, I have seen the French *Cotterie*
enamelled on a porcelain pipe at Leipsic, and on a golden snuffbox in the
museum of the Hermitage at St. Petersburg. There is a humorous modern
lithograph, representing a party of sapient-looking bibbers, assembled in
solemn conclave over a hogshead of Rhine wine in a cellar ; and the hint
for this—albeit, the grossness is softened down—is evidently taken from the
M. M. C.

from moderate conviviality abroad, sometimes partaking of the nature of the hilarious gambols known as " High Jinks." Brother, we must die. It needs not the digging Trappist to tell us so. It needs not the moralist with " *Disce mori !* " It needs not the looking-glass that shows us the wrinkled brow and grizzled locks. We must die ; and we are gravelled, and worn, and sick, and sorry ; and in the night we pray for morning, and in the morning cry out that it were night. But they need not be grim ghosts, those memories of the old pleasant follies and " High Jinks." They did not all belong to the folly and recklessness of wayward youth. They were jovial and exuberant, and merry and light-hearted ; trivial, certainly, and, maybe, undignified, as when you, John Kemble, rode the hippopotamus at early dawn among the cabbages in Covent Garden ; as when you, grave senator and reverend senior, danced the Irish jig over the crossed broomsticks ; as when you, now stately dowager, then sprightly maid of honour, dis- guised yourself as a buy-a-broom girl ; as when you, grave philosopher, condescended, " on that occasion only," to lead the donkey that was the Rosinante of a fifth of November " Guy." But you didn't do any harm. You didn't exactly bring your parents' grey hair with sorrow to the grave when you broke the half-crown's worth of crockeryware ; nor were you ever brought to the pass of biting your mamma's ear off on the Place de Grève, because she didn't flay you alive for partaking of apples which you had not precisely acquired according to the " vendors' and purchasers' " doctrines of wise Lord St. Leonards. I say, that I hope we shall not *all* be brought to judgment for *all* the rejoicings of our youth ;

for the assize would surely be too black, and shuddering Mercy would tear the calendar.

In 1732 there must have been "high jinks" on foot from time to time at the Bedford Coffee House, Covent Garden. Now, where was the Bedford Coffee House? Was it at that Bedford Hotel, under the piazza, so unceremoniously elbowed by that monstrous glass-house called the "Floral Hall"—the Bedford of which Mrs. Warner is so urbane a hostess? Or was it the "Bedford Head," in Maiden Lane, Govent Garden, a hostelry where to this day a club of bookworm men meet to lay the dust of ancient lore with frugal libations, and talk about Hogarth and Fielding, and Johnson, and the brave deeds and the brave men of the day that shall be no more? I confess that I incline to the "Bedford Head," and that I have purposely avoided taking counsel of London antiquaries more learned than myself on the point, lest I should be undeceived. Moreover, Tothall lived at the corner of Tavistock Court, Tavistock Street, which, as everybody knows, is over against Maiden Lane. It was nearer to Leicester Fields, where Hogarth dwelt, than the Bedford under the piazza, and HOGARTH and TOTHALL, with THORNHILL, FORREST and SCOTT, were the immortal FIVE who, on the morning of Saturday, the 27th of May, 1732, set out on a Kentish pilgrimage, of which the aim and end were "High Jinks."

A word as to the Pilgrims. A famous English writer in some lectures on the "English Humourists," familiar to us all, has described the pilgrimage as that of a "jolly party of tradesmen engaged at high jinks." Now, with the exception of Tothall, who had been pretty nearly everything, and a woollen draper among multifarious

other callings,* the party were all professional men.
What Hogarth was, you know. He had come to the days
when he could wear his sword and bag.   Thornhill was

---

* Tothall's career was a most curious one.   He was the son of an
apothecary, was left an orphan, taken care of by an uncle.   He ran away
to sea ; went to the West Indies, Newfoundland, and Honduras ; was on
one occasion captured by hostile Spaniards, and marched "up the country,"
with no other clothing but a woollen cap and a brown waistcoat—a costume
almost as primitive as that of an unhappy French governess taken prisoner
by some followers of Schamyl, in a raid on the Russians, and driven before
them to their mountain home, the poor lady having nothing on but a pair
of blue satin corsets.   Tothall had his picture painted in the brown waistcoat.   Coming afterwards to England, he entered the service of a woollen
draper, in Tavistock Court ; who, after some time, told him he was a very
honest fellow, and that as he the draper only sold cloth, Tothall might have
half the shop to sell shalloons and trimmings.   He lent him money to buy
stock, and recommended him to his chapmen.   By-and-by, a relative of
Tothall in the West Indies sent him a puncheon of rum as a present.   The
recipient was about to sell the alcohol for what it would fetch—perhaps to
the landlord of the Bedford Head—when his master interposed.   "I have no
use for my cellar," quoth this benevolent woollen draper.   "Do you open the
door to the street ; tap your puncheon, and draw it off in twopennyworths."
Spirit licences were not yet known.   Tothall followed the draper's advice,
speedily sold all his rum at a good profit ; sent to the West Indies for more,
and drove a merry trade in rum, shalloons, and trimmings, till it occurred
to the woollen draper to inform him one morning that he intended to retire,
that he might have all his stock at prime cost, and pay him as he could.
Why are there no such woollen drapers now-a-days ?   Between the shop
and the cellar Tothall contrived to realize a very considerable fortune.   All
this time, this odd man had been assiduously collecting fossils, minerals,
and shells, of which he had, at last, a handsome museum.   He retired to
Dover, and, true to his old adventurous habits, entered into large speculations,
in what his biographer modestly calls the "smuggling branch of business."
But a "byeboat," laden with horses, in which he was interested, having
been lost between Flushing and Ostend, and some other speculations turning
out disastrously, Tothall became in his later days somewhat straitened in his
circumstances.   Hogarth used frequently to visit him at a little village near
Dover, whither he retired, and where he died four years after our painter.
He left 1,500l. in cash, and his collection of shells, &c. sold for a handsome
sum.

Sir James's son and heir. He was afterwards sergeant-painter to the navy, and preserved a good estate in the west. Scott was a marine painter, said by Lord Orford to be second only to Vandevelde; and Forrest's poetic narrative of the Tour, in "Hudibrastic verse," is so fluent, and often so witty, as to show a capacity and a facility very uncommon in those days among trades-men. The curiosity is that these five accomplished men should have taken delight in diversions of the plainest and most inelegant kind. As my author quoted above justly remarks, this was indeed a "jolly party of trades-men," at least, of merrymakers who behaved as we should expect tradesmen to do; but I suspect that the real London tradesman of the time would have been frightened out of his life at such wild doings; and that these jovial Kentish jinks were engaged in by the five Bedfordians through sheer humorous eccentricity, tinged by that inherent coarseness and love of horseplay of the age, which we discover, not only in such holiday jaunts, but in such almost inconceivable frolics as that of George the Second, the Duke of Montague, with Heidegger at the masquerade; the escapade of Lord Middlesex and his friends of the Calves' Head Club, and the hideous practical joke played off by Pope on Curll. Educated men seemed to share in those days the yearning of the French actress—the *besoin de s'encanailler*—the desire to disport themselves in a pigsty, more or less Epicurean; and but for the knowledge of this prevalent low tone in cultivated society it is difficult to realize the fact of Hogarth going back to his lady wife, and Thornhill to the powdered and bewigged grandee, his papa.

Forrest's narrative of the tour, which began, as I

have said, on the twenty-seventh, and finished on the
thirty-first of May, is far too elaborate for me to give
anything beyond a very brief reflex of it here. I will
quote, however, the opening lines :—

> 'Twas first of morn on Saturday
> The seven and twentieth of May,
> When Hogarth, Thornhill, Tothall, Scott,
> And Forrest, who this journal wrote,
> From Covent Garden took departure,
> To see the world by land and water.

It appears that their hearts were light, and those
nether garments, now fallen almost into desuetude, save
among grooms, footmen, blackrods, and members of the
diplomatic service, were thin. They started, singing
after a carouse, during the small hours of the morning,
and went down the river to Billingsgate. At the noted
" Dark-house" they met the same sort of company as
Mr. Edward Ward introduces us to in the *London Spy*,
and Hogarth took a portrait, unfortunately not preserved,
of a waterside humourist, known as the "Duke of
Puddledock."

> Of Puddledock a porter grim,
> Whose portrait Hogarth in a whim
> Presented him in caricature,
> He pasted on the cellar door.

Thence they went to Gravesend in the tilt-boat with
a " mackrel gale," chanting lustily, and regaling on
" biscuit, beef, and gin." At Gravesend they put up at
" Mrs. Bramble's." They had previously seen at Purfleet
three men-of-war, the *Dursley Galley*, the *Gibraltar*, and
the *Tartar Pink*, the pilot of which last vessel begged
them to "lend him a cast." Thence they walked to
Rochester, and saw in the cathedral " th' unknown

person's monument." *Pendente lite,* they drank six pots
of ale. They saw " Watts' Charity," and eulogized its
hospitality, remarking only

> But the contagiously affected,
> And rogues and proctors are rejected,

marvelling much as to the origin of the distaste conceived by Master Watts against " proctors." For dinner
at the Crown at Strood they had " soles and flounders,
with crab sauce ; " a stuffed and roasted calf's head,
" with purt'nance minced and liver fried ; " and by way
of a second course, roast leg of mutton and green peas.
Peas were early; alas ! in May, '32.

> The cook was much commended for't,
> Fresh was the beer, and sound the port.

At Chatham they went aboard two men-of-war, the
Royal Sovereign and the *Marlborough.* In the churchyard at Hoo they found a curious epitaph, written by a
" servant maid turned poetaster," in honour of her master,
who had left her all his money, and which Forrest thus,
literally, transcribed—

> And. wHen. he. Died. you. plainly. see.
> Hee. freely. gave. al. to. Sara. passaWee.
> And. in. Doing. so. it. DoTh. prevail.
> that. Ion. him. can. well. besTowthis. Rayel
> on. Year. sarved. him. it. is well, none
> But. Thanks. beto. God. it. is. all. my One.

How they lay two in a bed, drawing lots who should
be the fifth, fortunate enough to sleep " without a chum ; "
how they were tormented with gnats, and tossed and
tumbled, and, waking up in the morning, told their dreams
and could make nothing of them ; how Hogarth and Scott
played at " Scotch-hop " in the Town-hall, Rochester ;

how they pelted and bemired one another in country lanes and churchyards; how they perambulated the "Isle of Greane" and the "Isle of Shepey," and came upon a party of men-o'-war's men, who had been left without provisions by their midshipman, and learnt how the same midshipman had afterwards got into dire disgrace for philandering with a married lady of Queens-borough; how they ate cockles with the sailors, and sent to the alehouse for beer to regale them; and treated a loquacious man of Queensborough to "t'other pot," whereat the loquacious man began to abuse the mayor of that mighty borough as a mere custom-house officer; how they found the Market-place

> Just big enough to hold the stocks
> And one if not two butchers' blocks;

how they abode at the "Swans," and the landlady threatened to have Scott up before the mayor; how they heard the famous Isle of Sheppey legend of "Horse Church" and the wicked Lord of Shorland, so graphi-cally narrated in our own days by Thomas Ingoldsby in the story beginning "'He won't,' said the Baron. 'Then bring me my boots;'" how at last they got back to Gravesend, put up at Mrs. Bramble's again, and returned per tilt-boat, very tired and jovial, to London. All these notable incidents are set down with a charming simplicity, and an unflagging humour and good nature. Forrest, as I have said, kept the journal. Hogarth and Scott illustrated it. Thornhill made the map, and Tothall was the treasurer. The original drawings, done with a pen and washed with indian ink, and not unlike some of old Rowlandson's rough sketches, are now in

the Print Room of the British Museum.   I believe this
very interesting memorial of an English artist, this
homely *Liber Veritatis*, was secured for our National
Collection at the cost of a hundred pounds.   Some of
the drawings are capital ; though all are of the very
slightest.   These boon companions were too much bent
on enjoying themselves to work very hard.   There is a
view of Queensborough Market-place and Hôtel de
Ville, the manner of taking the draught of which is thus
described :—

> Then to our Swans returning, there
> Was borrowed a great wooden chair,
> And plac'd it in the open street,
> Where in much state did Hogarth sit
> To draw the townhouse, church and steeple,
> Surrounded by a crowd of people.
> Tagrag and bobtail stood quite thick there
> And cried "What a sweet pretty picture !"

There is certainly nothing very elevated in good Mr.
Forrest's Hudibrastics ; yet the jingle of his verse is by
no means disagreeable ; and from his simple description
it is easy to form a definite notion of sturdy little Will
Hogarth "sitting in much state" in the great wooden
chair borrowed from the "Swans" at Queensborough,
and gravely sketching with the tagrag and bobtail
staring open-mouthed around him.

A still better word picture by Forrest illustrates
Hogarth's drawing of *Shaving in the Isle of Sheppey :*

> Till six o'clock we quiet lay
> And then got out for the whole day ;
> To fetch a barber out we send ;
> Stripp'd and in boots he doth attend,
> For he's a fisherman by trade ;
> Tann'd was his face, and shock his head ;

12

He flours our heads and trims our faces,
And the top barber of the place is ;
A bowl of milk and toasted bread
Are brought, of which, while Forrest eats,
To draw our picture Hogarth sits ;
Thornhill is in the barber's hands ;
Shaving himself, Will Tothall stands ;
While Scott is in a corner sitting,
And an unfinished sketch completing.

There is also a very droll tailpiece of Hogarth's design, and freely, vigorously and racily touched.

The "Hudibrastics," when the accounts were duly audited—and a rare chronicle these accounts are of pots of ale, cans of flip, bowls of punch, lobsters and tobacco —were handsomely bound to be preserved as a perpetual memorial of this famous expedition. By way of motto, Forrest prefixed to his poem a quotation of the inscription over Dulwich College porch, *Abi tu, et fac similiter.*

The great success of the *Harlot's Progress* had naturally incited William Hogarth with a strong and almost fierce desire to accomplish some other work of the same satirical force, of the same breadth of morality

BREAKFASTING &c

A . The Fisherman shaving

B . Mr Thornhill.

C . Mr Tothall shaving himself

D . Mr Hogarth drawing the Drawing.

E . Mr Forrest at Breakfast.

F . Mr Scott finishing a Drawing.

with that excellent performance. He determined that there should be on record a sequel, or at least a pendant to the drama whose lamentable action his pencil had just so poignantly narrated. He felt that it was in him, that it was his vocation, his duty to follow step by step the career of human vice, to point, with unerring finger, whither tend the crooked roads, to demonstrate as clearly as ever did mathematician—much more explicitly than ever did logician — that as surely as the wheels of the cart follow the hoofs of the horse, so surely will punishment follow sin. He was as yet but at the commencement of his trilogy: Clytemnestra might begin ; Orestes might succeed ; but the Eumenides had to come at last. He saw before him a whole ocean, seething, weltering, bubbling of pravities and impostures, and deadly lies, and evil passions. He heard the thorns crackling under the pot. He saw vice, not only stalking about with hungered looks, ragged garb and brandished bludgeon ; now robbing Dr. Mead's chariot in Holborn ; now stopping the Bristol mail ; now cutting Jonathan Wild's throat on the leads before the Sessions House, and being pressed to death for it ; now with sooty face and wild disguise of skins, stealing deer in the king's forests, and rioting in caves on surreptitious vension and smuggled Nantz ; * now being ducked for pocket-picking in the horse-pond behind the King's Mews, Charing Cross ; now cutting throats in night-cellars ; now going

---

* *Vide* the statutes at large for the " Black Act," by which poaching in disguise was made a felony, punishment death ; and the curious relation of the gentleman who fell among a gang of " Blacks," and was courteously entreated by them, and regaled at a rich supper, at which the solids were composed exclusively of venison, on condition, only, of never revealing the place of these sooty poachers' retreat.

filibustering and suffering death for piracy, to be afterwards gibbeted at Halfway Creek and the Triptoptrees ;
but Vice in embroidery and Mechlin lace, with a silver-
hilted sword, and a snuff-box enamelled by Rouquet, at
its side ; vice, painted and patched, whispering over fans,
painted with Hogarth's own " Progress " at Heidegger's
masquerade ; vice punting at the " Young Man's," stock-
jobbing in the Alley, brawling with porters and common
bullies at the Rose, chaffering with horse-jockeys at
Newmarket, clustered round the Cock-pit, applauding
Broughton the ex-yeoman of the guard, pugilist, and
lending its fine Holland shirt to Mr. Figg the prize-
fighter after a bout at back or broadsword,* dancing
attendance on the impudent and ugly German women,
for whom the kings of England forsook their lawful
wives, duelling in Hyde Park, and taking bribes in the
very lobby of the Parliament House.   William Hogarth
knew that he was enjoined to mark this duplex vice, to
burn it in the hand, to force it into the pillory, to pile
the hundredweights of his indignation upon it in his own
pressyard, to scathe and strangle it, and hang it as high
as Haman, to be the loathing and the scorn of better-
minded men.   Between the summer lodgings at South
Lambeth and other lodgings he took at Isleworth,
between the portraits and conversations, and the book-
plates and the benefit-tickets ; odds and ends of artists'
work, done in the way of business for the lords and
gentlemen who were good enough to employ him ;
shop-bills, " illustrating the commerce of Florence ;"
" breaking-up " tickets for Tiverton School ; scenes from

---

* Figg fought much more with the sword than with his fists.

Paradise Lost ; busts of Hesiod ; tickets for Figg the prize-fighter, for Milward, Jemmy Spiller, Joe Miller, and other comedians ; coats of arms for his friend George Lambert ; caricatures of Orator Henley ; benefit cards even for Harry Fielding, illustrating scenes from *Pasquin* and the *Mock Doctor ;* between high jinks and suburban jaunts, and pleasant evening strolls in Vauxhall Gardens ; between 1733 and 1735, he was planning, and maturing, and brooding over the *Rake's Progress.* The experiment was a dangerous one. The public are averse from tolerating *Paradise Regained* after *Paradise Lost,* the *Drunkard's Children* after the *Bottle,* the *Marriage of Figaro* after the *Barber of Seville.* And who has not yawned and rubbed his eyes over the second *Faust ?* But William Hogarth saw his way clearly before him, and was determined to pursue it. The pictures, eight in number, were painted by the end of 1733. In 1734, the proposals of subscription to the plates were issued. The subscription ticket was the well-known etching of the *Laughing Audience.* The sums were one guinea and a half for nine plates ; the ninth promised being *The Humours of a Fair*—no other than the far-famed *Southwark.*

Thus I sweep the stage, and sound the whistle for the curtain to draw up on the drama of *The Rake's Progress,* closing this paper with the form of receipt given by Hogarth to his subscribers :

> "Recd. Decr. 18th, of the Rt. Honble Lord Biron, half a guinea, being the first payment for nine plates, eight of which represents a *Rake's Progress,* and the ninth a *Fair,* which I promise to deliver at Michaelmas next, on receiving one guinea more. *Note.*—The *Fair* will be delivered at Christmas next, at sight of this receipt. The prints of the *Rake's Progress* will be two guineas, after the subscription is over."

> "WILLIAM HOGARTH."

VI.

The Rake's Progress : A Drama in Eight Acts.

AND what if all this should be but a Barmecide Feast ?
or worse, a meagre banquet of Dead Sea apples, husks
and draff, peelings, and outside leaves of lettuces, and
the like unpalatable food ?　I have talked largely, for I
don't know how many pages, of a succulent Hogarth
ordinary—of rich viands and rare wines ; and lo ! I have
nothing better to offer you than the skimmings of
skimmed milk, and the gyle of thrice-brewed malt.
Here is your mess of pottage ; here is your soup *à la
purée de pavé;* but I give you simply the paving-stone,
and have kept back the savoury stock of meat, and
spices, and pungent herbs.　Are my many good friends
to be fed with Æolic digammas, and shall I fill their
bellies with the east wind ?　Oh ! I can write out the
bill of fare well enough : white and brown soups,
hors-d'œuvres, entrées, roasts, *relévés,* dessert, coffee, and
chasse.　But, good Mr. Essayist, where is the dinner ? or
rather, *where are the plates ?*　Can there be anything
more meagre and unsatisfactory than the description of
a series of pictorial performances without the pictures
themselves ? and of what avail are these dissertations
upon William Hogarth, Painter and Engraver, without

some of Hogarth's pictures by way of illustration? Of little more tangible use, I fear, than the purse now empty, but which once held all those brave bank notes —of little more than a cask of home-brewed without a key, and with no gimlet handy—than the bill for a feast that is over and paid—than the gay hat and feathers which come home for the dear child who died yesterday. Have you ever opened a desk, and found a pair of cards, a large and a small one, tied together with a true-lover's knot in silver twist? These were for your own wedding; only that ceremony never came off as intended, as you know full well, grizzling over your gruel in those lonely chambers, with the laundress filching the contents of the caddy from under your nose, and muttering disparagement of yourself to the bootboy on the staircase.

I should have liked to possess an empire, and I have but a little Elba of Essay. I should have wished my bald prose to serve but as a framework to Hogarth's rich pregnant pictures. I revel in dreams of a vast edition, a big book that you might knock down an enemy with—nay, barricade your door withal against the button-holding world. Isn't there a size called "elephant folio?" "Ho! there, thou Barmecidean cook! Send me up such an elephantine Hogarth of my own, full of plates, line for line, touch for touch, tint for tint, of the master's handling. Serve me swiftly a *catalogue raisonné* of all my hero's pictures and all his engravings, to his minutest snuff-box achievements and pen-and-ink scratchings. Let me whet my palate with footnotes as with Spanish olives, and give me a varied appendix by way of dessert." The Barmecide says this, and claps his hands, and flourishes his table napkin ; but the cook doesn't serve up anything worthy of a name of a feast, hot or cold. Shamefaced, I glanced at a few tiny woodcuts which chequer these pages, and admit that at my banquet there have been little better beyond hand-clapping and napkin-flourishing, with some sparse halfpenny loaves, and latten spoons and forks, and a plated cruetstand. What happened to the Barmecide who boasted of his hot joints ? Alas ! *he had his ears boxed*. My own lobes tingle at the apologue. What happens to the finger-post which points out the way, and goeth not itself any way ? It is consulted, and passed by in indifference. And what is the doom of the showman whose exhibition is always "going to begin," and never does begin at all ? The public at last grow tired ; pouch up their pence, or wisely expend them at the next booth, where there is a real live armadillo and a spotted girl whom one can really pinch. Only—let this stand on record for all explanation and excuse— were I to give you even the sketchiest copy of every one of Hogarth's pictures to illustrate these Essays on his life and character, you would have to wait until the year 1870 for the delivery of volume the first of my elephant folio. For the writer's life is very short, and the engraver's art is very long. *Cras mihi*, it may be, O dear friends and brothers gone before ! and many a man vainly hoping to sit under his own umbrageous fig-tree and his own vine, finds a chill strike to his marrow, for indeed he is sitting in the cold shade of the cypress and the yew.

I had some thoughts of issuing modest proposals for a subscription—I think ten thousand pounds would be sufficient—to enable me to illuminate a copious biography of Hogarth, with facsimiles of his performances. You should see how the price of steel plates would rise forthwith in the market, and how I would set all the etching-needles and graving-tools of our Cousenses, our Lewises, our Barlows, to work. I had some thoughts of advertising for a patron—a nobleman preferred. I find the descendants of Lorenzo de' Medici numerous enough, and supplying the needy from their golden-balled palaces with funds to any amount; but alas! the Medici only lend at interest, and on tangible security. So, for the present, these papers must be without plates, and the drama of the RAKE'S PROGRESS must be performed without dresses, scenery, properties, decorations, or even a shovelful of blue fire.

Do we need a prologue to scene the first? Here are a few lines that may serve, from Mr. Pope's epistle to Lord Bathurst :—

> Who sees pale Mammon pine amidst his store
> Sees but a backward steward for the poor :
> This year a reservoir to keep and spare ;
> The next a fountain, spouting through his heir.*

---

* I admire the originality of the image by which a spendthrift is compared to a conduit-pipe ; but, as often happens with Pope, his exquisite polish and musical rise and fall often conceal a careless, an illogical, and sometimes a mischievous argument. If "pale Mammon" be but a "backward steward to the poor," keeping and sparing in a reservoir which will afterwards spout up in his squandercash heir's *grandes eaux !* there is no such great harm done. The poor are only kept out of their dues for a time, and come to their own at last. If Pope's moral be taken *tale quale*, alternate avarice and improvidence must be in the main very good things, and charity only lies fallow for a time to produce a more abundant harvest. Yet I have little doubt that had Pope been philosophizing in prose instead of verse he would have drawn a very different conclusion. Would it not be more rational to inculcate the position that excessive frugality and excessive

And again : the reverend Doctor Hoadly's epigraph :—

> O vanity of Age untoward,
> Ever spleeny, ever froward !
> Why those bolts and massy chains—
> Squint Suspicion's jealous pains ?
> Why, thy toilsome journey o'er,
> Lay'st thou in a useless store ?
> Hope along with Time is flown—
> Nor canst thou reap of field thou'st sown.

It is all very true. Why, indeed ? Yet the old
gentleman who was the reservoir, and has now left all to
his heir, at the sign of the Fountain, has only done as
Harpagon, and Gripewell, and Vulture Hopkins, and
John Elwes, Esquire, delighted to do. The Rake's papa
saved thousands of candle-ends. Young Squander
comes and burns them at either extremity, setting the
welkin in a blaze.

Let me adopt a nomenclature that for the nonce
may serve the purposes of showmanship. You see that
Ralph Grindall Mucklethrift Moneypenny, Esq., of
Foreclose Court, near Parchment-Regis, Bondshire,
somewhere in the west of England it may be, is

---

lavishness are both equally pernicious ? The miser keeps money out of
circulation, stints his household, starves himself, and grinds the faces of the
poor. The prodigal spends his long-hoarded gold, indeed, with a free
hand ; but to whom does it go ? To sharpers, and bullies, and bona-robas,
and rascal mountebacks, fiddlers, squallers, and tavern-drawers. It is as
on the Derby day, lobsters, pigeon pies, and half-emptied champagne flasks
are flung to the rapscallionry of pseudo-Bohemia and Ethiopia. Hogarth
was a sounder philosopher than Pope. No honest man profits by the rake's
fortune. It was all got over Lucifer's back, and it is all spent under his
abdomen. *Ce que vient par la flûte, s'en va par le tambour.* In contra-
distinction to this, we see that when Francis Goodchild, the industrious
apprentice, attains wealth, he feeds Lazarus blind and Lazarus crippled at
his gate.

gathered to his fathers. He leaves all to his son
Thomas, who speedily obtains the royal permission to
assume the name and arms of Rakewell. His mamma
was one of the Rakewells in Staffordshire, a family
which in their time have entertained several crowned
heads ; and Tom's maternal grandfather left him a snug
estate to swell the fortune—mainly a ready-money one
—left him by his old scrivening father.

So Tom has come into his property, and stands in
the musty parlour of his father's house, eager, trembling,
almost fevered with that odd sensation of Possession.
Even princes, heirs-apparent, for years expectant of a
crown, have been thus feverishly nervous on the great
day when the old king has turned his face to the wall,
and the courtiers have come trooping through the
antechambers to pay homage and lip-service to the new
monarch. So Frederick, who was to be called Great,
was feverish and nervous when the Hof Kammerer told
him that the drunken old corporal his father was dead,
would never more thrash subjects with his cane, or
scourge precentors' daughters, and that he, the bullied,
despised Fritz, was " König von Preussen." And I have
heard of a duke, who the day after he had ceased to be
a marquis by courtesy, scribbled his ducal signature
some two hundred and fifty times over his blotting-pad.
The old miser's memorandum-book lies on the ground.
Hogarth makes entry for him of the date when "my
son Tom came from Oxford," when he "dined at the
French ordinary"—treating Tom, doubtless,—and when
he "put off his bad shilling." Young Thomas has done
with Oxford and all its humours. He may dine at
whatever ordinary he chooses ; and if he does not " put

off his bad shilling," he will at least put off a great many
good guineas of his own.

For all the guineas are his, and the moidores, and
pieces of eight, even to the hoard of worn Jacobuses
which come tumbling from the rooftree (even as they
did when the Heir of Lynn was about to hang himself)
as the servant nails the black hangings to the cornice.
A bale of black cloth has come from the draper's, and
awaits hanging in its due place. How it would have
twisted the heartstrings of the deceased curmudgeon to
see this waste of stout Yorkshire in vain trappings ; and
how he would have invoked the gibbet law of Halifax
against those who were "backbarend" and "handhabend"
with that precious store of well-teazled broadcloth !
The old man was the architect of his own fortunes—
chiefly built of cheese and mousetraps, with parchment
dressings—you may be sure ; but the undertakers have
found out a scutcheon for him to deck his funeral pomps
withal. The bearings are, significantly, "on a field
sable, three vices proper;" motto, "Beware." Like
almost everything our Hogarth does, the motto is as a
two-edged sword, and cuts both ways. The motto is
better word-play than the patrician *Ver non semper
viret.* The hard-screwed vices express not only the
tenacity of the old man's love of gold ; and the motto
acts not only as a caution to prodigals against falling
into the clutches of a usurer ; but, to my thinking, there
is a counter allusion to the "vices" of human nature ;
and that the "Beware" may also be taken as a counsel
to young Tom.

Already this young man had sore need of warning.
Look at that pair of sorrowing women—mother and

daughter — in the right-hand corner of the picture. Tom has wronged the girl, cruelly; that is painfully manifest. Young Tom Moneypenny, screwed down to a starvation allowance by his papa, may have promised marriage to this poor mantua-maker—the miser's house-keeper's pretty daughter, perhaps ; but Thomas Rakewell, Esq., could not think of contracting so degrading an alliance. So he strives to cover that broken heart with a golden plaster. A handful of guineas must surely atone for the mere breach of a solemn oath. Tom gives freely enough, and the girl cries and points to the ring the traitor has bought her, while the mother—a virago every inch of her—scolds and objurgates.

What does it matter—this tiny capful of wind on the great idle Lake of Pleasure ? Tom's steward—the harsh-visaged man with the pen in his mouth—thinks that it *does* matter; and that the richer is the heir, the greater care he should have of his ready money. He places his hand on a bag of gold which Master Tom has by him for present emergencies, and would prevent further disbursements if he could. The expression of his face, the mere action of the hand on the money-bag, half in remonstrance, half in the instinct of avarice—for he is a true disciple of the old money-spinner deceased— are very eloquent.

The heir thinks merely to trim his barque by casting this golden ballast overboard :—so *vogue la galère.* Sir Sans Pitié the False has disdainfully flung a handful of ducats to the damsel he has betrayed, and ridden away Tom has other things than distressed damsels to think of. The tailor is measuring him for his fine new clothes.

The steward tells him dazzling tales of the India bonds, the mortgages, leases and releases that he inherits. Before him stretches in glittering perspective the Pro-. mised Land of Pleasure. The era of pinching and pining is over, and Plenty comes swaggering in with a full horn. A decrepit old woman comes to light a fire, for the first time these many years, in the fireplace, of which the grate is dull, and the bars rusty. Soon the faggots will crackle and leap up into a rare blaze : it would be as well to burn that apronful of love-letters beginning, " To Mrs. Sarah Young—My dearest life," which the exaspe- rated old mother displays to the false-swearer. The fire had need blaze away, even if it made a bonfire of every memento of the old man's penuriousness. He saved everything. There is a cupboard full of old clothes, worn-out boots, and the dilapidated cauls of periwigs. The lamp outside his door was smashed in a frolic by the Mohocks. The miser brought the wreck of iron and glass indoors, and saved it. He was bidden to Venture Hopkins, or some equally famous usurer's funeral. The miser purloined the gravedigger's spade, hid it under his cloak, and brought it home, to save it. He had bought a handsome Bible at the price of wastepaper. The sole of his shoe wanted mending ; and you see, in the fore- ground, how he has pieced it with a portion of the cover of the holy volume. He kept a cat which he nine-tenths starved. You see the wretched animal mewing over a chest crammed with massy plate, and wishing, doubtless, that the chased silver was wholesome paunch. There is a Flemish picture on the wall—the usual miser gloating over the usual money-sacks ; but I will warrant the painting was not there merely for ornament: It must

have served a turn many and many a time to eke out
the little cash, and the great discount in a bill. A rusty
spur, a pair of horn spectacle-frames without glasses, the
old man's furred cap, his crutch, his walking-cane, a pair
of battered swords he kept for fear of robbers, and a
long-disused jack and spit, removed from the fireplace
and thrown by in a cupboard, where they are hoarded
as old iron—attest with eloquence difficult to be improved, all the self-torturing avarice of this poor, wealthy,
griping wretch. Let us close the scene upon his sordid
memory, and follow the fortunes of his heir.*

---

* Gilpin—*Essay on Prints*—greatly and justly admires the perspective
of this picture ; and it may be termed, without pedantry, an ingenious
isometrical projection. ·Thomas Cook, engraver, author of *Hogarth
Restored* (London, 1813), and who himself engraved many unpublished
Hogarths, speaks of the Rake's face, in this first stage of his history, as
"marked by that uneasy, unmeaning vacancy, which seems, by nature,
the characteristic of a dupe." But I rather discern in poor young Tom's
countenance the simplicity, the eagerness, and the carelessness of youth, as
yet unmarred by the stamp of cynical sinfulness. The features are eminently
beautiful ; and although he has already been a profligate, and ruined this
unhappy Sarah Young, I fancy I can trace a struggle between conscience
and shame, and the recklessness of the nascent spendthrift. Tom does not
wholly belong to the Evil One yet, else he would be content with laughing
at his victim, and would not take the trouble to give her any money. It is
likewise the opinion of Thomas Cook, that the harsh-visaged man with the
pen, whom I described as the miser's steward, is "a pettifogging attorney,"
and when he lays his hands on the bag of gold, is actuated by "propensities
too ˙ ͟n attributed to certain practisers of the law," and "seizing the
earliest opportunity of robbing his employer ;" but I believe in the steward's
fidelity, and only think him to be remonstrating on the folly of spending
money at all. Such men love gold, not for the sake of what it will purchase,
but for its own sake,—because it is gold. When Lucrece Borgia, in Victor
Hugo's play, asks Gubetta why he borrows money from the young nobles,
he being so much richer than they,—he makes answer, "*Pardieu! madame,
pour en avoir.*" To *have* money, and, having some, to have *more*. "All
the baccy in the world," and then—"more baccy," was the sailor's notion
of perfect happiness and unlimited riches.

Thomas is himself again in Act the Second of this
tragi-comedy, "*The Rake's Levée.*" He lives in a splendid
suite of apartments—say in Pall Mall, or in Soho Square,
or in Great Queen Street, Lincoln's Inn. We don't see
the ceiling in the picture; else, I daresay, we should find
it painted with the story of Danaë, or that of the Golden
Fleece. A splendid picture, in a frame as splendid, of
the *Judgment of Paris*, is the principal ornament of the
grand saloon; but that it has been bought merely for
show, and not through any love for art, is plain from its
pair of pendants; portraits of gamecocks in gaudy frames.
An arched doorway exhibits beyond a gaudy antecham-
ber, where the humbler class of courtiers cool their heels.
There is a French tailor; a poet—yes, a poet, who reads
one of his own epistles to wile away the time; and a
milliner. Now the milliner—you know her by the long
cardboard-box under her arm—is, I can't help thinking,
our old friend, the deceived Sarah Young. Has the
golden ointment healed her heart? Has she accepted
the Rake's money, and gone into business for herself?
Not at a mean frock-shop as Hogarth's own sisters did,
selling (see engraved card) "ye best and most fashionable
ready-made frocks, stript dimity and flanel, blue and
canvas frocks, and blue-coat boys' Dra^{rs}. Likewise
tickens and Hollands at ye piece." But rather as a
fashionable *modiste* in the New Exchange, like that
celebrated "white milliner," the Duchess of Tyrconnell,
or "Mrs. Holt," who lived at the "Two Olive Posts in
ye Broad part of the Strand," for whom Hogarth also
engraved a card, and who sold "Lustrings, Sattins,
Padesois, Velvets, Damasks, Fans, Legorne hats, Violin
strings, Books of Essences, Venice treacle, Balsomes;"

and in a back warehouse (!) "all sorts of Italian wines, Florence cordials, Oyl, Olives, Anchovies, Capers, Vermicelli, Saussidges, Parmesan cheese, and Naples soap." Sarah Young, with that odd, half-vindictive, half-affectionate hankering after the man who has deceived her—a hankering by no means uncommon to her sex—has solicited the high honour of being milliner in ordinary to his worship Thomas Rakewell, Esq.—for gentlemen had female milliners in 1735 ; just as ladies had staymakers and "taylors" of the ruder sex. Sarah, then, furnishes Thomas with his bands of Valenciennes and Point de Dunquerque, with his ruffles and laced nightcaps, with essences and ribbons for his hair. And you may be certain that Thomas, who has quite forgotten those fervent billets in which she was his "dearest life," does not forget, while condescending to patronize, to run a long bill with her. Will Sarah turn out to be Nemesis ? Will this deceived white milliner become *Alba cura*, jump up behind Tom's chariot, and bid the coachman drive to Styx Old Stairs, where his worship will take water, in Charon's barge—like young Bibo—for Tartarus ? Ah, no ! A vulgar melodramatist would, with much speed, have brought about this consummation ; but William Hogarth knew better. Five thousand times better .did he know the inexhaustible love, and tenderness, and longsuffering, and mercy, that are for ever welling, even from the bruised heart of a betrayed woman.

Such love and tenderness are lost upon the graceless prodigal. Three years have elapsed. The uncouth, but not quite hardened hobbledehoy has cast off his awkwardness and his conscience, and has all the allures of a

fine gentleman. He holds levées. His mode of life
may be quoted from Brampton's *Man of Taste* :—

> Without Italian, and without an ear,
> To Bononcini's music I adhere.
> To boon companions I my time would give,
> With players, pimps, and parasites I'd live ;
> I would with jockeys from Newmarket dine,
> And to rough riders give my choicest wine ;
> My evenings all I would with sharpers spend,
> And make the thief-taker my bosom friend ;
> In Figg, the prizefighter, the day delight,
> And sup with Colley Cibber every night.

Cioé, I would hotly dispute concerning Verdi and
Donizetti, and go into ecstasies over the sixpenny
libretto books, not knowing one word of Italian. I
would affect to despise the grand old music of the
English school, and give a guinea a lesson to some
lantern-jawed sallowface, who, before he turned music-
master, was a barber at Bologna. I would stop late in
my club billiard-rooms and smoking-rooms, and have
my toadies and my convenient men. Yes, I would dine
with Newmarket jockeys, and give rough riders Clos
Vougeot ; and look in at night at the subscription
hazard-tables ; and sometimes, for fun, go the rounds of
Thieves' Kitchens and Rats' Castles, under the guidance
and guardianship of Inspector Bull's-eye. I should be
sure to attend the "international" prizefights, and be
full of solicitude as to the designs of the Staleybridge
Chicken upon the vacant belt ; and I might sup with
the low comedian at night, and make the man who sings
nigger-songs tipsy with champagne. And upon my
word, I, Thomas Rakewell, suppositious prodigal, must
be 125 years old ; for in this present year, 1860, I am
precisely the same Thomas Rakewell, and indulge in

precisely the same refined and agreeable pleasures that marked my *Progress* in 1735.

"Thou hast it now," Thomas ; "King, Cawdor, Glamis all." In the grand saloon the Rake receives his courtiers of the first class. There is the fencing-master, with his "saha!" his carte and his tierce, and his *raison demonstrative*.* There is the *Improver of Gardens*, designed by Hogarth for a certain Bridgeman, "a worshipper of the modern style, who attempted to create landscape, to realize painting, and to improve nature"—in short, an archetype of "Capability Brown." There is the kneeling Horse Jockey, the descendant of Cromwell's Dick Pace, of "coffin mare" celebrity, who holds a silver race-cup, inscribed, "Won at Epsom by Silly Tom," a very appropriate name for Squire Rakewell's "Crack." Observe the turned-up shade to the jockey's cap, his easy tunic, the loose turnover tops to his boots, and the tremendous weight of his whip.† There is the hired bravo, the Sparafucile, the Saltabadil to this young monarch *qui s'amuse*—who kills or cudgels in town or country, with promptitude and despatch—with his bloated form, black

---

* The fencing-master is intended for the portrait of one Dubois, a *maître d'armes* of much renown. He was killed in a duel with one of the same name. See *Grub Street Journal* (May 16, 1734). "Yesterday, between two and three in the afternoon, a duel was fought in Marylebone fields, between Mr. Dubois, a Frenchman, and Mr. Dubois, an Irishman, both fencing-masters, the former of which was run through the body, but walked a considerable way from the place, and is now under the hands of an able surgeon, who hath great hopes of his recovery." But afterwards, in the same journal, under date of May 23 : "Yesterday morning, died Mr. Dubois, of a wound he received in a duel."

† "Feather weights" were unknown in those early days of the turf. Heats were not ridden by pigmies ; and race-horses were strong, muscular, large-limbed animals, not satin-skinned, greyhound-like, hot-house plants.

wig, dingy laced hat, and a patch over his nose. He has
his hand, curiously, on his *right* side, as if he didn't know
where his hand was ; but he knows well enough where
to lay his right hand : namely, on the hilt of his hanger,
as he enters into the stereotype protestations of fidelity.
He has brought a characteristic letter of recommenda-
tion to his new patron :—" Sir, the captain is a man of
honour, and his sword may serve you.   Yours, Wᵐ Stab."
The foolish, sensuous rake, in 'broidered slippers and
richly laced morning gown and cap, seems much inclined
to take the honourable captain into his employ ; from
which we may glean, that, fond as he may be of midnight
frolics, beating the watch, roasting tradesmen, terrifying
women and so forth, active courage is not among the
characteristics of Thomas Rakewell, Esq., and that he
needs the bravo's brawny arm to protect him in his
pranks, and give impunity to his impertinences.

There is a blower on the French-horn present too ;
and a heavy, somewhat good-natured looking man with
a couple of quarter-staves, whom we may take for Figg,
the pugilist.*

---

* There is some difficulty in "making out" likenesses in a period when
almost everybody went clean shaven, and wore a wig ; but comparing the
bewigged pugilist in the levée scene with the bare-polled prizefighter holding
the broadsword, who stands on the platform, in the card etched by Simpson,
after a design by Hogarth, for James Figg, there can be little doubt, I think,
that both are meant for the same person.   The inscription describes Figg
as "master of yᵉ noble science of defence ;" and states that he dwelt " on
yᵉ right hand in Oxford Road, near Adam and Eve Court ;" and that
"he teaches gentlemen yᵉ use of yᵉ small backsword and quarter-staff, at
home and abroad."   There is not a word said about fisticuffs or the
"gloves."   Figg appears to have been in the "zenith of his glory" about
1731.   His portrait was also painted by Ellis, a man who imitated Hogarth
in small "conversations ;" and the Ellis-Figg portrait was engraved in

The prominent figure standing to the left of the Rake is Essex, the dancing-master. He is even a greater

---

mezzotint by Faber, and published in October of the year just mentioned. It is not at all uncommon, now, to see daubs in the curiosity-shops about Leicester-Square, which purport to be "original" portraits of Figg, by Hogarth. The admirers of Messrs. Sayers and Heenan may find delectation in the following flight towards Parnassus anent this distinguished Mr. Figg :—

> The mighty combatant, the first in fame,
> The lasting glory of his native shame (?)
> Rash and unthinking men, at length be wise ;
> Consult your safety, and resign the prize :
> Nor tempt superior force, but timely fly
> The vigour of his arm, the quickness of his eye.

In the name of the prophet—Figg ! Captain John Godfrey, in his quarto pamphlet on *The Useful Science of Defence* (1747), calls Figg "the Atlas of the sword ;" "and may he long," the captain continues, "remain the gladiating statue ! In him strength, resolution, and unparalleled judgment conspired to form a matchless master. There was a majesty shone in his countenance and blazed in all his actions beyond all I ever saw." And yet the captain was old enough to have seen Marlborough, and Peterborough, and Eugène, and Tallard, and Vendôme. Perhaps those heroes, although their actions were certainly "blazing," were not very "majestic" as to their countenances. Chetwood, in his *History of the Stage*, tells us that Figg informed him that he had not bought a shirt for twenty years, but had sold some dozens. The aristocracy were his purveyors of body-linen. In the sixth volume of Dodsley's *Collection of Fugitive Pieces*, there are some verses by the witty Doctor Byrom of a sword contest between Figg and Sutton, in which the first was victorious. Figg appeared on the stage calm and sedate, "with a fresh shaven pate." They wore "armigers" too. Figg's arm was encircled with a blue ribbon ; Sutton's with a red one. The fortune of the day was for a long time suspended, till Figg hit his opponent a stroke on the knee, and so disabled him. At his amphitheatre in the Oxford Road he engaged with not only Sutton, but "William Holmes and Felix MacGuire, the two first (Hibernicè) and most profound swordsmen of the kingdom of Ireland. 'Tis not," the advertisement sets forth, "the accidental blow which Mr. Holmes received on his metacarpus the last time he fought with Mr. Figg has cooled his courage, or given room to Mr. MacGuire to decline his interest. An impression of Figg's card has been sold for eight guineas.

dandy than Tom Rakewell. Laced coat and ruffles, monstrous cuffs, resplendent wig, silk stockings and diamond buckles, deck his radiant person ; but for that unmistakable self-satisfied smirk, and that ridiculously diminutive " kit," and that exquisitely pointed toe, you might mistake the predecessor of Vestris and D'Egville for a dancing-master. It is fated that the Rake— whether he have rings on his fingers, or bells on his toes, or not—shall have, for the present, music wherever he goes. Besides the twanging of the French horn—the probabilities are a little violated by its professor presuming to sound that instrument while his worship, Squire Thomas, is conferring with Captain Saltabadil— besides the squeaking of Mr. Essex's kit, we have the strumming of a harpsichord, touched by the figure with the enormous periwig, who sits with his back to the audience. He is trying over a new opera, *The Rape of the Sabines*.* The *dramatis personæ* appear on the fly-leaf, and include the name of Senesino. But *majora canamus !* over the back of the maestro's chair there hangs, to trail at length far over the ground, a document, resembling several " yards of songs " tacked to a bill of costs in a Chancery suit, and inscribed with an enumeration of the gorgeous presents bestowed on the Italian opera-singer, Farinelli, by the nobility and gentry

---

* The figure of the maestro at the harpsichord has by some commentators been held to be Handel, but there is no evidence to go to the jury. It must certainly be remembered that he who was afterwards to write the *Messiah* was at one period of his career manager of the Italian Opera ; but I don't think it likely that he would spend his mornings at Tom Rakewell's levées. Besides, Brampton makes *his* rake say, " To Bononcini's music I adhere." B. and H. were sworn foes.

of this kingdom. The extremity of the schedule half covers an engraving, representing a lady of fashion kneeling at an altar erected before the statue of the illustrious soprano ; and exclaiming, label-wise, " One God, one Farinelli," an impious ejaculation attributed to some aristocratic female devotee of the signor. Poor Farinelli ! He was the friend of princes, and abounded in diamond snuff-boxes, but his singing, after all, must have resembled the tootle-tooing of a flute.

This, then, is the morning's reflection bearing on the previous night's entertainment of T. R., Esq. It must be admitted that while evidences of vanity and frivolity are plentiful enough, young Tom's pursuits do not, as yet, appear outrageously vicious. On that long schedule over the chair you read that Thomas Rakewell, Esq., has presented a golden snuff-box, chased with the story of Orpheus charming the brutes, to Farinelli. By the way, why shouldn't the periwigged unknown at the harpsichord be the signor himself ? There is nothing so very unpardonable in making such gifts. At least, the apologist may urge, there are no soda-water bottles, betting books, ends of cigars—(were those vanities then invented ?)—about, to mark the sensual, unprofitable mode of life adopted by this deluded young man. Tom seems, at the worst, to be simply wasting his time ; and the student of Fielding, when he has well considered Hogarth's levée, will turn to the description of a fashionable Do-nothing's day, as set forth in *Joseph Andrews* : " In the morning I arose, took my great stick, and walked out in my green frock, with my hair in papers (a groan from Adams), and sauntered about till ten. Went to the auction ; told Lady —— she had a dirty face ;

laughed heartily at something Captain —— said,—I can't remember what, for I did not very well hear it; whispered Lord ——; bowed to the Duke of ——; and was going to bid for a snuff-box, but did not, for fear I should have had it. From two to four dressed myself. (A groan.) Four to six dined. (A groan.) Six to eight coffee-house? eight to nine Drury Lane playhouse; nine to ten Lincoln's Inn Fields "—you see Fielding does not make Mr. Abraham Adams groan at the mention of coffee-houses and theatres—" Ten to twelve drawing-room. (A great groan.) At which Adams said with some vehemence, ' Sir, this is below the life of an animal, hardly above vegetation.' "

And so it is; but worse is to follow; vice active in lieu of vice passive. Prompter, sound the whistle; and shift the scene, ye carpenters. We come to the third tableau of the *Rake's Progress.*

Orgie: and, I am afraid the less said about it the better; yet there must be some definite record made of this stage in Tom's journey; and after all, I am writing about William Hogarth's works and time; about the suckling of fools indeed, but *not* the chronicles of small beer. Truth must out, and Tom is going to the dogs with dreadful swiftness. Act three represents a very different scene of dissipation to the dull sensuality of the topers in the *Modern Midnight Conversation,* for alas! woman, vicious, and impudent, and fallen, but still, under Hogarth's pencil, angelically beautiful, is there. Tom is far gone in foreign wines, drunk on the splendid and disreputable premises he condescends to patronize. There are nine ladies, two ballad-singers, and a drawer (in the background) visible, but only two gentlemen.

Tom has just been robbed of his watch by the fair one who declares she adores him. Fair one Number 1 passes the stolen property to fair one Number 2; and fair one Number 3—a very hideous negress indeed—looks on with a grin of approval. Two fair ones have quarrelled, and one is squirting aqua-vitæ from her mouth at her adversary; the shot is a good one, and the range is long, at least three feet. In the background another daughter of Folly is setting fire to a map of the world. A rich mirror of Venice glass has been smashed in the scuffle; but Thomas will pay for all, or will halve the damage with that other intoxicated gentleman, whose wig falling off reveals his neat black crop beneath. He is quite imbecile, and is as a sheep for the shearers. The portraits of the twelve Cæsars grace this abode of revelry; while the Kitcat effigy of mine host, Pontac, looks down in plethoric serenity on the agreeable scene. Mine host, you have the best of it; the triumph of the fair ones is short-lived; the beadles of Bridewell wait for them, and there is hemp galore to beat. After all—for apoplexy, an excise information, or a man killed at an orgie, may put a stop to Pontac's profits—those ragged minstrels and ballad-singers, who come bawling and twanging in, may derive most benefit from the joyous company and the gay life. *They last*, these scrapers and caterwaulers; so do the beggars. We go to India, and returning, find our old vagabond acquaintances as ragged as ever, and yet not older, so it seems. They watch the procession defile, the panorama unroll, the farce play itself through; they watch and grin, and shout, and call us noble captains, and fair ladies, and have their share of our loose coppers, and see us all out.

Our friends die, but the vagabonds remain and flourish. And I *have* seen the seed of the righteous begging their bread.*

I cannot be more explicit in describing young Thomas's evening entertainment, beyond hinting that, to judge from the trophies in the foreground, he has been to a masquerade, and in a conflict with some semi-paralytic watchman—where is Captain Saltabadil?—has carried off the staff and lantern of the guardian of the night. Many more pages could be devoted to the consideration of the Pontacian symposium ; but I can't tell all the things that are on the tip of my tongue. I can't tell them, at least, on Cornhill. There is reverence due to young readers. You must wait until the advent of my elephant folio. Meanwhile, go you to Hogarth's own picture, and study its sad details.

It is to be noted as an intentional feature of this young man's career, that from the first he is, as to the belongings of his own sex, Alone. The unlucky lad is an orphan, nay, most probably, has never known a mother's care. I can't discover in his after career, until his marriage, that he has any friends, nay, that any living soul save Mrs. Sarah Young, the milliner, cares anything

---

* The Cæsars,—only six of them are visible, but we may be permitted to assume the existence of the remaining half-dozen,—have been barbarously mutilated. The heads have been cut bodily from the canvas, with one exception, Nero. To complete the propriety of the exemption there should surely have been added to the Cæsars a *silhouette*, at least, of Elagabalus. Pray note the face and figure of the woman ballad-singer yelling out the "Black Joke," the melody of which questionable ditty was selected by Thomas Moore whereto to set the curiously antithetical words beginning "Sublime was the warning that liberty spoke." I think the air is also known by the title of the "Sprig of shamrock so green."

about him. He has, even, no associates, young and wild as himself; and knows nobody beyond tavern-drawers, prize-fighters, and buffoons. He is solitary in the midst of all this revelry and this vice. Probably Hogarth so isolated him to concentrate the tragic interest of the drama in his person; and yet, I think, some thought prepense must have moved him to teach us that a pocketful of money, lavishly spent, won't buy us friends, or even companions, more reputable than Captain Saltabadil, or Lieutenant Sparafucile, or "Yrs. Wm Stab."

Yet Thomas Rakewell, Esq., goes to Court. All kinds of queer people could make their bow at St. James's a century and a quarter ago; and a birthday reception was almost as incongruous a medley as one of those New Years' night balls at the Czar's Winter Palace, to which almost every man in St. Petersburg who can manage to raise a dress-coat and a pair of patent leather boots, was invited. Moreover, in 1735, there were two excellent recipes for becoming a man of fashion: to wear fine clothes, and to frequent the coffee-houses. Now-a-days, dress has ceased to denote rank, and clubs and the ballot have done away with coffee-house life. Where can a man " drop in " now, and boast that he has mingled with " the wits? " Bah! the wits themselves have departed in peace. Grub Street is pulled down, and Buttons's, Wills's, Toms's, are shadows.

Nevertheless, Thomas, in raiment of most astounding splendour, shall go to Court. So wills it Hogarth, in Act the Fourth of the *Rake's Progress*. It is the 1st of March, the birthday of Queen Caroline, and likewise St. David's day. With his usual happy ingenuity,

Hogarth has fixed the date by the introduction of a Welsh gentleman (doubtless a lineal descendant of Captain Fluellen), who—a prodigious leek adorning his hat—is marching proudly along St. James's Street. This Cambro-Briton carries his hands in a muff—a somewhat strange ornament for a gentleman; but muffs were much worn at this time. You may see a beau with a muff in Hogarth's *Taste in High Life;* and I remember that Voltaire, in his *Siècle de Louis Quinze*, tell us, that when Damiens attempted to assassinate the well-beloved king, the courtiers, in consequence of the intense cold, had their hands thrust in enormous muffs.

Tom, embroidered, laced, and powdered up to the eyes, goes to Court in a sedan-chair. It is a hired one, No. 41, and the hinder chairman, by the leek in his hat, would also appear to be a Welshman. The rake's affairs have been going but badly lately. He is deeply dipped. He has made ducks and drakes of all the ready money, all the India bonds and mortgages, all the leases and re-leases. He has been shaking his elbow, my dear. Hogarth insists very plainly on the gambling element in his career. In front of his sedan a group of blackguard boys are gambling on the flags of St. James's Street. Two shoeblacks are deep in dice. Two other ragged little losels—one a newshawker, it would appear by the post-horn in his girdle, and who carries a voting-ticket in his hat; the other absurdly accoutred in the dilapidated periwig of some adult gambler gone to grief—are equally deep in cards. The hand visible to the spectator—that of the boy in the wig—shows only *black* pips: and on a post you read the word "black." On the other hand a flash of lightning breaks through the

stormy sky,* and points direct to *White's* notorious
gaming-house. The allusion is passably significant. It
is, doubtless, at White's that Tom has gambled away the
paternal thousands; but, be it as it may, it is in St.
James's Street, going to the birthday drawing-room,
that the rake feels the first practical effect of the heraldic
monition—"Beware!" The sheriff of Middlesex has
been long running up and down in his bailiwick seeking
for Tom; and now two catchpoles march up to the
sedan-chair, and capture the body of Thomas Rakewell,
him to have and to hold at the suit of our sovereign
Lord the King and somebody else—very possibly the
tailor who had made that fine suit of laced clothes for him.
The poor wretch, at best but a faint-hearted shirker of
responsibilities, is quite overwhelmed and cowed at his
arrest. Not yet, however, is he to languish in the Fleet
or the Marshalsea. Mrs. Sarah Young, the milliner,
happens to be passing with her bandbox. Her tender
heart is touched at the sight of the perfidious Tom's
misery. Bless her for a good woman! She lays her
hand on the catchpole's arm. She "stays harsh justice
in its mid career;". she whips out a washleather bag
full of money, and I declare that she pays Tom's·debt
and costs, and very presumably gives the catchpoles a
guinea for themselves.

Thomas, there is yet time. Thomas, you may make
Sarah Young an honest woman, assist her in the millinery business, and become a reputable citizen, occasionally indulging in connubial junketings at Sadler's Wells,

---

* The sky, and indeed the whole background of the fourth tableau, are
very badly engraved, and evidently, not by Hogarth.

or at the Bell at Edmonton. There is time. The veiled lady comes on the eve of that fatal supper to warn the libertine, Don Juan. The Commendatore knocks a loud rap at the front door before he comes upstairs. Even Sganarelle was saved—although he lost his wages. He quaked and repented amid the terrors of that Feast of Stone. Turn' again, Thomas ; ere thou herdest with swine. Alas ! I think the wretched youth might have turned indeed, if he had had a father or mother. He had none, and there was no fatted calf at home. There was Sarah Young ; and ——

Thus he requites her in Act the Fifth—the last act in most dramas ; but there are more to come in Tom's life history. Released from the catchpole's claws, the ungrateful Rakewell, now become mercenary, hunts up what is called a "City fortune." A rich old maid, dreadfully ugly, and with a decided cast in her eye, is foolish enough to marry him ; and married the badly-assorted pair are in Marylebone Church. See them at the altar. The parson is purblind, the clerk is gaunt and hungry-looking. The rake has grown unhealthily fat. The bride is very splendid and hideous. Not so the little charity-boy, who adjusts the hassock for her to kneel upon. He has a pretty, innocent face, but his clothes are patched and ragged, as if the governors of the Charitable Grinders, to whose school he belongs, didn't treat him very liberally. Indeed, there is a woeful want of charity visible in the whole proceeding. Arachne has been busy with the poor-box ; and an over-grown spider's web has been woven over the orifice of that charitable coffer. A crack runs through the ninth commandment on the tablet within the communion-rails. Two dogs are snarling at one another.* In the distant aisle, the pew-openers and almswomen are squabbling, and even coming to blows—clapperclawing one another with great fury—over the largess given by the bridegroom ; while—can I believe my eyes ?—there appears, meekly kneeling as bridesmaid, and holding up the bride's train, a comely young woman, who bears a remarkable resemblance to Mrs. Sarah Young. Surely, it is somewhat overdoing charity and longsuffering for her to officiate at the marriage of this wrinkled harridan with the man she has loved. Perhaps the likeness may be accidental ; or, perhaps, it may be acceptable as a supportable hypothesis that Sarah, deprived of her capital by her generosity to the rake in his distress, has been compelled to give up the millinery business, and go into service as lady's-maid to the squinting spinster, even as Lydia became handmaiden to the widow Green. Her mistress being married, she accompanies her to church, and tells not her love, but suffers, and loves on unrepiningly.

The money Rakewell got by this marriage of perjury goes very soon in the pandemonium where his first patrimony was wasted. He gambles it away. The scene of the gaming-house is terrible. Artistically, it is one of the finest compositions ever designed by a painter. The rake, now haggard and battered, bare-

---

* The presence of these animals in the sacred edifice has been objected to as an anomaly ; but it must be remembered that church doors stood open somewhat wider than at present in Hogarth's time, and that it was one of the specified duties of the beadle to "WHIP THE DOGS OUT OF THE CHURCH." The beadle in Hogarth's picture is probably busied in counting his gains on the church-steps.

pated, carelessly arrayed, frantic at his losses, kneels
with uplifted arm and clenched fist, uttering vain impre-
cations to Heaven. He is ruined, body and bones. A
drunken lord hugs a bully who steals his silver-hilted
sword. Another *magnifico*, sumptuously attired, is
borrowing money of an ancient usurer in rags ;—he
knew Tom's father well, but would not lend the beggared
profligate a guinea now. Of all the dreadful company
the money-lender is sober, cool, and collected, and
makes a neat entry in his memoranda of his loan to my
lord One man has gone to sleep ; another, an old
gambler, seems stupefied by his reverses, and cannot
hear the waiter-lad who brings him a glass of liquor, and
bawls in his ear for payment. It is but a squalid kind
of Hades, and there is no trust. A fierce black dog—
he is the usurer's watch-dog Tearem, you may be sure
—leaps up at the blaspheming rake, and adds by his
yelling to the outcry of this demoniacal crew. A sharper,
whose face we cannot see, but whose flabby, covetous
hand is strangely suggestive, takes advantage of a
sudden alarm to purloin the stakes on the table. Do
you know what the alarm is ? It is Fire. Some crazed
desperado has been brandishing a flambeau. The
wainscot catches. The watch come bursting in, and
Hades is in flames !

The race of "silly Tom," begun at Epsom, is nearly
run. Tattenham Corner has been turned long ago, and
he is fast approaching the post and the judge's chair.
But he has a couple more stands to pass. Behold the
penultimate in Act the Seventh of this eventful history.
Tom is a hopeless captive for debt in the Fleet Prison.
He has squandered the "city fortune" of his squinting

wife. The gold is gone; but the oblique-eyed lady remains to plague and torture him with her face and her reproaches. She visits him in prison, only to scold and abuse. Thomas is on his last legs. He has turned dramatic author, and has written a play, which he has sent to Manager Rich, and which Manager Rich won't have. "Sir,—I have read your play, and find it will not *doe*. Yours, J. R." Such is the impresario's curt form of refusal. The keeper—a crafty-looking successor of the far-famed Bambridge, with his big key and his yawning account-book, glozes over the shoulder of the penniless spendthrift, and demands "garnish." The boy from the neighbouring tavern won't leave the pot of porter unless he is paid for it. Trust is dead; and the manuscript of the rejected play would not bring two-pence, even as waste paper.

Hither, unalterable in her devotion, comes the poor wronged milliner to comfort the ruined man. Unhappily her visit is paid at the time when the vixen lady with the squint is present. There is a passage of arms, or rather of words, between the two. The ex-old maid has the best of the encounter over the ex-young one. Sarah faints; the legitimate Mrs. Rakewell shaking her fist at, and vituperating her. Some pity is to be found even in this abode of woe. A miserable inmate assists the fainting Sarah. Poor wretch! he has every mark of having long been an inhabitant of this dismal mansion. From his pocket is pendent a scroll, on which is written: "A scheme to pay the National Debt. By J. L., now a prisoner in the Fleet." All his attention is given to the debts of the Commonwealth. His own private liabilities he has forgotten. Sarah has a child with her—Tom's child, alas!—and the cries of this infant serve—for you really hear them, as it were—to heighten the sad interest of the scene. On the tester of a bed are a huge pair of wings, doubtless the crack-brained invention of some prisoner who has striven to while away the weary hours of his confinement by vain attempts to imitate Dædalus; but there is a chemist in the background happily absorbed in contemplating his retort, and caring nothing for all the noise and squalor and wretchedness around him. We will drop the curtain, if you please.

To raise it again in Act the Eighth, and last; in one of the wards of Bedlam. Tom Rakewell has gone stark staring mad, and ends here—here among the maniacs that gibber, and those that howl, and those that fancy themselves kings and popes. He ends here on straw, naked and clawing himself, and manacled. But Sarah Young, the woman whom he has wronged, is with him to the last, and comforts and cherishes him; and— Heaven be merciful to us all!—so ends the *Rake's Progress*; a drama in Eight Acts, as I have designated it, and assuredly, one of the saddest and most forcible dramas that was ever conceived by human brain, or executed by human hand. I have dwelt at this length upon it, because I think it exhibits, in the superlative degree, the development of those qualities in art and in philosophy which have made William Hogarth so justly famous.

VII.

A History of Hard Work.

Is there anything in the world that cannot be accomplished by sheer hard work? Grant to any man, high or low, a sound natural capacity, and the essential faculties of insight and appreciation—or, if you will, call them discernment and judgment—and may he not aspire, with a reasonable degree of certainty, to the very grandest prizes which the Heads of the Houses of Life have to confer? May he not say to his Will: " You are my steed, I mean to saddle and bridle you. I shall spare neither whip nor spur, and you must carry me to the great goal. Be your name Hare or Tortoise, you and I must win the race. I know full well that I must go into training for such a tremendous heat. I must rise at five in the morning, and sleep short hours upon hard beds. I must live on the simplest and scantiest fare. I must conciliate and be servile, until I can command and be tyrannical. I must be always learning something, always doing something, always saving something. I must never look back, even though behind me may be a poor man crying out that I have ridden over his one ewe lamb, or a widow weeping for the trampling of her tender vines under my horse's hoofs. My motto must not be '*Excelsior,*' but rather Cæsar Borgia's '*Avánti !*' or Blucher's '*Vorwärts ;*' for the rewards of this world lie straight ahead, not far above, and must be tilted at, not clambered for. And if I have a firm seat, and a hard hand, and a steady eye, shall I not succeed? My hair may be powdered grey with the dust of the race; but shall I not ride in some day, the crowd crying—*Tandem triumphans?* Shall I not be crowned with laurels in the capitol— foremost poet of the age? Shall I not be the great painter: my hire a thousand guineas for six inches of coloured canvas? Shall I not have discovered the longitude and squared the circle. Shall I not be Rothschild, to hold crowns in pawn, and ticket sceptres in fasces as though they were fire-irons? Shall I not be borne on the shields of the legionaries, and saluted as Emperor of the Eujaxrians, King of Politicopolis, and Protector of the Confederation of the Scamander?"

Many a man asks himself these questions; and digging his rowels into the sides of his stern Intent, rides away with his knees well set and his hand on his hip, defiant. What Cæsar, and Napoleon, and Frederick, and Newton, and Bayle, and Milton, and Buonarotti, and Pascal, and Wolsey, and Ximenes, and Washington, and Francia, and Ganganelli, and Flaxman, and Callot did —you see I dip my hand in the lucky-bag and draw out the numbers as they come—was by pure and simple hard work: the labour of the hand as well as the brain. Believe me that nothing is unavailing towards the great end, so long as it is work. The making of sundials and toy windmills helped Isaac of Grantham towards the *Principia*. Bacon was not wasting his time when he

wrote about laying out gardens. Brougham took something by his motion when he sat down to furnish nearly
an entire number of the *Edinburgh Review*. Leonardo
was not wholly idle when he promulgated his rules for
drawing "monsters:"—lions' flanks, fishes' tails, and
"*mulier formosa superne.*" Burke found his account in
writing summaries for the *Annual Register*, and Canning
in making jokes for the *Anti-Jacobin*. All these things
"tell up." They are columned, and figured, and entered
to our credit; and some day the balance is declared,
and we draw the splendid capital.

And the reward—is it certain? Is it always splendid?
Does every studious sub-lieutenant of artillery become
an emperor? Is the mastership of the Mint waiting for
every mathematician? Ah, vain and fallacious argument! Ah, sorry reckoning without our host! Here
is the day-room of a country workhouse, and here over
the scanty fire is a paralytic, slavering dotard nearly a
hundred years of age. Hard work! Giles Clover, of
the old men's ward, was working hard when New York
and Virginia were English colonies. He had tilled the
earth so long, that just before the spade dropped from
his palsied hand he was digging a grave for his great-
grandchild. His neighbour there, the patriarch of
eighty, has helped to clear away the crumbling ruins of
the house the bricks of which he worked so hard to
mould the clay for. Hard work! Look at that dod-
dering old fellow in the scarlet blanketing creeping along
the King's Road, Chelsea. He was at Valenciennes, at
Walcheren, at Maida, at Vittoria, at Waterloo. He was
in garrison at St. Helena in 1821, and lent his strong
shoulder to carry the body of Napoleon to the grave.

But he will be thankful, poor pensioner, for a halfpenny to buy snuff, and his granddaughter goes out washing, to furnish him with extra beer. Hard work! Look at the pale-faced curate of St. Lazarus. He is full of Greek, and mathematics, and the Fathers. He marries, and buries, and baptizes, and preaches, and overlooks the schools, and walks twenty miles a day to visit the sick. And he has just written a begging letter to the benevolent society which supplies the clergy with old clothes. Perhaps these men, with all their industry, were dull. When genius is allied to perseverance, the golden mean must be reached indeed. Must it? Alack! the reckoning of the host is still better than ours. He comes with a smile, and taps us on the shoulder, and says, " Oh, ho! you are becoming famous, are you? You shall go to a padded room, and howl for the rest of your days. And you who have heaped up riches, and have such a swollen cheque-book? Here is a little pin, with which I just perforate your skull. You tumble down in apoplexy, and farewell money-bags. And you, Monsieur le Duc, with a field-marshal's bâton you once carried in your knapsack? A tiny pellet of lead from a flintlock musket fired by a raw recruit will arrange all *your* affairs. And you, potent, and grave and wise, who sit in the king's council and rule the destinies of millions, —ah! I have but to place a little pebble beneath the pastern of your park hackney, and lo! he will stumble and fall, and four men with a stretcher will carry you home to die."

Should these grim reminders cause men to shrink and faint, and lose their faith in the powers of Will and Hard Work? Never, I hope. Should the fame that

Hamilton gained by a speech, and Shenstone by a quaint imitation, or Campbell and Thomson by a volume of blank verse, cause us to drift into the *far niente*, to sit down contented with the success of a lucky hit, and allow the game to go on while we lie in bed, and are fed with a spoon like Fenton; or, with our hands in our pockets, gnaw at the peaches on the walls, like the writer of the *Seasons?* Not yet, I trust. The grandest and noblest monuments in the world are those of hard work. Look at the *Decline and Fall.* Look at the great porch of Notre Dame de Paris. Look at Bayle's *Dictionary.* Look at the lines of Torres Vedras. Look at the *Divine Comedy.* Look at Holman Hunt's *Doctors in the Temple.* Every one of these elaborately magnificent performances—you see I have been playing at loto again, and trusted to the chances of the lucky-bag— might have remained mere sketches, crude and vigorous, perhaps, as Coleridge's *Kubla Khan*, or as that strange Titan-daub of the lady at the pianoforte in this year's Academy's exhibition (1860), but dreamy, unsubstantial, and unsatisfactory, without hard work. Therefore I drink to hard work, with a will and on my knees; and if ever I am sentenced to six months' imprisonment with hard labour, I will try to become an expert even at the treadmill or the crank, satisfied that some good will come of it some day.

I remember with a friend, once, staring at the great golden dome of St. Izaak's church, at Petersburg, as it blazed in the sunset, and striving to calculate how many bottles of champagne, ball-dresses, diamond bracelets, carriages and horses, marriage settlements, were spread over that glittering cupola. But in a healthier frame of mind I began to ponder upon the immensity of human labour concentrated in that stately edifice. There were the men who beat the gold out into flimsy leaves, who spread it on the dome, who hewed the marble from the quarries, and polished and dragged it, and set it up, who formed those wondrous mosaics, and wrought those glowing paintings, who made the mould and cast the bronze for the statues, who hung the bells and laid the pavement, and illuminated the barbaric screen of the Ikonostast. Thousands of serfs and artisans were pressed, or poorly paid, to do this work. Numbers of brickmakers will build a pyramid, or wall all Babylon round ; yet that concentrated immensity is always astounding. How much more should I wonder at the pyramid of hard work that lies before me in the giant folio of William Hogarth's works! There are 157 plates in the book, and yet many of his minor works are not here. How the man must have pored and peered, and stooped to grave these millions of lines and dots on the hard metal ! A large proportion of these performances was preceded by a sketch, a drawing, a finished oil picture. Every engraving required its separate drawing, tracing, retracing on copper, etching, biting in, engraving deeper, touching up and finishing. Granted that for the later plates assistants were called in. Still, the vast mass of the stupendous work is by one man's hand. It was *his* province alone to conceive, to determine, to plan the picture, to discover and to arrange the models. No falling off, no weakness, is apparent, from the *Rake's Progress* to the very end of his own honest career. He died in harness ; and the strength, the wit, the humour, and the philosophy of the *Bathos* thunder forth a lie to

Wilkes and Churchill, in their sneers at his dotage and his infirmity.

When an artist is in the full tide and swing of his productive power,—when his early struggles for bread are over, and he is married and pays rent and taxes, and being known, can command an adequate, if not a generous remuneration for his daily labour,—his life, if his lot fortunately be cast in a peaceful and civilized country, must necessarily be uneventful. Young Robert Strange, roaming about the Highlands in '45, with his "craig in peril," engraving banknotes for the Pretender, and sheltering himself beneath ladies' hoops from the hot pursuit of Duke William's soldiers, was a very wild and picturesque Bohemian. So was Callot, scampering from fair to fair in Italy, with Egyptians, vagabonds, and mountebanks. So was David, screeching applause at the *Serment du Jeu de Paume*, and rushing home to transfer the oath to canvas ; or, as some of the libellers assert, sitting at his easel at the scaffold's foot, and copying with red fidelity the facial contortions of those who died by the guillotine. But Strange becomes grave and portly Sir Robert, engraver to his Majesty, a worthy knight-bachelor, with a grand collection of antique prints and drawings, dwelling in his own house in King Street, Covent Garden. And you shall hardly recognize the erratic young companion of the Romany Rye, in the handsome, thoughtful cavalier in his point-lace, velvet justaucorps, and swaling plume to his beaver — the noble Jacques Callot, who lives near the Luxembourg, and draws martyrologies to the great delight of the *Petits Pères*, and employs " *M. Israel son amy* " to grave his etching more forcibly. And who shall not marvel at the transformation of the ranting-club man of '93, long-haired, tricolour-sashed, nine-tenths *sans-culotte*, into M. le Baron Louis David, Grand Officer of the Legion of Honour, who calls in his chariot to beg sittings from his Eminence the Cardinal, and his Grandeur the Arch-Chancellor, and Monseigneur the Archbishop, and messieurs the marshals, the senators, and the councillors of State, for the portraits that are to be introduced into the colossal picture of the coronation of his Majesty the Emperor, destined for the Salle du Sacre of Versailles?

William Hogarth's earliest life had not been, as you have seen, very fruitful in incident. No desperate adventures had chequered his path. No doubt but that in his case, as in that of every child of humanity, " the days passed and did not resemble each other;" but still the days glided by without duels in Hyde Park or the fields behind Montagu House, without gallantries with my Lady Bellaston or Madame la Comtesse des Quatres Vents, without committals to the Tower for participation in Jacobite plots. I daresay there were days when the crust to the goose-pie was somewhat hard and flaky and the Derby ale was sour; when Mistress Hogarth's temper was none of the sweetest, when a slight commotion in the painting-room was created by the outrageous behaviour of Mr. Shard ;* when my lord

* Hogarth, save in the portraits of Wilkes and Churchill—in the which, if Lord Ellenborough's dictum is to be accepted, the magnitude of the libel must be estimated in proportion to its truth—was seldom malevolently personal. Still, his pictures must be as full as faces, as true to their proto-types in life as Mrs. Salmon's waxen effigy of "Ann Sigg on Crutches," which stood at the door of the Salmonian museum by the Inner Temple Gate, near Gosling's banking-house. "Ann Sigg on Crutches" was as well known to London loiterers as Charles at Charing or the bell-strikers

would not pay for his picture, or when William's own temper was ruffled at the sight of some vile wood piracy of the *Rake's Progress*. It may sometimes have happened, also, that William took t'other bottle, had a curtain lecture at night, and a headache the next morning. There may have been wintry days, when it was too dark to paint, and sunshiny days, when palette and maulstick were flung by with a jolly laugh; and the painter with his wife, or with some of the wags from the "Bedford," were off to take the air and their pleasure. There may have been days when a shortness of ready money reigned in the house in Leicester Fields. Such domestic incidents may have ruffled from time to time the placid stream of the honest life of an English working man. Even courtly Sir Joshua, in *his* painting room on the other side of Leicester Fields, may not have been

---

at St. Dunstan's; and Ann Sigg, a noted beggar, used to hobble past the wax-work show every day; but she never turned on her crutches to inspect her counterfeit presentment, either ignorant of or disdaining to acknowledge its existence. Not so philosophically sensible was one Mr. Shard, son of Sir Isaac Shard, a rare money-spinner and money-clutcher. In Hogarth's picture of the *Miser's Feast* (?) he is said to have introduced a portrait of this Sir Isaac, which made much mirth. Comes fresh from the university and the grand tour, Mr. Shard, junior, a young gentleman of fine parts, but a hot temper. Hogarth, as was common with painters then (and is still with the Roman and Florentine artists), had a sort of show-room in which his finished pictures were exhibited. The young university blood asks the person who shows the pictures for whom such and such a lean, pinched face is intended, and on being told that it is thought to be uncommonly like one Sir Isaac Shard, he "straightway draws his sword and slashes the canvas." It does not appear that Hogarth took any steps to resent this outrage; and one malignant biographer chuckles with much glee over his forbearance. I have queried the *Miser's Feast*, in relating this anecdote, because I am unaware of the existence of such a picture. Some critics are of opinion that the steward or pettifogger who guards the money-bag in Act I. of the *Rake's Progress*, was the obnoxious portrait slashed by young Mr. Shard.

exempt from such transient puffs of adverse winds : but .
in the main, I think the tenor of William Hogarth's life
from 1735 to 1745—when the Jacobite rebellion left, in
some degree, its mark upon his life and work—was
eminently smooth and even.   Nor can I imagine any
condition of existence much happier than this tranquil
work-a-day life of an English painter.   Ah ! it is very
fine to be Sir Thomas, scampering off to congresses to
limn popes and emperors and plenipotentiaries, to stand
in one's grand saloon in tights and opera hat, receiving
the flower of the peerage—but with that dreadful man
in possession sitting in the parlour all the while.   It is
very dignified, no doubt, to be Barry, fiercely warring
the Academy, entertaining Senator Burke with Spartan
banquets of beefsteaks and porter, and dying at last in
a dingy back parlour, just too late to enjoy a meagre
annuity.   It is wilder and more picturesque to .be a
jovial Bohemian, and paint pigs in a spunging-house like
George Morland, or to be stark mad and a believer in
the " ghosts of fleas " and the connection of " William
Pitt and the New Jerusalem," like Blake ; but I think
the balance of happiness is in favour of such quiet,
unostentatious working lives as those led by William
Hogarth and Joshua Reynolds ; by the equable Westall,
and that stainless soul, Flaxman ; by honest David
Wilkie, and our good painter LESLIE, just taken from
us.* Surely it is reckoned in their favour : the blameless,
spotless life, without turbulence, without intrigue, without place-seeking : the life devoted, from its dawn to its
close, to the worship of nature in her most beautiful

* This was written in 1860.   Leslie died 5th May, 1859.

forms. And, O ye precisians! who are apt to descry a positive naughtiness in the somewhat lavishly developed carnations and luscious *morbidezza* of William Etty, do you know the squanderer of gorgeous hues lived the life of a hermit in his bachelor chambers in Buckingham Street, Strand? and that the dignified spinster, his lady-sister, found pleasure in seeking out the fairest models that money would persuade to sit, for her William to paint?

I have called this section of my attempt, a history of hard work; and although I must defer a long meditated dissertation on Hogarth's oil pictures * which would open a widely different field of contemplation, the pages that follow will not be unprofitably devoted to a careful consideration of the works engraved by W. H. between the stand-points of the *Rake's Progress* and the *Marriage à la Mode.* Gentlemen collectors, therefore, will you be so good as to open your portfolios and

---

* Walpole and Allan Cunningham have said nearly all of Hogarth's merits in oil-painting that can be said; and the latest edition of the *Anecdotes of Painting* gives a commendably liberal list of the pedigree and present locality of the principal oil pictures and sketches by Hogarth extant. This list, however, is susceptible of many additions. It is quite as easy to fix upon an authentic W. H., as upon a veracious Gerard Douw. His *touch* was almost unique—a broad, firm, predetermined mark of the brush— and to imitate it without the possibility of detection, even in these halcyon days of picture forgery, would argue the possession of artistic qualities on the part of the forger well nigh equal to those of Hogarth himself. But I reserve bibliographical, genealogical, chalcographic, and auctioneer's lore about Hogarth's pictures for a more convenient occasion, staying now only to acknowledge the kindness of half a dozen courteous correspondents from Bristol, who tell me that the Hogarthian pictures which formerly adorned the chancel of St. Mary Redcliffe's fine old church, were purchased by Mr. Thomas Proctor, of Wall's Court, near Bristol, and by him presented to the Fine Arts Academy at Clifton (Bristol). I am glad to hear that the pictures have suffered nothing in the way of "restoration."

adjust your glasses while your humble cicerone tries to tell you what he has been able to find out respecting a few more of the *dramatis personæ* in the *Human Comedy* of the comic Dante?

A few words may be spared for that capital free-handed etching of the *Laughing Audience* which I have already mentioned as delivered with the subscription-ticket to the life-drama of Thomas Rakewell, Esq. It is a suitably humorous prologue to that tragi-comedy. Taken as an etching it is executed entirely *con brio*, and without — save in the background of the box — any symptom of the employment of mechanical line or rule. All is round, rich, and flexible ; and the easier is the artist's hand, the more lucid, I think, is the exposition of his thought. It is, pray observe, the audience in the pit, not those in the boxes of the theatre, who are laughing. They, good people, have paid their money to be amused, and are determined to have their three shillings' worth.* Their business cares are over for the

---

* Three shillings would appear to have been the statutory price of entrance to the pit of Covent Garden, Lincoln's Inn Fields, and Drury Lane Theatres. I find " 3*s.* " marked in pen and ink on a medallion in the benefit-ticket engraved by Hogarth for Milward, the comedian. Those executed for Jemmy Spiller (the original Filch), " Macheath " Walker, Fielding, and Joe Miller, have merely " Pitt " written in, but no price. The beneficiaries probably asked what they liked — having previously purchased the tickets from the management—and took what they could get. In respect to the Georgian theatres, I should be glad to be enlightened on the point as to whether the footmen of the nobility and gentry—for whose use the gallery was reserved, and against whose fighting and gambling there, managers Rich, Highmore, and Cibber used so piteously to protest— paid for their admission. I don't think they did, seeing that the footmen's turbulence led to a managerial enactment that they should only be admitted "after the fourth act." Again, as to paying at the doors. In a stray paper of Fielding's, I find the shabby conduct of a Temple Buck censured,

LAUGHING AUDIENCE.

15

day; and they will laugh, and laugh heartily, or know the reason why. There are just eleven of these merry groundlings, and they exhibit almost every phase of the risible faculty. There is the old lady's sly chuckle— you know what I mean: the "Ah! he's a wicked one," and "Go along with you!" chuckle, accompanied by a wag of the good old soul's head; the laugh of the man who is obliged to put his hand to his forehead and screw his eyelids tight—the laugh of him who fairly cries for mirth; the grateful grin of the deaf man *who sees the joke*, albeit he hears it not; the jolly "Boo-hoo!" of the fat matron, whose sides, I am sure, must be aching; the gruff "Ha-ha!" of the big man, who doesn't laugh often, but when he does, laughs with goodwill; the charming, good-natured, "all-overish" smile of the fresh and comely young lass; the broad bursting laugh of the stout old gentleman, who has been laughing any time these sixty years; and the silly "Hee-hee!" of the fool, who is wise enough, however, to know that it is better to laugh than cry: all these are deliciously portrayed. After blue pill, or a bill that has been presented, always look at the *Laughing Audience*. In the background even you shall see a man with a peaked nose, and a normally dissatisfied countenance. I am afraid that he has the toothache by twinges, or that his affairs are not going prosperously. Yet even he laughs *sous cape*, under his bent brows and his wig. I only wonder that William Hogarth did not introduce a laughing child to crown

---

who takes advantage of the fourth act to go away without paying. Could there have been anything like theatrical credit in those unsophisticated days? or did the first crude scheme of "half price" give the spectator a right of election as to which half of the performance he should witness?

the gaiety of the scene. Laugh on, ye honest folks, and clap Milward or Jemmy Spiller to the echo! I never hear a sour phiz groan out that this world is a vale of tears, but I think upon the *Laughing Audience;* and often, as I sit in the fourth row of the Haymarket pit, I hear the loud cachinnations of the comfortable old ladies— substantial dividend-drawers and tradesmen's wives, who always pay, and would despise a "horder" as much as they do half-price, and who have come all the way from Camberwell or Dalston to laugh at Mr. Buckstone. And then more reverently do I recall the eloquent words of the great author of the *Golden Grove*, who in a sermon bids us rejoice and be merry at due times and seasons, and tells us that we have a Creator so kind and good, "that we cannot please Him unless we be infinitely pleased ourselves." If we are never to be joyful, O Sourphiz! why, if you please, do the lambs skip and the babies smile in their sleep, *and the very dogs laugh?* I believe that in the way of lineage I am more an ancient Roman than a Dane; but if Sourphiz be in the right, and this *is* a vale of tears—save when in Heaven's wisdom the rain and the dew fall on us—I am a Dutchman, doubly distilled.

Mark this, notwithstanding, that the musicians in the orchestra do not laugh. These rosin-bows have other things to think of. To scrape the intestines of the cat with the hair of the horse night after night, for a wage of twenty-shillings a week, is no laughing matter. The fiddlers and fifers have grown stale and accustomed to the witticisms of Messrs. Milward and Spiller; and when they have forty bars rest they yawn and take snuff, and do not laugh. Let us hope that their merriment is reserved for the time when they draw their salaries and go home to a tripe supper, a mug of punch, and the society of their wives and families.   Nor are the young ladies, who are the descendants of Orange Moll, and supply those golden fruit from pottle-shaped baskets, much given to laughter.   'Tis their vocation to pluck the beaux in the boxes by the sleeve and simulate a pleased interest in their bald chat.   The beaux, of whom there are a pair most exquisitely attired, are sniggering and simpering, but not laughing.*   They are very magnificent grandees, dining at Lebeck's or Pontack's,†

---

* So Mons. Mephistopheles laughs in Goethe's Faust and Scheffer's pictures, and so Iago, when he sings his little song in Cyprus to tipsy Cassio.   And the Prophet, in the sacred writings, has his "bitter laugh." There is an appalling little Latin treatise, happily rare, written by some monastic Mephistopheles who had the misfortune to wear human flesh with some cold blood in it, and a friar's cowl over all.   It is called the *Risus Sardonicus*, and contains such agreeable passages as "Aha ! you think that eternal punishment is merely figurative, do you ?   Hee-hee ! wait a little." And then he goes on to expatiate on the brimstone, and the molten pitch, and the burning marl—always with his "bitter laugh."   Ugh ! the cynic.

† I make my beaux dine at Pontack's — with a *k*, through malice prepense.   You know that in the *Rake's Progress* young Tom holds high festival at *P.'s*.   In my simplicity I imagined Pontac to have been a living "mine host" actually contemporary with Thomas Rakewell, but I have since been better informed.   Pontack's was at the old White Bear in Abchurch Lane.   It was destroyed in the Great Fire, and rebuilt as a French restaurant by one Monsieur Pontack, a Frenchman, "son of the President of Bordeaux, owner of a district whence are imported into England some of the most celebrated claret."   Proud of his descent, he set up a portrait of his presidential sire in official costume as a sign.   The Fellows of the Royal Society, after the Fire, moved to the "Pontack's Head," and held their anniversary dinner there.   In George II.'s reign, Pontack's, which had changed proprietors several times, was spoken of as a "guinea ordinary," where you could get a "ragout of fatted snails," and "chickens not two hours from the shell."   The loose company depicted in the *Progress* would fix something like an imputation of evil manners on this celebrated tavern ;

and using the Turk's Head o'nights; but they would
think it infinitely beneath them to laugh.*

Passing over a companion etching to the above—a
set of bewigged choristers singing from the oratorio of
Judith—let me come to the large and elaborate
engraving from Hogarth's picture of *Southwark Fair* :
the plate was, you will remember, included in the
subscription for the *Rake's Progress*. I saw the oil
painting in the Art Treasures Exhibition at Manchester
in 1857, and a magnificent work it is—second only in my
opinion to the *March to Finchley*. The scene, which is

---

yet we read that on Thursday, January 15, 1736, a date that exactly suits
my purpose—" William Pepys, banker in Lombard Street, was married at
St. Clement's Church, in the Strand, to Mrs. Susannah Austin, who lately
kept Pontack's, where, with universal esteem, she acquired a considerable
fortune." Perhaps the eulogy came from Grub Street, even as the sign
came from Harp Alley. See *Evelyn's Diary*, 1683 and 1694, *passim ;* the
Metamorphoses of the Town, 1731 ; the *Weekly Oracle*, 1736 ; and specially
my fountain-head of Pontackian information, the remarkably learned and
curious *Catalogue of London Traders, 'I avern and Coffee-house Tokens*, in
the Beaufoy collection, printed for the corporation of London (to whose
library the collection was presented), and written by Mr. Jacob H. Burn.
1855.

* In the *Laughing Audience*, the barrier dividing the orchestra from the
pit is garnished with iron spikes. In an era of theatrical anarchy, when
the groundlings not unfrequently invaded the stage, such precautions were
by no means needless ; but to the credit of the French, the management of
the Royal Opera in Paris were the first to remove these somewhat barbarous
chevaux-de-frise. Towards the close of King William III.'s reign, a young
English nobleman, visiting Paris and the Opera, had a quarrel with a French
gentleman. Being a "muscular Christian," he seized his adversary round
the waist, and pitched him bodily from the box tier into the orchestra.
The poor Frenchman fell on the spikes, and was well nigh impaled ; and
after this mishap, the authorities took away the spikes from the barrier, but
placed two extra sentinels in the pit. There had already been soldiers on
the stage. For the pit sentries, see Sterne's capital story of the little
hunchback at the opera in the *Sentimental Journey*.

literally crammed with life, incident, animation, and
varied character, is artistically remarkable for the
exquisite beauty of the central figure, the young woman
with the Amazon hat and plume who beats the drum :
not one of Lely's *Beauties*, and scarcely Rubens' *Chapeau
de Paille*, can surpass the face and form of " *La Belle au
Tambour* " in fresh, ruddy, pulpy comeliness. Mark the
astonishment of the two bumpkins who are gazing at this
parchment-drubbing beauty ; one, awed by her charms,
has pulled off his hat. His mate wonders "with a
foolish face of praise." The legend recounts that
Hogarth, passing once through the fair, saw the original
of the beautiful drummer being grossly maltreated—
poor child !—by some ruffian. The legend goes on to
tell, and I delight in believing it, that Bill Hogarth—
one must call him Bill when he uses his fists—beat the
scoundrel soundly, and took pity on the young drummer-
girl, whose fair face served him as a model in many
of his after pictures. I hope Jane Thornhill wasn't
jealous.

There is an astonishing impression of Sound prevail-
ing in this picture. It is a painted noise. It is an
English Donnybrook ; and the only object quiet in the
scene is the bell in the turret ·of the church. The
platform erected for the strolling players who are
performing the " Fall of Bajazet " gives way ; and down
come poles and boards, Bajazet, Roxalana, grand
viziers, scimitars, turbans, Kislar-agas and all the
borough-orientalisms of the managers, Messrs. Cibber
and Bullock. The country squire with a whip in one
hand and another locked in the arm of a young girl,
stares in mute astonishment at the gay doings around

him, and a pickpocket takes a natural advantage of his
amazement to ease him of his pocket-handkerchief.
The Amazon with the drum has among her admirers,
likewise, two individuals, whose sober attire and starched
visages would point them out as members of Whitfield's
congregation in Moorfields.

Here are all the "humours of a fair," indeed;
mountebanks, fiddlers, players, and buffoons; rogues
and proctors, sharpers and dupes, and those that live
by bullying honest folk—

> Maint poudré qui n'a pas d'argent,
> Maint sabreur qui craint le sergent,
>   Maint fanfaron qui toujours tremble,

as sings Monsieur Scarron, "*Malade de la Reine*," of the
humours of a Parisian crowd.   Here is the "sergent," in
the form of a ruthless constable who collars Alexander
the Great—or a poor player, at least, who is about to
strut and fret his hour on the stage, made up in the
likeness of that hero—on some charge for which he will
have to find good and sufficient bail.   The captor is a
constable or headborough—not a sheriff's officer or
catchpole, to judge by his brass-tipped staff.   He has
his follower with him, a truculent ruffian, who brandishes
a bludgeon over the head of the hapless Alexander of
Macedon.   Or, stay: Can the plumed, periwigged, and
buskined conqueror in the grasp of the constable be
intended for Hector of Troy?   I see that against the
church tower in the middle distance they have reared a
stage and a huge show-cloth, which, with its vast
wooden horse giving ingress to Greeks, tells of the
history of *Troy Taken.**   There are other show-

---

* A "droll," devised by the indefatigable compasser of "motions,"

cloths displayed, depicting *Adam and Eve*, and *Punch wheeling his Wife to the Evil One ;* but the most remarkable effort in this branch of art—now alas! fallen into decay and desuetude,—is the monstrous cartoon to the spectator's left, swinging high and secure above the *Fall of Bajazet.*

A history of a theatrical squabble, almost as momentous as the O. P. Row of 1810, or the Coletti and Tamburini revolt of our own times, is there set forth. The *Stage Mutineers, or a Playhouse to Let,* a tragi-comico-farcical ballad opera, published in 1733, will throw some light on this dramatic insurrection. Bankes' poetical epistle on the event states that Theophilus Cibber had stirred up a portion of the Drury Lane company to rebellion, and they accordingly seceded to the "little theatre in the Haymarket."

The show-cloth in Hogarth's picture is mainly copied from a large etching descriptive of the dispute by John Laguerre, the scene-painter. The mutineers include portraits of the ringleader, Theo. Cibber as Pistol, and of Harper as Falstaff ; and a naïf commentator informs me that the lady waving the flag is " intended for the portraiture of the notorious Mistress Doll Tearsheet." The simple man imagined, no doubt, that Mistress Doll—" what stuff wilt have a kirtle of ? I shall receive money on Thursday,"—was a character as real as Mother Needham or Mary Moffat. Poor Doll ! it was full three centuries before the Southwark Fair, that the beadles, the " famished correctioners," dragged her to durance vile, there to have " whipping

<hr>

Elkanah Settle. *Troy Taken* was a great favourite at the fairs, and in 1707 was even printed.

cheer enough," and all because she was a friend of Dame
Quickley.*

Raree shows, wax-work shows, the "royal," and the
"whole court of France," Faux's dexterity of hand, and
acrobat swinging on the *corde volante ;* † a poor demented,
tumbling Icarus of a creature, "flying" from the church
steeple ; a fiery prise-fighter, broad-sword in hand, his
bare pate covered with hideous scars and patches, and
mounted on a wall-eyed steed—can this have been
Holmes of "metacarpal" fame, or the renowned Felix
Maguire ?—a black-boy (in attendance on the Amazon)
blasting a clarion ; a little bagpiper, a military monkey,

---

* The figure in the corner of the Hogarth-Laguerre show-cloth is meant
for Colley Cibber, who had just sold his share in Drury Lane Theatre to
Highmore. The purchase-money was 6,000*l.* The man in his shirt-sleeves
is Ellis, the scene-painter of the T. R. D. L. Over the Druryites is the
inscription, "We'll starve 'em out." Over the Haymarket mutineers runs
the legend, "We eat." I conjecture that alleged insufficient salaries and
illiberal treatment were at the bottom of this, as of most theatrical revolts.
A word as to Manager Highmore. He was a gentleman, and originally
possessed a considerable fortune, but managed to dissipate it all between
Drury Lane and White's gaming-house. Laguerre, indorsed by Hogarth,
seems to sneer at Highmore's assumption of gentility in the figure of the
monkey perched on the signboard of the "Rose Tavern," and with the
label, "I am a gentleman." Highmore failed as a manager ; and he then,
with little more success, turned actor. In 1743, according to an ingenious
well-wisher of his, "he completed the climax by publishing a poem entitled
Dettingen, which proved him a very indifferent writer." Poor broken-
down Highmore !

† The swinger was Signor Violante, an eminent performer, both on the
tight and slack rope. The Icarus descending from the steeple is the famous
Mr. Cadman, who performed the same feat at the church of St. Martin's-
in-the-Fields, from the steeple of which, by means of a running line, of
course, he actually descended into the King's Mews. He tried the same
experiment at Shrewsbury, but the rope breaking, he was dashed to pieces.
Who does not remember the lamentable end, in our own day, of Scott, the
American diver, and poor Gale, the aëronaut ?

a set of " fantoccini " on a foot-board, a Savoyard music-grinder, a galantee show, with a dwarf drummer, a woman kneeling with a tray and dice-box, just as the fellows with their three cards kneel on the hill that leads to Epsom racecourse : a knot of silly gamblers, a tavern bar, beneath the crashing platform of the " Fall of Bajazet," for which, and breakages for flagons and glasses, Messrs. Cibber and Bullock, proprietors, will have to pay a heavy bill : these, and the close-packed throng, and the green fields and Surrey Hills in the distance, make up the wonderful life-picture called *Southwark Fair.* Greenwich I have seen, and Chalk Farm, and Bartlemy ; but Southwark Fair was abolished, I believe, before the close of the last century.

The print of the *Sleeping Congregation*, to which I now pass, purports to have been invented, designed, engraved and published, by William Hogarth, pursuant to an Act of Parliament in 1736. Many of his best works were so engraved from a mere sketch, unhappily lost to us ; were it otherwise, it is to be hoped that our national collection would be much richer, and that the gallery of every wealthy private collector would contain at least one original Hogarth, in oil or water colours. The few pictures he left are easily traced ; and to tabulate them will be hereafter my task. He rarely executed replicas. There was no Giulio Romano to emulate, as a disciple, this Rafaelle of Leicester Fields ; but, on the other hand, the cupidity of picture-dealers, baffled by the paucity of genuine works from his hand, took refuge in barefaced fraud, and works by Hayman and Narcissus Laroon, and crowds of inferior would-be humourists, were, and are to this day, advertised as paintings by William Hogarth.

The *Sleeping Congregation* is just the reverse to the droll medal of which the *Laughing Audience* is the obverse. Hogarth, ordinarily a decorous man in his theology, has been guilty—humorous and apposite as is the quotation of the preacher's text—of a censurable piece of irreverence : the same that prompted the French eating-house keeper to adopt as a derivative for his new-fangled restaurant, the *Ego restorabo vos* of the Vulgate. The clergyman is, however, very fine : a hard-mouthed, short-sighted, droning-voiced divine, one of those uncomfortable preachers of whom the old Scotch lady, in Dean Ramsay's book, remarks, " If there's an ill text in a' the Bible, that creetur's sure to tak' it." The huge sounding-board above him seems to proclaim his deficiency in sonorous delivery, and the need there is for affording adventitious wings to his voice. The fat, sensuous, beef-witted and carnal-minded clerk, who screws his eyes with a furtive leer towards the sleeping girl— one of the most beautiful of Hogarth's female creations —is conceived in the purest spirit of comedy. There is a wonderful fat man snoring in the left-hand corner, his pudgy hand hanging over the pew, whom only William could have discovered and transferred to copperplate. The old women in their peaked hats, the slumberers in the gallery, the lanky cherubs who hold up the Royal arms, the heraldic lion in the same emblazonment, the very hats and hatchments, have a sleep-impressing, sleep-provoking look. So the Church slept in Hogarth's time, and was neglected or sneered at, and the parson drowsed on in his wig and cassock ; while in Moorfields or in Tottenham Court Road, or far away on the wild moors of Devon, and in the almost unknown regions of the

Anglo-Phœnician stannaries, among the Cornish miners, earnest albeit fanatic men, who disdained cassocks and wore "their own hair loose and unpowdered," were crying out how Eutychus slept, and how he fell from the third loft, and was taken up dead. But the Church has become the *Sleeper Awakened* since then.

The *Distressed Poet:* ah! the distressed poet! Here is a picture one can almost gloat over. It is meant to be droll. It is funny enough in its incidents and character; but there pervades the piece, to my mind, a tinge of sympathy and sadness most pitiful yet charming to consider. No poet, surely, of ancient or of modern times —were he Codrus or Camoens, François Villon or Elkanah Settle, Savage or Johnson, in the days when he was writing *London* and wore the horseman's coat, and wolfed his victuals behind the screen that veiled him from the genteel guests at Cave's dinner-table—could have been more distressed than this creature of Hogarth's fancy—the fancy blended with the sad and stern experience which he must have acquired of the sorrows of the Muse's sons. Many and many a time must William have mounted the crazy stairs to garrets or to cocklofts in Blood-bowl Court or Hanging-sword Alley, or, perchance, to dens on the coffee-room flight of the Fleet, to confer with distressed poets about the frontispieces to the translations they were executing for scrivener's wages, or for the volumes of poems they had persuaded booksellers to publish for a pound a sheet. The date of the print is 1740. Mr. Thomson has been petted and caressed by the great—falling among the Philistines, nevertheless, in spunging-houses, sometimes; Mr. Pope is waxing feeble, but he is famous and prosperous, and

has ever a lord for a friend, and a bottle to give him.
Mr. Pope can afford, uncudgelled, to sneer at old Sarah
of Marlborough, and to blacken never too immaculate
Lady Mary. He comes to town from 'Twitnam' in his
little coach, and a lane is made for him by the admiring
spectators at the auctions which he frequents. The
sentimental maunderer, Young, has done his best to
yelp and whine himself into preferment, and his *Night
Thoughts* have had chiefly reference to the degree of
obsequiousness to be observed at the levée in the morning. Mr. Fielding is a gentleman, and is "hail fellow
well met" at White's and the Rose with St. James's
beaux and Temple bucks, but his affairs are wofully
embarrassed, and he does not disdain to pocket the
receipts of a benefit night at the playhouse—as though
he were Jemmy Spiller or Macheath Walker. And even
the successful poets—Pope, and Gray, and Shenstone
excepted—were, according to Lord Macaulay, sometimes reduced to the low ebb of the bard who was "glad
to obtain, by pawning his best coat, the means of dining
on tripe at a cook-shop underground, where he could
wipe his hands after his greasy meal on the back of a
Newfoundland dog." Before 1740, Samuel Johnson had
written that same stern, strong poem of *London*, and
had gotten ten guineas for the copyright thereof. He
was lucky even to get that, seeing that one publisher
had advised him to abandon literature, take a porter's
knot, and carry trunks. He slept on bulks, and amidst
the hot ashes of lime-kilns and glass-houses. "He was
repeatedly provoked into striking those who had taken
liberties with him." He was scrofulous and hypochon-
driacal, and without a change of clothes or body linen.

Hogarth's "Distressed Poet" is quite as penniless, but
not quite so wretched as Johnson, or so reckless as
Savage. The poor fellow has a wife : not ugly, coarse,
and a shrew, as I am afraid the Johnsonian "Tetty" was,
but a tender, loving young woman ; very fair and delicate
to look at in her poor patched garments. Codrus is hard
at work at his table beneath the window in the lean-to
roof of the garret. He racks his brains for rhymes in
a poem on "Riches." Above him hangs, all torn,
tattered, and rat-begnawed, "A View of the Gold Mines
of Peru."* You see two of the consolations of his misery
on the window-sill—a pipe and an oval box of Kirton's
best tobacco. Another consolation, a little baby, is crying
lustily in the bed. A cat and her kittens have made a
comfortable couch on his coat. His sword, without a
scabbard, and the blade somewhat bent, lies on the floor.
It is evident that he can dress in gallant array sometimes ;
but it is to be feared that the last time he went out with
his sword by his side, he got either into a squabble for
the wall, or a broil at a coffee-house or in a night-cellar,

---

* In the earlier "states" of the *Distressed Poet*, the "gold mines of
Peru" do not appear. In their place is the copy of an engraving representing Pope beating Curll. A mine of very curious disquisition is opened
in the subject of the various states of the engravings of W. H., and in
which consists their extreme value to modern collectors. Alterations—often
of considerable magnitude and importance—become visible on comparison
of different impressions of Hogarth's plates. Notably, these changes are
found in the *Rake's Progress* (plate iv.) ; in the *Four Parts of the Day*
[Evening] ; in the four plates of *An Election* (scene i.) ; in *Beer Street and
Gin Lane*. Most of the alterations were from afterthought, and in
correction by Hogarth himself ; but after his death, another important
work, *Credulity, Superstition, and Fanaticism*, was audaciously garbled and
parodied, to suit the circumstances of the Johanna Southcote mania, by
Samuel Ireland.

and came home with his weapon thus damaged. House-hold utensils, mops and brooms, pails, and such matters are scattered here and there; there is not a vestige of looking-glass; but over the chimney, with the Bible, teacups and saucers, the loaf, and the little saucepan for the baby's pap, there is a target studded with bosses, and which has evidently come from the property-room of some theatre for which the poet has written.* Squalid, hopeless poverty is everywhere visible. The washing is done at home, as you may see from the sleeves and ruffles and bibs hung to dry over a line. A fencer's foil has been degraded into serving as a poker. There is a capacious cupboard quite empty. The walls are naked; the roof is not watertight. A little pewter porter measure stands on the chair by the bed-side; but when we remember the wealth of flagons, and rummers, and noggins, with which Hogarth heaps the foreground of some of the scenes in his Progresses, we may opine, either that the poet is too distressed to be a good

---

* Here a learned commentator assures me that I am in error, and that the instrument I assume to be a target is, in reality, a "dare for larks," or circular board with pieces of looking-glass inserted, used, on sunshiny days, for the purpose of "daring" or "dazing" larks from their high soaring flight to within a distance convenient for shooting or netting them. I never saw any dares for larks in this country, but they are common enough abroad, where they are yet used by sportsmen and bird-fanciers to decoy larks. The "dare" I have seen resembles a cocked hat—or *chapeau bras*—in form, and is studded with bits of looking-glass, not convex, but cut in facets inwards, like the theatrical ornament cast in zinc, and called a "logie." The setting is painted bright red, and the facets turn on pivots, and being set in motion by a string attached to the foot, the larks are sufficiently "dared," and come quite close over the fascinating toy. I don't see what such an instrument should do in the garret of the *Distressed Poet*, and adhere to my target theory.

customer to the tavern, or that his trust, like Rakewell's, is defunct, or that his potations are moderate.

A Welsh milkwoman—an exceedingly good-looking, although strapping young person, the model, indeed, of a Blowsybella in Gay's *Pastorals*, has come to dun the unhappy stanza-hammerer for a milk-score. That strong-lunged baby takes so much pap! The milkwoman is comfortably dressed. She wears high-heeled shoes and a coachwheel hat, and her petticoat is, doubtless, of the stoutest homespun dyed in grain. She brandishes the awful tally; she expatiates on every notch on the board; she *will* have her pound of flesh, or her handful of coppers, for her pint of milk. I think I hear the poet's pretty young wife striving to assuage the wrath of this angry milkwoman. Look at Mrs. Codrus' simple, loving, lovable face—Fielding's Amelia all over. Surely a glance at that visage is enough, O you seller of milk! It seems to say, "Think how clever my husband is. Even lords with blue ribands have complimented him. See how hard he works. He has been up all night, finishing that heroic poem, for which, when completed, Mr. Osborne has promised him two pounds five shillings, a copy of Montaigne's *Essays*, and an order on his tailor for a new coat. Indeed, we are sorely pushed. Our baby has been very ill, and stands in need of all the nourishment we can give it. Even our landlady has been kind, and forbears to trouble us for the rent. Besides, Mr. Codrus has a tragedy, which he has sent to the managers, and ——" And while she pours out these plaintive apologies the little woman is hard at work. She is a gentleman's daughter, I daresay. She has been tenderly nurtured. She thinks her husband the bravest, kindest, cleverest of mankind ; and, upon my word, she is mending his smallclothes.

Perhaps the milkwoman was touched by the pretty face and soft voice, and forbore to dun any more that day. But the milkwoman's dog has decidedly no pity for distressed poets, and putting his ugly head from behind her skirt, seizes with ravenous jaws on the scanty remains of yesterday's dinner, which had been put by on a plate.

Just about this time, 1740-1741, young Mr. Horace Walpole is travelling in Italy. He writes to his friend Mr. West, that he has passed a place called Radicofani. " Coming down a steep hill with two miserable hackneys, one fell under the chaise, and while we were disengaging him, a chaise came by with a person in a red cloak, a white handkerchief on its head, and a black hat ; we thought it a fat old woman, but it spoke in a shrill little pipe, and proved itself to be Senesino." This Senesino, a *soprano*, clever enough in his shrill piping, was the friendly rival of Farinelli. Both realized immense fortunes in England. I don't so much grumble at Mr. Codrus's wretched earnings, or at the ten guineas which Johnson (really) received for *London ;* but I may in justice notice Mr. Walpole's statement, that an Italian, the Abbé Vanneschi, and a certain Rolli, were paid three hundred guineas for the libretto of an opera. As to the singers, Monticelli and the Visconti had a thousand guineas for a season : Amorevoli had eight hundred and fifty, the "Moscovita" six hundred, including "secret services"—and I am entirely of the opinion of Doctor Pangloss concerning this being the very best of possible worlds.

So, I daresay, thought William Hogarth, when he could get enough bread and cheese for his hard work. You have heard already of the *Four Parts of the Day*, as having been designed by Hogarth for Jonathan Tyers of Vauxhall Gardens. The auctioneers have persisted in proclaiming the pictures at old Vauxhall to have been by W. H. ; but I repeat that they were not, and were probably the work of Frank Hayman or of John Laguerre. Hogarth, however, subsequently completed a set of four finished oil pictures from his first sketches. Two, *Morning* and *Noon*, were sold to the Duke of Ancaster for fifty-seven guineas. The *Evening* and *Night* were purchased by Sir William Heathcote for sixty-four guineas. The Abbé Vanneschi and the eminent Rolli would have turned up their noses at such remuneration. In 1738-9, the *Four Parts of the Day* were published in a series of plates of large dimensions, engraved mostly by Hogarth, but sometimes with the assistance of the Frenchman Baron.

Amidst these constant labours, culminating in 1741 in the *Enraged Musician* and the *Strolling Actresses Dressing in a Barn*, Hogarth could find leisure for the production of his large oil picture, *The Pool of Bethesda*, of which perhaps the less said the better. Why did he not attempt something in the style of the *Brünnen des Jungen* of Lucas Crannach ? At all events, a plea may be put in for the painter, for that he presented the *Pool of Bethesda*, together with his equally unsatisfactory painting of *The Good Samaritan*, to St. Bartholomew's Hospital. This generous donation took place not very long after he had published a very stinging caricature called *The Company of Undertakers*, reflecting with some

severity on the chief notabilities of the medical profession.
The work is one of his broad, bold etchings ; the motto,
Et plurima mortis imago. The heads, monstrous periwigs and all, are supposed to be portraits ; and it is
probable that the originals of the gold-headed canes
represented are to this day reverently preserved in the
Museum of the College of Physicians. Many of the
portraits are, of course, through lapse of time, no longer
recognizable ; but tradition points to the counterfeit
presentments of the Chevalier John Taylor, the oculist,
who was called " Liar Taylor," from a romancing account
of his life and adventures which he published ; of Dr.
Joshua Ward, commonly called " Spot Ward," from the
"port-wine face" with which he was afflicted; of Dr. Pierce
Dod, of St. Bartholomew's ; and of Dr. Bamber. The
corpulent figure in the centre, with a bone in its hand,
is designed for a *female* doctor, Mrs. Mapp, daughter
to one Wallin. She was otherwise known as " Crazy
Sally," and used to travel about the country, re-setting
dislocations by sheer strength of arm. The doctor in
harlequin's attire has been conjectured—but only conjectured—to be a quiz on Sir Hans Sloane.

William Hogarth was now forty-three years of age,
married, but childless ; busy, cheerful, and foremost man
among English artists, and with another kind of personal
celebrity entirely and exclusively his own. He never
became rich, but his gains were large ; and he prospered,
as he deserved, exceedingly. I rejoice that another
chapter yet remains to me wherein to depict my hero
in his golden prime. Then, alas ! must come the sere
and yellow leaf,—which comes to all.

VIII.

The Shadow of the Forty-five.

IN the days of which I am writing, the English nation were much given to the eating of beef. There is a philosophy of meat, as well as of every other kind of matter ; and they who philosophize in a right spirit shall not fail to trace many symptoms of the influence of a beef diet upon William Hogarth. This was a man who despised soups, and set at nought the kickshaws of Lebeck and Pontack, of Recbell and Macklin's ordinaries. It was so ordered that Hogarth should not rise above the level of the English middle class, then hearty admirers of beef and other fleshmeats,—they had not degenerated into a liking for warmed-up stews served in electrotyped side dishes—and although when he became famous he was often bidden to great feasts, such as lord mayors' dinners, benchers' tables at Lincoln's Inn, Oxford commemoration banquets, and loyal Train Band gatherings at the King's Arms, the ordering of those repasts was always intimately connected with ribs of beef, sirloins and briskets, shoulders of veal, venison pasties, and pies made from the humbles of a deer. These entertainments, too, were of a public nature ; and though some noble patrons of Hogarth, — some Boyne, or

Ancaster, or Castlemaine, or Arthur Onslow—may, from time to time, have asked him to dinner in Piccadilly or Soho, it is not likely that he enjoyed himself to any great extent at those symposia of the aristocratic meagre and the refined frivolous.* Horace Walpole records that he'once sat next to Hogarth at dinner, and that he was either sulky or embarrassed, and would or could say nothing. The latter I take to have been the case, for the painter was the very opposite to a churl or a hypochon-

---

* Dining out, even at the tables of the great, was not a very refined proceeding in Hogarth's time. When Dr. King dined with the Duke of Ormonde, Lords Marr, Jersey, Lansdown, Bishop Atterbury, and other magnificoes, the company were not deterred by the presence of a prelate of the Church of England from entering into a "jocular discourse concerning short prayers." At another dinner-table, that of Cardinal Polignac at Rome, his eminence, observing that Dr. King drank only water, told him that he had entertained five hundred of his countrymen during his embassy to the Pontifical court, and that he, the doctor, was the only water-drinking Englishman he had yet met with. When Pope dined with Lord Burlington, he could not relish his dinner until his host had ordered a large glass of cherry-brandy to be set before him, by way of a dram. Moreover, when you had the honour to be invited to my lord's table, you had, to a certain extent, to pay for your dinner, for the impudent and extortionate lacqueys in the hall expected large donations, or "vails." There is a good story of one Lord Poor—query, De la Poer?—a Roman Catholic peer of Ireland, who excused himself from dining oftener with the Duke of Ormonde on the ground that "he could not afford it ;" but added that if his grace would be kind enough to put a guinea in his hand at the conclusion of the banquet he should be happy to come. This was done, and Lord Poor was after-wards a frequent visitor at the duke's house in St. James's Square. But Lord Taafe, likewise in the peerage of Ireland, and who had been a general officer in the Austrian service, more resolutely set his face against "vails," always attending his guests to the door himself, and when they made offer to put money into the servants' hands, preventing them, saying : "If you do give, give it to me, for it was I who did buy the dinner." Be it men-tioned, likewise, to the honour of William Hogarth, that he would not allow his domestics to take any fee or reward from visitors who came to sit for their portraits.

driac, and by universal testimony was a sprightly, jovial, chirruping little man. The gravest accusation brought against him by those who were obliged to hate because they envied him, was that he was parsimonious. The only evidence that can be adduced in support of this charge is, on the one hand, that he had a habit of paying ready money and never getting into debt, and that, on the other, he *would* have his due from the printsellers and the people who bought plates and pictures from him. For the remainder, any imputation of avarice must fall utterly to the ground when we remember his charities ; and he left so little, that five years after his death, his widow was poor.

To return to the roasting-spit, and to my hero in his relation with butcher's meat. Throughout his works you will find a careful attention to, and laudable admiration of good, sound, hearty eating and drinking— tempered, however, by a poignant censure of gormandizing and immoderate libations. What mounds of beef, hecatombs of poultry, pyramids of pies and tartlets are consumed at the mayor's feast in *Industry and Idleness !* What a tremendous gorge is that in the first scene of the *Election !* Look at the leg of mutton so triumphantly brandished in *Beer Street.* Admire the vastiness of that roast beef of Old England in the *Gates of Calais.* Consider the huge pie which the pretty girl is bringing home from the bakehouse in *Noon* of the *Four Parts of the Day.* Observe the jovial fare of the soldiers who carouse at the table in the print of *England,* while the sergeant is measuring the bumpkin against his halbert, and the Giotto-like grenadier is scrawling a caricature on the wall of the French king. Hogarth was a man who, so soon as he could dine at all, dined every day and dined well. He did not eschew punch ; he had no grudge against the generous wines of Portugal ; but his faith was in the mighty, potent, and nourishing fermentation of malt and hops—in the "jolly good ale and old," that Bishop Hill sang so jolly a song about, in the Black Burgundy of Humphrey Parsons, and the Titanesque Entire of Harwood :—in beer. This liquid, which is, by the way, much esteemed by foreigners visiting England, and which I find mentioned in the Italian libretto to the opera of *Marta* as a potation—

> Che il Britanno rende altier—
>
> Which makes the Briton haughty (!)

was evidently a decided favourite with William. All his good and honest people drink beer, and plentifully, from the hugest of tankards and cans. His rascals and his rogues quaff French wines and strong waters. His vicious characters fare thinly and badly. The miserly alderman in the *Marriage à la Mode* is about to breakfast on an egg stuck in a monticule of rice. There is certainly a pig's cheek, cold, on the table, but like the empty silver tankard it is merely there for show ; has been up to the table half a dozen times, and gone down, untouched, and so would depart again, but for the wary dog which, half-starved at most times, takes advantage of the commotion created by death, to distend his ribs with pork, to him unwonted.

In his simple, straightforward way of thinking, it was evidently my painter's creed that virtuous people have hearty appetites and a good digestion. The French hold otherwise. "A good stomach and a bad heart," is

their favourite gastronomic paradox.   But Hogarth
makes his dissipated countess take nothing for breakfast but tea and a starveling slice of bread-and-
butter ; and *Kate*, with her Hebrew admirer, can indulge
in nothing more substantial than well-frothed chocolate
in eggshell porcelain.   Very different are these unsatisfactory refreshments to the solid meat breakfasts and
ponderous dinners consumed by the pilgrims who started
one morning from the Bedford Head, and took the
tilt-boat for Gravesend, *en route* for Sheerness.   I can
imagine the horror which the sturdy little beefeater of
Leicester Fields must have entertained for such a pinch-
stomach as John Lord Hervey, who " never eat beef, nor
horse, nor any of those things," * who breakfasted on
an emetic, dined on a biscuit, and regaled himself once
a week with an apple.

The hard work, of which I sketched the history in
the preceding section, was continued by William
Hogarth, and without intermission, throughout the
reign of George II.   His popularity had not only
become general, but it was safe.   He could have many
imitators, but no rivals.   The airy patronage accorded
to him by the aristocracy pleased them more than it did
him.   He had little to gain from commerce with the
great.   His great stay and holdfast were in the steady
patronage and encouragement of the affluent middle
classes.   Vicious noblemen may have dreaded his satire ;
and Hogarth was certainly not averse from administering
a stinging stripe to the Charterises, the Whartons, or
the Baltimores, whom he saw passing and misconducting

---

* An impertinence, since, and erroneously, attributed to Brummell.   I
daresay both beaux ate beefsteaks in private.

themselves ; but to render the satirist justice, it seemed to him perfectly a matter of indifference whether his satire were directed against barons or against beggars. He curried favour neither in the ante-chamber of Chesterfield, nor in the cellar of Mother Midnight. If an oligarchy, haughty, ignorant, and dissolute, are treated with merited severity in the *Marriage à la Mode*, the ruffianly vices of the soldiery, the coarse and hardened cruelty of the lowest mob, the smug sanctimoniousness of precisians, the coarse self-indulgence of the citizens, are treated with equal and impartial severity. Hogarth quite as much disdained to glorify the virtues of a mechanic, because he had ten children and only one shirt, as to denounce a lord, because he possessed ten thousand acres and a blue ribbon. At least he was free from the most irrational and degrading vice of modern satire : the alternate blackening and whitening of persons occupying different grades in society, for the simple reason that they were born to occupy those grades. Is it a chimney-sweeper's fault that he is sooty, and hasn't a pocket-handkerchief, and lives in Hampshire Hog Lane, and cannot aspirate his *h*'s ? Is it a gentleman's fault that he has parts and accomplishments, and a historic name and forty thousand a year ? Did we make ourselves, or choose for ourselves ? Are we any the better or the worse in our degree, or is there any need that we should fling stones at one another, because you, O my Aristarchus, were educated at the University of Oxford, and I at the University of France, or at Leyden, or Göttingen, or at the One Tun Ragged School ? Hogarth meted out justice to all classes alike ; and the depraved earl or the tipsy parson could not very well complain of seeing himself gibbeted when the next victim might be Taylor the eye-doctor, or Philip-in-the-Tub. But the anchor which held Hogarth fastest to the public favour was the sincere and deliberate belief—prevalent among the serious and the substantial orders—that his works were in the highest degree moral, and that they conduced to the inculcation of piety and virtue. Pope has stigmatized vice in deathless couplets. We shudder and turn away sickened from Sporus and his gilded wings, from Curio and Atossa, from grubby Lady Mary and greedy Sir Balaam. We can scarcely help despising even while we pity the ragged fry of hacks who grovel in Grub Street or flounder in the Blackfriars' mud of the *Dunciad ;* but it is impossible for the most superficial student of those wonderful exercitations to overcome the impression that all Pope's satire subserves some mean and paltry purpose ; that he hated the rascals he flagellated, and wished to be revenged on them ; and, on the other side, one can as little trust the high-flown panegyric which he bestows on the pro-blematically perfect Man of Ross,* as the adulation with which he bestains Bolingbroke, a genius and a wit certainly, but whom all men know,—and whom the moral Pope must have known—to have been as politically false as Fouché, and as debauched as Mirabeau, and as unbelieving as Arouet. The acute and accomplished admired Pope ; the dull and the foolish wondered at and dreaded him ; but all the world understood and believed in Hogarth. I have said, that his surest anchorage was in the middle class, and that they had faith in him as a

---

* One of whose merits in Pope's eyes may have been that he spelt his name " Kyrle," and not " Curll," as the hated Edmund was wont to do.

moral teacher. All you who have seen his collected works know how coarse are many of the representations and the allusions in his tableaux. Were that elephant folio dream of mine to become a reality, it would be impossible, in this nineteenth century, to publish exact reproductions of all Hogarth's engravings. Modern taste would revolt at, and spurn them. So are there things in *Pamela*, in *Clarissa Harlowe*, in Defoe's *Religious Courtship*, in Brooke's *Fool of Quality*, in the chaste essays of Addison and Steele even, which it would be expedient, in our state of society, not to reprint. Official persons were obliged, the other day, to expurgate the Royal Proclamation against Vice and Immorality, for the reason that there were words in it not fit for genteel ears. A hundred years ago such scruples did not exist. A spade was called a spade ; and the plain-spokenness of such a moralist as Hogarth was welcomed and applauded by clergymen, by schoolmasters, by pure matrons, by sober tradesmen, and decorous fathers of families. The series of *Industry and Idleness* was subscribed for by pious citizens, and the prints hung up in counting-rooms and workshops as an encouragement to the virtuous and a warning to the wicked, and scriptural texts were carefully selected by clerical friends to accompany the pictures of orgies at the Blood-Bowl House and carnivals at Tyburn. The entreaties that were made to him to publish appendices to the *Marriage à la Mode*, in the shape of a *Happy Marriage*, are on a parallel with the solicitations of the pious lady to Richardson, that he would cause Lovelace to be converted through the intermediary of a Doctor Christian. Both Hogarth and Richardson knew the world too well

to enter upon such tasks.   They saw the evil man
setting out on his course, and knew that he would
accomplish it to his destruction.

Hogarth, however, might have incurred peril of
lapsing into the drearily didactic had he been for ever
tracing out the fatal progresses of Rakes to Bedlam and
Kate Hackabouts to Bridewell, of frivolous earls and
countesses to duels and elopements, or of naughty boys
who play at pitch-and-toss on Sundays, or tease animals,
to the Tyburn gallows, or the dissecting-room in
Surgeon's Hall.   William's hard work was diversified by
a goodly stock of miscellaneous taskwork.   The purely
comic would sometimes assert itself, and his object
would then be to make you laugh and nothing more.

Thus, it is not apparent that he had any very grim
design in view in those admirable subjects, more than
once glanced at—the *Four Parts of the Day*.   He shows
you the abstract and brief chronicle of the time, and is
content with painting four inimitably graphic scenes of
life in London in 1738, without insisting on any particular
ethical text.   Let us see what this life in London is.
We begin with a dark, raw winter's morning in Covent
Garden Market.   There is Inigo Jones's "Barn;" and,
although oddly reversed (to the confusion of topographical
knowledge, in the engraving), the tall house, now Evans's
Hotel, and the commencement of King Street.   The
Piazza we do not see.   In front of the church is a sort
of shebeen or *barraque*, the noted Tom King's coffee-
house—whether so named from the highwayman, who
was the friend of Dick Turpin (and was shot by him), or
from some popular landlord, I am unable to determine.
The clock points to five minutes to eight.   A rigid old

maid of pinched and nipped appearance, but patched
and beribboned and befanned, as though in the desperate
hope that some beau who had been on the royster all
night would suddenly repent and offer her his hand and
heart, is going to *matins*, followed by a shivering little
foot-page, who carries her prayer-book. Inside Tom
King's there has been, as usual, a mad broil. Periwigs
are flying about. Swords are crossed with cudgels, and
the drawers are divided between fears for their sconces
and anxiety to know who is to pay the reckoning for
that last half-guinea bowl. Two stumpy little school-
boys in enormous hats are cowering along on their way
to school. It is so cold that they will find it almost a
mercy to have their palms warmed with the ferule. The
snow lies thick on the housetops, and the vagrant
hangers-on to the market have lit a fire with refuse
wood, and are warming one blue hand, begging piteously,
meanwhile, with the other. More beaux and bloods
have rambled into the market, their rich dresses all
disordered, to make staggering love to apple-women and
sempstresses going to their work. Early as it is, the
touters in the employ of the quack, Dr. Rock, are abroad,
and carry placards vaunting the doctor's cures, impu-
dently headed by the royal arms. There is a foreground
of carrots, turnips, and cabbage-leaves. Change the
dresses ; clear away Tom King's coffee-house, and trans-
plant its roysterers to some low tavern in the immediate
neighbourhood, and Hogarth's *Life in London* is enacted
every summer and winter morning in our present Covent
Garden Market. But the scene changes. We are at
high *Noon*. It is Sunday, and a congregation are coming
out of church, or rather chapel ; for, although the tall

spire of St. Martin's looms close by, our congregations are issuing from a brick meeting-house of the French Huguenot persuasion. A Parisian beau of the first water—on week days he is probably an enameller or a water-gilder in Bear or Spur Street,—is prattling to a coquettish lady in a sack, much apparently to the annoyance of an attenuated gentleman, not unlike M. de Voltaire in middle age. He is the husband, I think, of the lady of the sack, and is jealous of her; for even Huguenots are susceptible of the green-eyed passion. They have a child with them,—an astonishing little mannikin made up as sprucely as a bushy wig, lace, embroidery, ruffles, buckles, a tiny sword, and a diminutive cane will allow him,—but who, for all his fine raiment, looks lovingly at a neighbouring puddle. Two ancient gossips are kissing one another. A demure widow, stiff-wimpled, glances with eyes half closed at the flirtation between the beau and the lady in the sack. The widow is not talking, but she is evidently *thinking*, scandal. In the background, see the tottering old almsmen creeping away home to the house of charity, erected by some rich silk factor, who managed to save something from the spoliation of the dragonades, and, after that, made a fortune in Soho or Spitalfields. And sweeping down the church steps, see the stern French Protestant pastor with Geneva bands and austere wig. Exiled, proscribed, and with but a barren benefice, he is yet as proud as the haughtiest prelate of the swollen Gallican church. He can bear persecution, the bitterest, —has borne it, is ready to bear it again,—but he never forgets that there was, years ago, a confessor of his creed, one Jean Chauvin, called Calvin; and woe betide the day when he himself shall become a persecutor, and get some new Servetus into his power ; for, of a surety, he will roast him at the stake.

There is no wasting going on to-day more fatal than that of meat, and yet there are wars and rumours of war about that. There is "good eating" at the sign of the "Baptist's Head," which is depicted duly decollated in a charger ; but next door, at the sign of the "Good Woman," who is painted, according to custom, headless, a gentleman and his wife in the first-floor front have had a furious quarrel respecting a baked shoulder of mutton with potatoes under it, and the lady has flung the joint and its appurtenances, dish and all, out of the window. Below, mishaps as momentous have occurred. A bold Blackamoor has stolen a kiss from a very pretty girl who is taking home a pie. A shock-headed boy has stumbled against a post with the dish of viands he is carrying. All is smashed : the boy yelps with dismay, and scratches his tangled poll at the idea of the practical remonstrances which may be addressed to him by his parents on his return home ; and a hungry little tatter-demalion of a girl at the post's foot, crouches prone to the pavement, and greedily crams herself with the scattered waifs and strays of victual. Pass on to *Evening*.

We are at Sadler's Wells tea and bun house,* and

---

* Soon after tea became the fashionable beverage, several gardens in the outskirts of London were opened as tea-gardens ; but the proprietors, finding the visitors wanted something else besides tea, accommodated them with ale, bottled beer, &c. In an old magazine, printed in the beginning of George III.'s reign, the writer, speaking of persons whose habit it was to resort to the various tea-gardens near London every Sunday, calculates them to amount to 200,000. Of these he considers that not one would go away without having spent 2*s*. 6*d*. ; and, consequently, the sum of 25,000*l*.

hard by the Sir Hugh Middleton Tavern. A lean citizen,
and his portly, gaily-bedizened wife, are taking the air
by the New River side. Amwell Street and reservoirs
as yet are not. The two elder children—boy and girl—
are squabbling and nagging one another, even as the
author of *The Mill on the Floss* tells us that children
carp and nag. The lean husband is entrusted with the
care of the youngest child, who is weakly and fatigued
besides, and with a rueful countenance he cuddles the
little innocent. This is not a happy marriage. There
is a charming aspect of rurality about the scene ; and I

---

would have been spent in the course of the day by this number of persons.
Sunday afternoon and evening were a perfect carnival for the lower classes,
and the " fields," as well as the tea-gardens, were crowded. " People who
sell fruit, &c., in the fields, preparing to shut up their stalls and joyfully
retire to the Geneva shops ; cold beef and carrot most vigorously attacked in
public houses by hungry acquaintances just come out of the fields.   .   .   .
The Court of Aldermen belonging to the Black Bull in Kentish Town
clearing the afternoon reckoning, that they may walk to London before
dark.   .   .   .   Divers companies of Jacobites censuring the ministers in
hedge publick houses, and by their discourse do mighty matters for the
Pretenders.   .   .   .   The drawers at Sadler's Wells and the Prospect
House near Islington, Jenny's Whim at Chelsea, the Spring Gardens at
Newington and Stepney, the Castle at Kentish Town, and the Angel at
Upper Holloway, each of them trying to cheat, not only the customers, but
even the person who has the care of the bar ; and every room in these
houses full of talk and smoke. Poor men, women, and children creeping
out of the fields, the first half drunk, the others tired and hungry.   .   .   .
Men who keep hay-farms about this metropolis ordering their servants to
prevent the too great devastation of new-mown hay by people who are
tumbling about the fields.   .   .   .   Poor honest women at their bedsides,
praying and coaxing their husbands to arise and take a walk with them in
the fields." These notabilia are from a very rare and curious tract, called
*Low Life ; or, One-Half of the World knows not how the other half Live,
in a true Description of a Sunday, as it is usually Spent within the Bills
of Mortality, calculated for the Twenty-first of June* (Whit Sunday).
The book is anonymous, but is dedicated to the "ingenious and ingenuous
·Mr. Hogarth."

would that Hogarth had spared us that little bit of
cynicism about the protuberance of the cow which is
being milked in the background. It is not meet that I
should be more explicit regarding the connection of the
cow with the lean tradesman's wig, than to refer you to
a Roman poet who tells us that there are twin gates
to Sleep, through which our dreams issue—and even
married tradesmen must sleep and dream,—and that one
of the gates is of ivory, and the other of horn.

And what of *Night?*—night, when "wicked dreams
abuse the curtained sleep." Hogarth shows us night in
its more jovial, reckless aspect, not in that murtherous,
purse-cutting, marauding guise of which Fielding, as a
Westminster justice, was so searchingly aware. Xantippe
is showering her favours from the window of the Rummer
Tavern. Two Freemasons—one said to be a portrait of
the well-known Justice De Veil—are staggering home
after a banquet of extraordinary liberality. By the oak
boughs decking the windows and the Freemasons' hats,
the night would seem to be that of the twenty-ninth
of May—Restoration Day. The equestrian statue of
Charles I. is shadowed in the distance, but the locality
does not at all resemble Charing Cross. In the extreme
background a house is in flames — the conflagration
probably due to one of the numerous bonfires on which
the Hanoverian government for years strove to put an
extinguisher, but which the populace, with all their
hatred of Popery, brass money, and wooden shoes, and
love for the Protestant succession, as resolutely kept
alight. Through an open window you see a fat man
undergoing the operation of shaving. He is probably
being dandified in honour of some tavern supper to

which he is invited, in celebration of Restoration Day. The date should, properly, be nearer Michaelmas or Ladyday ; for a tenant to whom the payment of rent has become irksome is removing his goods in a cart— "shooting the moon" by the light of the bonfires and the blazing house. To complete the scene, the "Salisbury Flying Coach" has broken down ; the off-wheel has tumbled into one of the pyres of rejoicing ; and the immured passengers are vainly entreating assistance at the hands of the inebriated watch.

I come now to the work, *Strolling Actresses Dressing in a Barn*,—"invented, painted, designed, and published by William Hogarth." The wisest authorities concur in according the very highest meed of praise to this splendid composition. Horace Walpole says of it, that "for wit and imagination, without any other end, this is the best of all our artist's works ;" and the German, Lichtenberg, observes, "Never, perhaps, since the graver and pencil have been employed in the service of satire has so much lively humour been compressed within so small a compass as here." Indeed the picture-print is an exceedingly fine one ; and save that tragic interest is lacking, shows almost all that of which Hogarth was artistically, physically, and mentally capable. It has been suggested that the title *Strolling Actresses* is incomplete, and that "Actors" should be added ; but it is worthy of remark that the beau dressing has a face and figure of such feminine beauty, that Hogarth's model might well have been Peg Woffington, in that character of Sir Harry Wildair, in which she made the men jealous and the women fall in love with her ; or else William's famous Drum-Majoress from Southwark

17—2

fair, invested, " for this occasion only," with more than Amazonian grace. The children attired as cupids, demons, &c., may be accepted as of the epicene gender ; and the rest of the *dramatis personæ* are unquestionably women, either young or old. In the first impression of the plate the playbill informs the public that the part of Jupiter will be performed by " Mr. Bilk Village ;" but in later impressions the name is concealed by a deep shadow from another bill cast over it ; and the rest of the characters, so far as I can make them out with a magnifying glass, are all by Mrs. So-and-So. The manager is not represented here : and, indeed, decorum would forbid Mr. Lamp being present in the ladies' dressing-room, although the theatre was but a barn.

You must remember that this picture is, to a certain extent, an artistic *Dunciad*. It tears away a veil, it rolls up the curtain ; it shows all the squalor, misery, degradation of the player's life in Hogarth's time. It is repugnant to think that my William could be for once in his life so pusillanimous as to satirize women when he dared not depict men. Such, however, seems to have been the case. Moreover, the ladies are nearly all exquisitely beautiful ; and a woman will pardon almost any affront in the world so long as you respect her beauty. But once ignore her pretty countenance, and *gare aux ongles !* No sooner had the unhappy Essex been detected in making a face at his ruddled, wrinkled Royal Mistress, than his head was virtually off his shoulders. A woman may be beaten, starved, trampled on, betrayed, and she will forgive and smile ; but there is no forgiveness after such a deadly insult as was hurled by Clarendon in Castlemaine's pretty face : "Woman, you will one day become OLD."

And Hogarth may have feared the menfolk of the side-scenes and the footlights, even had he drawn no portraits and named no names. Some periwig-pated fellow would have been sure to declare that he was libelled in Jupiter Bilk Village. I am given to understand that in this present era the players are peaceable gentry enough ; that Mr. Robson is by no means a fire-eater, and that Mr. Wigan is no shedder of man's blood. But in the days when Colley Cibber wrote his fantastic *Apology*, and long before, the actors had been a strange, wild, and somewhat desperate set. In James's time, Ben—he was, to be sure, an author as well as an actor, and both constitutionally and professionally choleric—was a very Pandarus of Troy, and always ready to measure swords with an opponent. The comedians of King Charles I. gallantly took service on the Royal side, and at Edgehill and Wiggan Lane did so slash and curry the buff jerkins of the Roundheads, as to diminish our wonder at all players being rigorously proscribed during the Protectorate. The stage-players of the Restoration and the following reigns were notorious swashbucklers. Actors had often to fight their way by dint of rapier up to the "leading business." Betterton fought half a dozen duels. Mountford, in a quarrel with Lord Mohun, was stabbed by one of the companions of that noble bravo. Powell cudgelled an insolent dandy at Wills' Coffee House. Hildebrand Horden, a young actor of great promise, quarrelled with a Colonel Burgess, who had been resident at Venice, fought with him and was slain ; and Macklin, who was always in

some difficulty or another, was tried at the Old Bailey
for killing a man in the playhouse dressing-room on
some farthing-token turmoil about a property wig.   No
wonder that Hogarth forbore—after his early escapades
of the *Beggar's Opera* and the players in *Southwark
Fair*—further to provoke so irascible a race.   'Twas all
very well to paint Walker in *Macheath* and Garrick in
Richard, or to etch benefit tickets for the gentlemen of
the Theatres Royal ; but 'ware hawk when he came to
twit them on their poverty and their rags !

In mere assumption, therefore, I take all the
company in the· barn to be of the non-combative sex.
The comedians are announced as " from London ; " the
piece to be performed is *The Devil to Pay in Heaven.*
Diana, Flora, Juno, Night, a Ghost, three witches, a
Tragedy Queen, two demons, Jupiter's eagle—who is
feeding a swaddled baby from a little pap-saucepan, super-
posed on a copy of the Act against Strolling Players,
which again is placed on a regal crown—the sun, moon,
and stars, two kittens, and a monkey, seem to be among
the characters.   The handsome youth, whom I conjecture
to be an Amazon, is to play Jupiter.   The eagle—with
a child's face peeping from beneath the beak—is feeding
the baby, perhaps Jupiter's baby, at his or her feet.
The central female figure, Flora, it would appear—
although from the extremely airy state of her drapery,
she is not susceptible of reproduction as a modern
example—must ever remain a cynosure to all sincere
admirers of William Hogarth.   Nothing can be more
gracefully beauteous than the composition and drawing
of this figure, the only exception to which (in addition
to aëriness of drapery) is that some aberration of the

laws of pneumatics must have disarranged and held in suspense the folds of the sole garment which the goddess Flora, at this stage of her toilet, condescends to wear. She is, indeed, too much preoccupied just now, to think of dressing ; and in the ardour of recitation—she is going through the grand tirade of the evening, and tramples on the very hoop that she will presently assume.   To make amends, her head is elaborately powdered, jewelled, and plumed, and her fair neck is encircled by a rich necklace, composed, without doubt, of stones as precious as any of those in the large hamper which serves as a dressing table for the *seconda donna*, and which, to judge by its distinguishing label, contains the regalia of the entire company.   Heroine number two, who is kneeling before this hamper, has reached the more advanced stage of having donned a petticoat of vast amplitude of material and rigid circumference of basket-work : a few rents, however, in the fabric, would appear to show that the hoop has seen some service. This lady is further sacrificing to the Graces, to the extent of greasing her locks with a tallow candle ; and on the hamper top, by the candle in its sconce, the shell that holds the carmine, and the comb that wants a tooth, lies ready to the heroine's hand that flour-dredger from whose perforated dome shall speedily issue the snowy shower so essential to the frosting of that fair head. See yet another heroine, beautiful, majestic, severe, as Belvidera, as Sophonisba, or as Lindamira, and not unlike Hogarth's own Sigismunda, duly equipped in veil and tiara and regal robe, and with certainly as comely a pair of hands and arms as any well-grown young woman could desire to have.   This is the Tragedy Queen.   She

is conning her part for the last time; but is not too
proud to rest her exquisite leg and foot on a wheel-
bench in order that a faithful comrade, the *suivante* in
the drama, may darn a rent in her stocking. Briefly
must the rest of the wondrous tableau be glanced at.
Look at the noble matron who holds a squalling and
clawing kitten, while the atrocious harridan near her
snips off the tip of the poor animal's tail with a pair of
scissors, and allows the blood to drip into a broken
basin. Is rose-pink, or, at least, red ochre so scarce
that real blood is necessary for the bedaubing of some
stage assassin? Why, Farmer Hodge, to whom the
barn belongs, would surely lend some of the red pigment
with which he ruddles his sheep. Jupiter—lady or
gentleman as the case may be—does not disdain to take
some comfort in the glass of celestial ichor, otherwise gin,
which a young lady attired as a mermaid pours from a
black bottle and hands to the Olympian potentate, a
daughter of Night looking on in pleased contemplation.
An ape in a corner is making himself comfortable with
the plumed helmet of Alexander the Great, and the
kittens are tranquilly playing with a regal orb and the
lyre of Apollo. A Virgin of the Sun (apparently, in
everyday life, mamma to Cupid) points with that deity's
bow to a pair of stockings hanging over a scene to dry;
and the obedient urchin, wigged, winged, and quivered,
ascends a ladder to fetch down the required hose. A
considerable portion of the company's body linen, all
more or less tattered, is suspended for drying purposes
over a prosaic clothe's-line. For the rest, drums,
trumpets, violoncellos, and the stage thunder; fragments
of scenery—now a forest and now a Roman temple; the

dips stuck in potatoes cut in halves that are to illumine
the stage and the auditory ; a classical altar with rams'
heads at the angles, and behind which the two demons
are contending as to who shall take the first draught from
a mighty tankard of home-brewed ; the child's crib, a
homely gridiron, an S.P.Q.R. standard, the palette,
pipkins, and brushes of the scene-painter, canvas clouds
and pasteboard griffins, Flora's car, and the union-jack,
make up the accessories in this curious medley.   The
originally agricultural character of the place is shown
by the flail hanging over the sheaves of straw, and
through a hole in the thatch, a gaping rustic stares at
the strange scene beneath him.   Poor mummers ; poor
rogues and vagabonds by Act of Parliament !   They
seem merry enough, for all their raggedness and all
their misery.

It was a very nice thing, in those days, to be Signor
Farinelli, or Senesino, or Faustina, or Cuzzoni.   It was
not so bad to write libretti, like the Abbé Vanneschi.
It was genteel and courtly to be an architect, author and
opera manager combined, like Sir John Vanbrugh.   It
was even tolerable to be the patentee of one of the great
houses, like Rich, with his diamond buckles, or Colley
Cibber, who was a fine gentleman and a macaroni, and
whom " all the town went to see," says Horace Walpole,
when, at seventy years of age, and at an honorarium of
fifty guineas a night, he condescended to play such
parts as Pandulph, in his own play of *Papal Tyranny*.
But at the time Hogarth was painting his wonderful
picture, the lot of an actor, even the most eminent, was
painful, was precarious, was replete with unspeakable
degradations.   A man against whom no stronger accu-

sation could be brought than that he lived by the honourable exercise of the talents which the Almighty had given him, was exposed to affronts the most brutal and the most wanton at the hands of every fool of quality, or of every rascal with a cockade in his hat who called himself captain. With the exception of the outrage on Dryden by the bravoes of Rochester, and that on Voltaire by the lacqueys of the duke he had offended, there is not on record a more cowardly and ruffianly transaction than the slaughter of poor Will Mountford by Captain Hill and the wretch Mohun, for the reason, forsooth, that Mrs. Bracegirdle chose to look with favour on him. It was to be expected that noblemen would hold players of but little account : it was bad enough to be excommunicated by the clergy, and vilified by the critics : but the players' humiliations did not end here ; and not an Irish ensign, not a beggarly son to some creeper of the backstairs, not a student of the inns of court, not a Somersetshire esquire whose grandfather was hanged for being at Sedgemoor, but thought himself infinitely superior to such men as Wilks, and Booth, and Doggett. It was long ere this irrational superciliousness declined ; even at this very day in which I write it is not eradicated. The wise, and learned, and pious Johnson, the gifted and polished Reynolds, the stately Warburton, the eloquent Burke, did not disdain the company and friendship of a play-actor ; but hearken to the terms in which a perchance War Office clerk addressed the Roscius of the English stage : "Vagabond ! keep to your pantomimes." It was thus that the party-writer, Junius, wrote to DAVID GARRICK ; and I doubt not but that had he been in Mr. Secretary Cecil's office two centuries before, he would, just as contemptuously, have apostrophized WILLIAM SHAKSPEARE.

If such was the status of the London actor, in what light was looked upon the wretched stroller, the Bilk Village, who wandered from fair to fair and from barn to barn, to rant the tirades of the drivelling Shadwell and the crazy Nat Lee, for the amusement of Lobbin Clout and Dorothy Draggletail. The stroller was a vagabond by law. The tipsy justices whom Gay satirized in the "What d'ye call it?" might send the constable after him, might lay him by the heels in the cage, and deliver his wife and daughters to the tender mercies of the beadle and the whipping-post. The unpatented player was *caput lupinum*. He was a social outlaw. He was driven from tithing to tithing, or clapped up in Bridewell, while quacks as impudent as Misaubin, and as extortionate as Rock, lived in ease and splendour, unmolested, battened on the plunder of the public, and drove about the town in gilded carriages. One can understand the bigoted French clergy demurring as to the Christian burial of Molière—had he not written *Tartuffe?* but it is difficult to comprehend what harm the English players had ever done to Church or State, or in what degree even the lowest strollers were inferior to the effete Italian mountebanks upon whom the English nobility delighted to heap gold in thousands.

The print of the *Enraged Musician* has been said by many to be capable, at most, of deafening those who looked upon it. It is, in truth, a noisier picture than *Southwark Fair;* but the noise it exhibits is less tolerable. There is no cheerful murmur, no busy hum, no babbling of human brooks; but rather one sustained, jarring, clanging, maddening " row." The unhappy musician, who is composing a *motett*, or scoring an overture, in his tranquil parlour, and—it being summer time—has left his window open, has every cause to be enraged and exasperated by this persistent concourse of discordant sounds. The raven himself would be hoarse were he to strive to croak down these hideous noises. There is a little girl springing her rattle; a needy knife-grinder plying his wheel and whistling meanwhile; a beggar-woman with a squalling bantling, excruciatingly swaddled, yelping out the ballad of the *Ladies' Fall;* * a pretty young milkwoman, with her open milk-pail on her head—not yoked with a brace of cans, as in our time—who is giving " milk O !" with all thè strength of her robust lungs; a dustman passes bawling with his cart; a small-coal man utters his lugubrious chant; a vendor of fish vaunts the freshness and succulence of his wares; a child, accoutred in all the absurdity of the reigning mode, and who might be twin-brother to the overdressed little urchin in *Noon*, is thwacking the parchment of a toy drum; from the chimney-top of a neighbouring house a sweep, having completed his task, gives utterance to his jödil, implying the crowning of the work by the end; it is the king's birthday, or some other national *fête*, and while the banner flaunts from the steeple, the joy-bells are vociferously ding-donging forth; and an additional contribution is made to this ear-piercing din by the vicinity of a whitesmith, one " John Long, Pewterer,"

---

* The " *Ladies' Fall* " was the harmonic predecessor of the " *Unfortunate Miss Bailey*."

whose journeymen are doubtless hammering away with might and main. One is puzzled to imagine what new phase of noise could have been devised by Hogarth to complete this atrocious *tintamarre.* He might have had, perhaps, a wedding-party next door to the musician's, and the marrowbones and cleavers outside congratulating the newly wedded couple with rough music.* The parish beadle might have been bellowing out an "Oh yes!" relative to purses stolen or pug-dog strayed ; a schoolmaster might have been thrashing a boy at an open window ; or a butcher ringing the nose of a pig in some outhouse close by. I see, however, that William, disregarding for once the proprieties of time, has sketched two members of the feline family vigorously caterwauling on the tiles. Observe that the musician is said to be "enraged," yet his ire takes no form more aggressive than is manifested by stopping his ears, clenching his fists, and making a wry face at his tormentors. If the disturbance continues, he may probably take a further revenge by snapping his violin strings, breaking his bow, or smashing one of the keys of his harpsichord ; but were the scene to have taken place in 1860, instead of 1740 ! I tremble to think of the exemplary vengeance which would be taken by the enraged musician on the miscreants who had done this violence to his tympanum. The needy knifegrinder

---

* The Marrowbones and Cleavers Societies' Books for the parish of St. George's, Hanover Square, are still extant, and in the one year, 1745, their earnings reach the amount of 380*l.*, all given in guineas by the aristocracy patronizing that Temple of Hymen. The gratuity became at last a perfect black mail, and the interference of the law became at last necessary to put a stop to an organized extortion.

would, for a certainty, be hauled before Justice Old-
mixon, and put in the stocks for a vagrant ; Bridewell
would be the doom of the pretty milkwoman, and the
birch or bread-and-water the fate of the little boy with
his drum, and the little girl with her rattle.   Rigorous
Acts of Parliament would be invoked against the
dustman and the industrial who sells small coal ; the
cats would be sent to the pieman, and the chimney-
sweep compelled to carry the penal and sable fasces of
Ramonage ; " John Long, Pewterer," would be indicted
as a nuisance, and the ballad-singer and hautboy-player
be sent for seven days to the House of Correction.   Oh !
for a week of despotism to put down itinerant musicians
and street noises ; and should we require a fortnight of
the despotism, I wonder, if the week were granted to
our desires ?

The *Enraged Musician* is stated to be a portrait of
Handel.   There is nothing to prove the assertion.   His
countenance does not at all resemble that of the
immortal composer of the *Messiah ;* and if we are to
take the *Harmonious Blacksmith* as a test of the power
of endurance of extraneous sounds possessed by George
Frederick Handel, he would more probably have
extracted something melodious from the odd *charivari*
going on before his window, than have been driven to
rage thereby.

Not to be passed over in mention of these one-act
dramas, such as the *Strolling Actresses, Southwark Fair*,
the *Distressed Poet*, the *Enraged Musician*, &c. &c., is
the oddly humourous picture called *Taste in High Life.*
It was painted by Hogarth as a commission from a
wealthy and eccentric lady residing at Kensington—a

TASTE IN HIGH LIFE.

Miss Edwards,—who, having been sharply satirized in society for her own personal oddities, took a sufficiently original vengeance, in commanding Hogarth to perpetuate with his pencil the preposterous absurdities of the dress worn by the most exalted society of her time.   There never has been, surely, before or since, a more ludicrous beau than the exquisite who is in raptures with the fine lady in the sack, over the diminutive cup and saucer they have just picked up at a sale.   Admire his cross-barred coat, his prodigious queue, his cuffs, his ruffles, the lady's muff he carries.   The beau is said to be intended for my Lord Portmore, in the dress he wore at the birthday drawing-room in 1742.   We have seen the magnificent accoutrement of Tom Rakewell, when, bound for St. James's on a birthday, he was dragged *
by unkind bailiffs from his sedan-chair.   We read in Walpole's letters with what solicitude the virtuoso Horace was possessed lest the birthday clothes which he had ordered of a tailor in Paris should fail him in his need. They had been bespoken a month, and he has heard nothing of them, he tells one of his correspondents, plaintively ; but none of these suits of attire, gorgeous, radiant as they may have been, could have equalled in

---

* Three fellows called Duel, Morice, and Hague, were the most notorious catchpoles, bailiffs, or sheriffs' officers in 1730-40.   The bailiffs were Christians after a sort ; the Jews, who were as yet not legally tolerated in England, could not officiate even as the lowest myrmidoms of the law ; and it was not until late in George III.'s time that the Israelites took to executing *ca sa*'s and *fi fa*'s.   Still the vocation of bailiff was, and had been for a long time, deemed infamous by the English people ; and Dutchmen and Flemings were often employed to do the shoulder-tapping branch of business.   Perhaps Messrs. Morice and Hague were of Low Country extraction.

transcendency the gala "full fig" of my Lord Portmore.
The fashionable lady is equally ineffable in her array.
Her younger companion is exquisitely dressed; the
black boy—designed, it is reported, for the celebrated
Ignatius Sancho in his sable youth—is an oriental dandy
of the first water; and the very monkey who is reading
the list of purchases made at the auction of articles of
virtù, is attired in the height of the fashion. Apart
from this picture being admirably drawn and composed,
and sparkling with very genuine humour—apart from its
containing a very stinging satire on the extravagance of
fashion in 1742, it is remarkable as a poignant burlesque
and lampoon on our own crinoline mania of 1855-60.
Just look at the monstrous hoops worn by two ladies.
That of the elder one is half concealed by her brocaded
sack; but the flagrancy of the younger lady's *panier* is
patent and palpable to the naked eye. She is chucking
the little black boy under the chin. Hogarth has, as
usual, symbolized a portion of his meaning in pictures
on the wall. There are pendants to these pictures of
"Taste," in portraits of celebrated male ballet-dancers
of the Italian theatre. This picture was, as I have
remarked, painted expressly for Miss Edwards. Either
she or Hogarth would never consent to an engraving
being taken from it; and it was not until after his
death that it was engraved—rather softly and cloudily—
in stipple or *taille douce*.

All these things were executed in the "shadow of
the Forty-five"—in the years immediately preceding
the great Jacobite outbreak in Scotland, which ended
in the defeat at Culloden, the flight of Charles Edward,
and the beheading of the rebel lords on Tower Hill. To

the Forty-five—its prologue, its drama, and its epilogue, —belong Hogarth's master-works of the *Marriage à la Mode*, the *March to Finchley*, and the portrait of *Lord Lovat;* and of those I must treat, even on the threshold of the scene from which I must soon depart altogether.

IX.

Tail-Piece.

IN twenty pages, or thereabouts, I have to glance at
nineteen years of the history of a man's life and works.
But the rough macadam of my path is smoothed and
levelled, comparatively, by the knowledge that the great
events in the career of my hero have been, if not fully
narrated, at least enumerated in their due order.   To
recapitulate a little.   You have seen William Hogarth
born, apprenticed to Mr. Gamble, taught graving and
design.   You have seen him teach himself to draw with
ease, to paint with grace and vigour.   You have watched
him learn to think, to use his knowledge of men and
cities, to cover Theocritus' sad face with the droll mask
of Democritus.   You have seen him marry his master's
daughter—Sir James's, not Ellis Gamble's ;—and were
this a novel, not a life-study, it would be fitting to end
the history just where the parson gives his benediction.
When a married pair are childless, and become prosperous, and the man renowned, and keep their coach
and their country-house, the fairy-tale peroration is
perhaps the most appropriate : " And they lived long
and happily, beloved by everybody."   But the childish
couch may be thorny, and there may be hyssop in the

cup of renown; and cannot poisonous laurel-water be distilled from the crisp leaves which the conqueror is crowned with? The fine coach may jolt, the wheels stick in the ruts sometimes. The country-house may be damp. There may be ratsbane in the creamiest porridge, and halters in the grandest pew. So until the end, telling of the evil and the good in an active life, I will, if you please, proceed: but be not impatient. A term is coming to your weariness and my prolixity. See how swiftly the sands are running, and how inexorably the clock-needles are moving towards the last minute of the last hour—moving sharply and cruelly, and like arrows wounding. *Vulnerant omnes, ultima necat*, is written on the dial. The bell will soon toll, and it will be time to split up this pen, and blot this sheet.

But as a shrewd devisor making his testamentary dispositions, let me first endeavour to set my artistic property in order: to see what rich treasures, as well as little waifs and strays of value, remain to make up the grand inheritance left by William Hogarth to his country. "All my messuages and tenements—all my plate, pictures, furniture, and linen—all my bonds and securities:"—well, the schedule is lengthy enough; but a few pages may suffice to let the reader know how much, pictorially, the good man died worth.

First, of that "Forty-five," whose shadow crossed my path as I journeyed towards the eighth stage of these travels in search of Hogarth. In the stormy time of the Jacobite troubles (1745-6-7—let the generic term be the "Forty-five,"—have not Stanhope and Chambers put their seal upon it, so?) Hogarth was busiest, cleverest, most prolific, and most popular. This jolly cabbage-

rose of the English garden of painting was in full bloom
and beauty and odour : yea, and the dried leaves in the
Hogarthian vase are redolent of sweet savours to this
day. As a man who took the keenest interest in the
transactions, manners, humours, and vices of his time,
William could scarcely help been affected, politically,
one way or the other, by that all-absorbing war of the
English succession. The painter who dwelt at the sign
of the "Golden Head" was a staunch Hanoverian, and
the political Hanoverian was in that day generally the
staunchest of Englishmen. Of the German kings who
were good enough to come from Herrenhausen, and sit
on our throne—the kings who were always scampering
over to Vaterland, who talked French at court, and
did not know enough of the English language to
deliver their own royal speeches, nay, scarcely knew to
what rank in the State their servants were eligible,*—
Hogarth could not have been a great admirer ; nor, I
should imagine, did the artist trouble himself much concerning the reputed descent of the Hanoverian monarchs
from ODIN (!), Radag, Frond, Freidger, *Wig* (!), &c. &c.
&c., as set forth in the pompous, lying *Brunswick
Genealogy*, published by the "person of quality" who
continued *Chamberlayne's State of England*. He simply
hated Jacobitism as the vast body of the middle classes
hated it, for the reason that, to his mind, the success of
the Stuart cause was associated with *soupe maigre*,

---

* When, in the early part of the second George's reign, a new Lord
Chancellor had to be appointed, the name of a certain great lawyer was
canvassed at the council board as fittest to hold the seals. "No ! no ! "
cried *König* George. "Gif me te man who read te tying sbeech zo
peautiful." He meant the Recorder of London, whose duty it was to
deliver the periodical report on the condemned criminals in Newgate.

fricasseed frogs, and foreign ascendancy, with surreptitious warming-pans, popery, brass-money, and wooden shoes. My dear romantic friends, I am afraid that in the " Forty-five " the " respectable classes " in England were almost to a man against the chivalrous Charles Edward. 'Tis distance, and that wonderful romance of " sixty years since "—a hundred and fifteen now—that lend enchantment to the view of " Bonny Prince Charlie." Even the noblemen who espoused his cause were either attainted titulars—as Perth, as Tullibardine, and as poor Charles Ratcliffe were—or else came to his standard as to an Adullam, wofully dipped, out at elbows, and discontented with the normal state of things, as were Kilmarnock and Balmerino.   The lowest mob in London was sometimes for the Elector, and sometimes for the Chevalier—mainly following with the fluctuations of the Geneva market ; but I think mob-Jacobitism in '45 must very much have resembled mob-chartism in our own '48.   The accounts of the preparations made for the defence of London, when the rebels reached Derby, form a curious parallel to the proceedings prior to that 10th of April which we all remember.   The stage carpenters of Covent Garden and Drury Lane sworn in as specials ; the Bank sandbagged and barricaded ; the Artillery Company under arms : the gentlemen of the Inns of Court breathing defiance to St. Germains and Rome from behind field-pieces and locked gates—all these read like prototypes of our little panic of the year of revolution.   Oxford was Jacobitical in 1745, but it pre-ferred drinking the king's health " over the water " in snug college rooms, to praying for King James, just before being turned off in that frightful Tyburn publicity.

There were plenty of rich Jacobite baronets and squires in Cheshire and Lancashire; but few cared to leave their heads on Tower Hill, while their broad acres went to enrich Greenwich Hospital. They remembered Derwentwater, and remained prudently quiet. I grant the noble, self-denying chivalry of the brave Scottish gentlemen who joined in this great quarrel—the heroism of such Paladins as Cameron of Lochiel, Cluny Macpherson, Clanronald, Macdonald of Keppoch, and the ducal Drummond of Perth; but on this side the Tweed—ah me! I fear that the people who had whole coats and small-clothes, and money in their pockets, were, in *posse* if not *in esse*, for King George. It is very nice and picturesque, now-a-days, to be a Jacobite in theory; it was not so pleasant in the "Forty-five" to be a Jacobite in practice —to lie in the condemned hold at Newgate, with seventy pounds weight of iron on your legs, and to be half strangled, wholly decapitated, disembowelled, and ultimately distributed piecemeal on spikes affixed to the gates and bridges of London, all in consequence of your political opinions. Cavalier Sir Walter Scott even remembered that Edward Waverley was his rich uncle's heir, and discreetly drew him out of the hempen circle of overt Jacobitism, just in time to succeed to the family estate, and marry pretty Rose Bradwardine.

There is something so suggestive of mendacity lingering about the very name of the IRELAND family, that I have been very chary, in the course of this undertaking, of quoting as an irrefragable authority any writings of the father of the notorious forger of *Vortigern*. I have been compelled to mention him from time to time, for Samuel Ireland has really written well and judiciously, as well as copiously, concerning the minor Hogarthiana. Now if Samuel is to be believed, Hogarth designed the headpiece or title for Henry Fielding's short-lived periodical, *The Jacobite's Journal : edited by John Trott Plaid, Esq.* The impression I have seen is from a woodcut, one of the vilest in drawing and execution that ever penetrated beyond Seven Dials. A monk is represented leading an ass, mounted on which are a man and woman in an absurd Scotch costume ; the plaid on the woman's dress being in saltire ×, and evidently produced by rough "crisscross" slashings on the surface of the block. This lady brandishes in one hand a sword ; and to the donkey's tail is appended a (seemingly) tavern sign, with three flower-de-luces on its field, and the name of " Harrington " as legend. Harrington may have been the host of some tavern which was the place of meeting of a more than ordinarily noted Jacobite club. From the Scotchman's mouth issues a scroll with "huzza !" in very big letters. He holds a glass of (presumably) whisky ; and to the ass's bridle is tacked a file of the *London Evening Post.**

---

* Here is a sample, in the shape of a suppositious diary of public events, from H. Fielding's other anti-Jacobite journal, *The True Patriot*, setting forth the dreadful results which London loyalists of the *bourgeois* class were taught to believe would inevitably follow from the restoration of the Stuarts. " *Jan.* 3.—Queen Anne's statue in St. Paul's Churchyard taken away, and a large crucifix erected in its room. *Jan.* 10.—Three anabaptists committed to Newgate for pulling down the crucifix. *Jan.* 12. —Being the first Sunday after Epiphany, Father Macdagger, the royal confessor, preached at St. James's—sworn afterwards of the Privy Council. Arrived, the French ambassador, with a numerous retinue. *Jan.* 26.—This day the *Gazette* informs us that Portsmouth, Berwick, and Plymouth, were delivered into the hands of French commissaries as cautionary towns ; and also twenty ships of the line, with their guns and rigging, pursuant to treaty.

London antiquaries may derive some edification from counting the spires—with St. Paul's dome in the midst— in the riverain view of London forming the background : which is, by the way, a curious counterpart of the well-known engraved heading to the *Illustrated London News*. It is not probable that W. H. did more than make the roughest sketch for this atrocious lignoon ; and I daresay he was ashamed even of his slight co-operation when the wretched thing chopped out was printed. The headpiece was discontinued after the twelfth number of the publication : the alleged reason being that it was not cut deep enough, and that the impressions were too faint.

The famous portrait-etching of Simon Lord Lovat must for ever connect William Hogarth with the " Forty-five." Not till the termination of that momentous struggle was this old coronetted fox trapped. I suppose there never was, in the annals of villany, such an ancient, disreputable reprobate as this said Simon Fraser. The Regent Orleans' Abbé Dubois was a sufficiently atrocious rogue. Don Francisco, otherwise Charteris, was bad enough. Both were cheats, and ruffians, and profligates, and the last was an usurer ; but the noble baron was all

---

27.—Tom Blatch, the small-coal man, committed to the Compter for a violent attack on Father Macdagger and three young friars who had assaulted his daughter Kate. . . . . . The writ *de hæretico combu-rendo* abolished. Father Poignardini an Italian Jesuit, made Privy Seal. Four heretics burnt in Smithfield, assisted in their last moments by Father O'Blaze, the Dominican. The pope's nuncio makes his public entry, met at the Royal Exchange by the Lord Mayor, a Frenchman. A grand office opened the same night in Drury Lane for the sale of pardons and indulgences. *March* 9.—My little boy Jacky taken ill of the itch. He had been on the parade with his godfather the day before, to see the Life Guards, and had just touched one of their plaids."

these, and something more. A finished scamp in early life, Captain Fraser narrowly escaped a capital conviction for a hideous outrage upon a lady whom he abducted and forced to marry him. He ratted to and from St. James's and St. Germain's a hundred times. He was as consummate a hypocrite as he was impudent a cynic. He lied and cozened, and played fast and loose with the English government, until he was nearly eighty years of age. At last they had him on the hip ; and the execu-tioner swept his wicked, clever, plotting old head off his decrepit shoulders.* He was as flowery as Barère, and as bloodthirsty as Fouquier Tinville. He was as treacherous as Reynard the Fox, and as astute as Macchiavelli. He was as malicious as Voltaire, and as depraved as Aretin, and as cruel as Claverhouse ; and he died with a high-flown Latin quotation in his mouth, "*Dulce et decorum est,*" &c. &c., just after he had given utterance to a heartless witticism — " the very fiend's arch-mock."

Old Simon had been in alternate correspondence with the Stuarts and the Guelphs for years ; but he was false to the last, and while protesting his unalterable devotion to King George's government, was sending his son, the Master of Lovat, with the Clan Fraser, to join the Pretender. He would doubtless have betrayed

---

* Immense crowds were collected on Tower Hill to see him executed. Amphitheatres of benches were erected, and seats were at a premium. As he was mounting the steps of the scaffold, the supports of one of the neigh-bouring stands gave way. Numbers of persons were thrown to the ground, and two were crushed to death. Says the moribund jester to the sheriff, who directed his attention to the terrible accident, " The mair mischief the better sport,"—an old Scotch proverb, and one that suited his lips better than "*dulce et decorum.*"

Charles Edward, had there been time; but Culloden
came, and Simon's last trump was played. He had fled
from his own house, Castle Downie, when affairs had
begun to look badly; had escaped from the Earl of
Loudoun, who manifested a strong inclination to detain
him a prisoner at Inverness; and had set up a Patmos
in the house of one Mr. Fraser, of Gortlich, in Strather-
rick, "whither he was wont to repair in summer-time
to drink the goat-whey." There the ruined, fugitive
Chevalier found the greyhaired rogue in terrible tribulation. He could say nothing but "Chop off my head,
chop off my head! my own family and all the great
clans are undone. Chop off my head!" We shall see
that his aspirations were attended to, presently. Simon
afterwards remarked that he had now nothing to trust
to but the humanity of the Duke of Cumberland ("of
whom his lordship," says my contemporary account,
"here took occasion to say several very handsome
things"). *Vieux Blagueur!* It was of no use. The
game was up. Simon was ultimately taken by the
duke's soldiers. He was found concealed in a hollow
tree in the middle of a pond, with two blankets wrapped
round his old legs. They brought him by easy stages
to London, making much of him as a captive of the
highest importance. He halted at St. Alban's, where,
it suiting his purpose to fall ill, he put up at the White
Hart Inn, groaning piteously. It so chanced that the
physician, Dr. Webster, called in to attend him, was one
of Hogarth's intimate friends. At Dr. Webster's invita-
tion, William posted down to St. Alban's, and was
introduced to the state-prisoner, who received him with
much cordiality, "even to the kiss fraternal"—not so

very pleasant an embrace at that moment, as Lord
Lovat was under the barber's hands. The old Judas!
with his kisses and slobberings. The painter had several
interviews with this venerable traitor, whose appetite,
notwithstanding his illness, for minced veal and burnt
brandy, reminds one of Mr. James Blomfield Rush's
solicitude, when confined in Norwich Gaol, for roast pig
"and plenty of plum sauce;" and Hogarth had ample
time to make the drawing from which, with great
celerity, he executed that amazing etching I speak of.
The prisoner is supposed to be counting on his fingers
the principal Highland chieftains, and the number of
claymores they could bring into the field before the
rebellion. Thus, "Lochiel had so many, Cluny Macpherson so many more," and the like. There are few
accessories to the portrait. Old Simon's coat and wig
— an astonishing wig — and buckled shoes, are quite
enough. There is not a wrinkle in his face, not a crease
in his ravenous-looking hands, but tells of cunning,
treachery, and lawless desire. The strangest thing about
this aged desperado was, that in addition to being witty,
he was an uncommonly jovial and good-tempered companion, was affable to his dependants, and bounteously
hospitable to all his *dhuinè-wassels*. He kept up a
grand, although rude, state, at Castle Downie, where
he maintained a bard to sing his praises in Gaelic, and
where claret for the gentry, and usquebaugh for the
commonalty, were continually flowing. Every Fraser
was free of the kail-kettle and the meal-tub at Castle
Downie. The clansmen pigged together at night in
stables and outhouses; and with a touching and characteristic spirit of impartiality, the lord of the castle

allowed his lady, while she lived, no other accommodation than her sleeping apartment, of which he resigned to her the full enjoyment, and where she lay, like the Margery Daw famed in nursery legend, on straw. Old Simon's affectionate conduct to his son, the Master of Lovat, whom, while he himself remained snugly in hiding, he bade march with his clansmen into the jaws of death, has already been alluded to. "Diabolical cunning, monstrous impiety!" exclaimed Sir William Young, one of the managers appointed by the Commons to prosecute the impeachment against him, when he came to touch upon that episode in the prisoner's career.

When the portrait was etched, a bookseller offered its weight in gold for the copper-plate.* Lovat was quite as popular a criminal as Thurtell or as Palmer. The impressions could not be taken off with sufficient rapidity to supply the anxious purchasers, though the rolling-press was at work day and night for eight or ten days. For several weeks Hogarth received money at the rate of twelve pounds a day for prints of his etching. Shortly after Lovat's execution (in 1747) a mezzotinto engraving was published, said to be from a sketch by Hogarth, and having for title *Lovat's Ghost on Pilgrimage.* The scene is a cemetery by moonlight. A headless figure, in the habit of a Capuchin monk, a staff in his hand, barefooted, is wandering through the Garden of Death, "his old feet stumbling at graves:" supported by his sinister arm is the mocking, satyr-like head of

---

* The plate may have weighed two pounds and a half. Allow 45*l.* per pound as the price of gold : this would give 112*l.* 10*s.*

Lovat, wigless now, and trunkless. The inscription to the plate is trivial enough :—

> Doomed for my crimes in pilgrimage to roam,
> With weary steps I seek my native home.

To the right of the headless monk is a vault, on one side of which you read—" This monument was erected by *Simon* Lord Fraser of Lovat," &c., and on another side is a bas-relief representing a skull and crossbones, a skeleton, an hour-glass, and the headman's axe, with these words beneath—" To the memory of *Thomas* Lord Fraser of Lovat." This monument has puzzled me. It was *Simon*, not Thomas, who was beheaded. Anon, I thought I could discern a sly touch of Hogarthian humour in the inscription. The old lord, it is clear, deliberately intended to sacrifice his son in case of the failure of the Jacobite undertaking. As it happened, the Master of Lovat escaped, while the lord was executed ; and Hogarth may have intended to hint how the biter was bitten, when old Simon erected a monument in anticipation of the probable end of his son, not foreseeing his own fate. But then Thomas Fraser was but the " master," the heir-apparent to the barony of Lovat ; he never succeeded to the title : so here my conjectures break down.*

Firmly, indissolubly to the " Forty-five," although not completed until three or four years afterwards, belong the plate and the picture of the *March of the Guards towards Scotland in the year* 1745, more familiarly known as *The March to Finchley*. It is well known that

---

* The attainder was reversed by our gracious Queen Victoria about the time of her coronation, and there is now a worthy Simon Fraser Lord Lovat.

Hogarth intended to dedicate the engraving to King George II., and a proof before letters was consequently taken to St. James's to be submitted to the descendant of Odin and Wig. A British nobleman was good enough to bring this work of art for the inspection of the Duke of Cumberland's august papa. The following dialogue is said to have taken place on the occasion :—

Descendant of Odin and Wig.—" Who is dis Hogart ?"

British Nobleman.—" May it please your Majesty, a painter."

D. of C.'s august papa.—" Bah ! I do hate bainting and boetry doo. Dos dis vellow mean to laugh at my garts ? "

British Nobleman (modestly, and yet with a complacent consciousness that he is saying a neat thing). — " The piece, my liege, must undoubtedly be considered as a burlesque."

Descendant of Odin and Wig.—" *Was sagst Du ?* A bainter purlesque mein zoldiers ! He teserves to be bicketed for his inzolence ! Dake de drompery out of my zight. (*Exit the D. of C.'s august papa in a huff. The British nobleman returns crestfallen to Leicester Fields, and, telling Hogarth of the ill-success of his mission, asks him to dinner that very evening to make amends.*)

To make himself amends, sturdy William Hogarth sat down to his yet unlettered plate, and with furious graver proceeded to dedicate the *March to Finchley* to " His Majesty the King of Prussia, an Encourager of Arts and Sciences," adding a big note of admiration (sarcastic dog !) and a tremendous flourish. I don't know what notice, if any, the flute-playing friend of the devout

Voltaire, and the "Protestant Hero" of English evan-gelical circles, took of this dedication; but I am afraid that *his* papa, Mr. Carlyle's Friedrich Wilhelm, would have marked *his* sense of the "bainter's" familiarity, not only by subjecting him to the punishment of the picket, but by belabouring him with his beloved cane, could he have got William to Potsdam.

There is something to be said on both sides regarding this historical misunderstanding between the king and the artist. Hogarth was certainly the greatest English painter of the time; and, moreover, as Sir James Thornhill's son-in-law, thought he had some claim to that which he subsequently enjoyed—the royal patron-age. He was in the right to feel himself aggrieved at being contemptuously snubbed and ignored; but, on the other hand, it was somewhat too much to expect the King of England, as a king, to bestow his favour on a production in which the soldiers who had just saved the crown from tumbling off his head were depicted under the most ludicrous and degrading circumstances. The guards who march to Finchley are a riotous and tipsy mob. The drummer staggers, the grenadiers are wallowing in the kennel; the rear rank are exchanging disorderly endearments with inebriated females; the sergeant is battering right and left with his halberts, and very nearly the only sober person in the tableau is the pretty little fifer-boy tootle-tooing away in the corner. Now, only imagine that in the year 1854, Messrs. John Leech and Richard Doyle had conspired to produce a graphic, humorous cartoon, called the *March of the Guards towards Gallipoli*. Imagine that these jocose draughts-men had drawn the Fusiliers and Coldstreams in all kinds of absurd and ignoble attitudes—beating the police with their belts, for instance, depriving the toll-taker on Waterloo Bridge of his copper-bottomed aprons, bartering their bearskins and cartouch-boxes for drink, blackening the eyes of their relations, and so forth. Imagine our two artists going up to Buckingham Palace, and coolly begging her Majesty's gracious permission to inscribe this facetious libel with her royal name! What would the first Lady in Christendom have said to such a request? What would his Royal Highness have thought? I daresay our art-loving Queen and Prince have a right royal "tall" copy of Hogarth's works on some snug shelf in their library; but in these genteeler days the aberrations of the Guards and other British warriors should figure only in the police reports. The battle and camp pictures of Wouvermans and Vandermeulens would not do now. We are grown more refined. Battles are fought in white kid gloves, and the camp at Aldershott gets into the *Court Circular*.

For very many reasons—the chief and plainest being, that I am uttering my last dying speech on Cornhill, having been convicted of a barbarous attempt on the life of William Hogarth, deceased, and that I am even now traversing the cart, and after taking leave, though feeling loth to depart,—my notices of the remaining things that make up Hogarth's WORK can be little more than a curt *catalogue raisonné*. Let me mention them:—

Mr. Garrick in the Character of Richard the Third.—The original picture was commissioned by a munificent Yorkshire squire, Mr. Duncombe, of Duncombe Park. The price paid was the then handsome one of 200*l*.

Hogarth shows us the tent-scene. The great tragedian, in a spurious kind of Elizabethan costume, is starting from his conscience-haunted couch. The head is very characteristic ; the outstretched hand wonderfully well drawn, and full of expression ; but the frame is burly and muscular enough for the body of a Lifeguardsman. In this great hulking, cowardly tyrant, we quite lose the notion of " little Davy." On the long and cordial friendship that existed between Hogarth and Garrick, I may not dwell minutely. 'Tis just right, however, to mention that William made the design for Garrick's chair, as President of the Shakspeare Club. The chair was of mahogany, richly carved ; and at the back was a bust of the poet, carved by Hogarth from the Statford-on-Avon Mulberry-Tree. What has become of this chair? Who is the fortunate possessor of this renowned mulberry-cum-mahogany-tree that brings together three such good men and true as Shakspeare, Garrick, and Hogarth ? *

---

* Garrick chanced to visit Hogarth one morning when the artist was engaged in his painting-room ; and being about to retire hastily, " old Ben Ives," the servant, called out to him to stay a moment, as he had something to show him, which he was sure would please him. He took Garrick into the parlour, and showed him an exquisite chalk drawing, personifying Diana (but the original model has not been discovered), and exclaimed, with something like rapture : " There, sir, there's a head ! they say my master can't paint a portrait. Look at that head." I know not which is the most gratifying feature in this story : the faithful servant praising his master's work, or the fact that he grew grey and became " old Ben Ives " in his service. Among the Hogarth anecdotes, few are so well known as that giving Garrick the credit for having sate for a posthumous portrait of Fielding, and by his extraordinary powers of facial mimicry, "making-up" a capital model of his deceased friend. If this be true, Garrick must have surpassed, as a mime, that famous harlequin who used to imitate a man eating fruit, and from whose mere gestures and grimaces, you could at once

For a little interlude, called the *Farmer's Return*,. good-naturedly written by Garrick for Mrs. Pritchard's benefit, Hogarth drew, first a rough chalk *ébauche*, and next a beautifully finished crayon study, light and graceful, and which was engraved by Basire, and appended as frontispiece to the printed copy of the interlude. It is chronicled in this place, as Garrick passes rapidly across my stage; but in point of chronology, the *Farmer's Return* is one of the latest of Hogarth's works, being dated 1761, just after the coronation of George the Third. Garrick is drawn smoking a pipe. His flapped hat, leathern belt and buckle, ample collar, and buff boots, make him look far more like the stage Falstaff than a farmer, and thus accoutred, he contrasts remarkably with that type of the British agriculturist with whom Gilray (about thirty years afterwards) made us so familiar. The *Farmer's Return* seems to have been a kind of "monopolylogue," to use the classic verbiage of "entertainment-givers;"

---

tell the fruit he was pretending to eat ; now he was pulling currants from the stalk, now sucking an orange, now biting an unripe pear, now swallowing a cherry, and now exhausting a gooseberry. Then there is the account of Garrick sitting to Hogarth for his own picture, and mischievously giving so many varied casts of expression to his countenance, that the painter at last threw down his brush in a pet, and declared he could do no more, unconsciously imitating the Irish swineherd, who declared that he had counted all his porcine charge save one little pig ; but that he "jumped about so that he couldn't count him." A better authenticated story than any of these is the relation of a trifling unpleasantness between Hogarth and Garrick, about the latter's portrait, for which he had given W. H. several sittings. David declared that the picture wasn't like him—perhaps he didn't think it handsome enough. Then they fell out about the price, and finally Hogarth drew his brush across the face, and turned the picture to the wall of his studio. Long years afterwards, the widow Hogarth sent the picture as a gift to the widow Garrick.

and the versatile David sang a song, described the humours of the coronation, and gave " imitations" of the Cock Lane Ghost.

The *Marriage à la Mode* (1745-6)* is to those whom

---

* Note specially in the *Marriage à la Mode*, in Scene I., the pride of the old lord shown in the coronet broidered on his crutch, and his ostentatious prodigality in the unfinished wing of his palace seen through the open window, begun through arrogance, left unfinished through lack of funds. Observe Miss in her teens twirling the ring on her handkerchief ; the beau bridegroom admiring himself in the glass ; the dogs coupled together, and the handsome *roué* barrister mending his pen. He must have been a special pleader, and have confined himself to chamber practice : was called in probably to draw Viscount Squanderfield's marriage settlement : wears, as you see, his wig and gown in private life ; precisely as the clergy wore their bands and cassocks. In Scene II., note the *one* receipted bill on the attenuated steward's file ; the crowded, costly, tasteless ornaments on the mantelpiece ; the yawning servant in the vista of the huge saloon, tardily getting through his household work, and telling plainly of late hours overnight at Squanderfield House. The perspective in this scene is very masterly. In Scene III., there is much to be noted, but little that can be dilated upon, beyond the admirably expressive faces of the actors, and the *perfect* drawing and pose of the quack doctor. In Scene IV., mark the contrast between the portrait of the grave divine on the wall, and the sensuous copies from Italian pictures ; the basketful of expensive trumpery bought *au poids d'or* at an auction, and over which the black-boy is grinning ; the humours of a masquerade painted on the screen ; the fat dilettante quavering from the music-book ; the inimitable beau drinking coffee with his hair in papers ; the country cousin who has gone to sleep ; the French hairdresser,—and pray, who is the lady with the red hair, the morning wrapper, and the Pamela hat ? The old lord is dead by this time. Hogarth quietly announces the event by the bed in the alcove being surmounted by an earl's coronet. In Scene V. mark the wondrous *falling* attitude of the murdered earl, who is absolutely dying—hush ! he falls, he is dead—in this scene, as is the Pierrot in M. Gérome's masterpiece, *Le Duel après le Bal.* No blood is needed to tell that the bowl is for ever shattered, and the wheel broken at the cistern. The hues of the dying man's face exactly fulfil the famous description of the *Facies Hippocratica.* Light and shade in this scene most excellent ; but none of the engravings (the originals by Ravenet) come up to the rich tones of the oil pictures. In Scene the last, observe the capital view of Old London Bridge, with the

(without offence, I hope) I may call the lay admirers of Hogarth, decidedly the most widely known and appreciated of this artist's works. We have been familiar with this terribly picturesque drama for years in its picture form at the National Gallery, and latterly at the delightful and admirably conducted South Kensington Museum. The six tableaux have been engraved over and over again in every variety of size and substance —from the lordly line engraving to the humble woodblock. Fortunately, too, while Hogarth's satire is in this performance at its keenest and most scathing point, there is an absence throughout of the literal coarseness which, unhappily, confines so many of his works to the library portfolio. The truth is indeed told in the midnight murder scene—but only by that man in the background, and that pamphlet on the floor; and the sole plate in the series in which Vice in its most dreadful form is sub-understood, is, luckily, to the young and ignorant, inexplicable. The million see little beyond Doctor Misaubin receiving patients in his laboratory, amid skeletons and stuffed crocodiles, and machines for

houses on it ; the aldermanic pride shown in the stained glass escutcheon on the window-pane ; his thriftiness in the Dutch pictures on the wall ; his prudence in the row of firebuckets in the vestibule ; his niggardliness in the meagre breakfast, and the half-starved ravenous dog, and the lean servant-man, whom the doctor collars and trounces for bringing in the "last dying speech and confession of Counsellor Silvertongue ;" his love of solitary conviviality in the punchbowl and tobacco-pipes in the cupboard ; his insatiable avarice in that act of his in drawing the ring from the finger of his dying daughter. The agony and remorse in the poor countess are tremendous. The old nurse, for all her hard lineaments, is tender and kindly. The little girl held up to kiss her mother is weakly and rachitic ; one of her poor legs strapped up in irons. The sins of the fathers are visited upon the children !

curing dislocation of the shoulder. The *Marriage* is a grand work to ponder over. I chafe and fret to think I must dismiss it in a dozen lines, instead of a dozen pages. This is no three-volume novel of fashionable life, written by my lord's footman, or my lady's maid, but an actual living drama, put on the stage by a man who had seen all his characters act their parts in the great world. Hogarth was no courtier, no beggar of dedications, nor haunter of antechambers; yet I do not think that a Chesterfield or a Bonnell Thornton could have detected any important solecism in etiquette among the great personages here delineated. The people in the earl's saloon and the countess's drawing-room are as true to nature as are those in the alderman's house by London Bridge, the quack's study, or the fatal bedroom at the " Key " in Chandos Street. Costumes and accessories are all in perfect keeping. You may ask whence Hogarth drew this intimate acquaintance with the manners of Piccadilly and Hanover Square—he who was born in a back yard of the Old Bailey, and served his apprentice-ship to the silversmith in Cranbourn Alley ? I answer, that the man was gifted with a wonderful power of observation and perception ; that nothing escaped him, and that he had taken stock of, and accurately remem-bered all the minutiæ of the high life above stairs which he must have seen when noblemen sat to him for their portraits, and he painted " conversation pieces" and " assemblies " of noble families. Nor should it be forgotten that, haughty and magnificent as were the British aristocracy of the " Forty-five," they could bend, now and again, to artists most gracefully. 'Twas not alone Pope who was privileged to crack a bottle with

Bolingbroke, or Swift who was Harley's " dear Jonathan."
The uncouth manners of Johnson, indeed, may have
repelled Chesterfield ; but Hogarth's simple, sturdy,
plain-spoken ways do not seem to have stood in his way
—with the memorable exception of his quarrel with the
ugly lord to whose portrait he threatened to add a tail
—in his intercourse with the proudest patricians.   The
great Lord Mansfield knew and loved him.   So did
Lord Temple.   And that best of Irishmen, Lord Charlemont, writing years after the painter's death, speaks of
William Hogarth as his personal friend, whose memory
he holds in honour, and whose reputation he will not
suffer to be assailed.

Industry and Idleness.—This " domestic drama " has
been, from its moral tendency, almost infinitely multiplied.*   A few years since, a handsomely framed set of

---

* Here is the scheme, in Hogarth's own words, for *Industry and Idleness:* "Exemplified in the conduct of two fellow-'prentices, where the one
by taking good courses, and pursuing those points for which he was put
apprentice, becomes a valuable man, and an ornament to his country ; while
the other, giving way to idleness, natually falls into poverty, and most
commonly ends fatally, as is expressed in the last print.   As these prints
were intended more for use than ornament, they were done in a way that
might bring them within the purchase of those whom they might most
concern ; and lest any part should be mistaken, a description of each print
is engraved thereon."   Again, Hogarth scribbled some memoranda which
he seems to have addressed to the person whom he wished to continue the
descriptions of his plates commenced by Rouquet.   "These twelve plates
were calculated for the instruction of young people, and everything addressed
to them is fully described in words as well as figures, yet to foreigners a
translation of the mottoes, the intention of the story, and some little
description of each print, may be necessary.   To this may be added a slight
account of our customs, as, boys being generally bound for seven years, &c.
Suppose the whole story describing in episode the nature of a night-cellar,
a marrowbone concert, a Lord Mayor's show, &c.   These prints I have
found sell much more rapidly at Christmas than at any other season."

the prints formed an attractive ornament of the office of the Chamberlain of London. The two careers, now parallel, now meeting, now diverging, of Francis Good-child and Thomas Idle, are so well known, that a minute recapitulation of their features would be trite and weari-some. Tom is the model scamp; sleeps at his loom, reads flash ballads, and *Moll Flanders;* is caned by the beadle for diceing on a tombstone; is sent to sea; comes back; turns thief; sees the worst of all bad company; is betrayed to the thief-catchers in a night-cellar for the forty-pounds blood-money; is arraigned at Guildhall before his quondam fellow-'prentice, and finishes at Tyburn with his shoes on and a halter round his neck. His reverence the ordinary follows, as in duty bound, in his coach, the procession to Tyburn; but it is an enthusiastic disciple of Wesley who sits by the convict's side in the fatal cart. As to Francis Goodchild, he is the model Lord Mayor and British merchant, of the approved Gresham and Whittington pattern. He learns his trade; reads the excellent old ballad of *The Valiant Apprentice;* works hard; pleases his master; marries that worthy tradesman's daughter; makes a fortune; serves all the civic offices with intelligence and dignity; dispenses hospitality to the poor—aided by his stout footmen, and encouraged by his virtuous spouse—in a very free-handed manner; makes out Tom Idle's mittimus —with a sigh, but makes it out, notwithstanding; and is at last elected king of the city.*

One side of Hogarth's drama has been made into a kind of stage-play : *George Barnwell.* The appropriate texts of Scripture, forming the commentary on each plate, were selected by Hogarth's worthy friend, the Rev. Arnold King.

* Note that the firm of "West and Goodchild" dwelt near Fish Street Hill. In the distance you see the Monument ; and Hogarth—I really must

" After the *March to Finchley*," says Hogarth, " the
first plate I engraved was the *Roast Beef of Old England,*

---

call him " Protestant Bill " for once—has taken care to give prominence to
the old fibbing inscription on the pedestal (since in common decency,
obliterated), touching "this Protestant city" having been destroyed by the
malice of the " Popish faction." Mr. Goodchild performs his Samaritan
duties in an elegant morning gown and silk nightcap.　Beggars are not
excluded from his bounty.　Cripples and *culs de jatte* are laden with broken
victuals, and the marrowbones and cleavers liberally fee'd.　Observe that
the Lord Mayor's banquet took place, not at the Guildhall, but in the hall
of one of the great companies.　Ladies sat down to table ; and the entertainment was held by daylight.　From the superscription of the letter
which one of the ward beadles has just had handed to him, and which he
is pompously scrutinizing, it would seem that the chief magistrate of
London was not always dubbed "right honourable." The missive is ⋅
addressed to the Worshipful Francis Goodchild, Esq.　Note that the forks
at table have but two prongs.　The perspective in the night-cellar seems to
be altogether faulty.　There are at least half-a-dozen points of sight.　The
guests are unutterably hideous : nearly all Hogarth's wicked people are
noseless.　The body of a murdered man is being flung down a trap-door—
a little phase in the manners of the time which, but for the discoveries made
when that old house in West Street, Smithfield, was pulled down some
years ago, might seem exaggerated.　Among the ruffians in the night-cellar
is a soldier of the Footguards, who at this time were very little better than
footpads.　In the Tyburn tableau the convict wears a nightcap, and has the
usual bouquet at his breast.　The place of execution is quite in the open
fields ; and the hangman, stretched on the cross-beams of the gallows,
lazily watches with pipe in mouth the arrival of the procession.　Note the
pigeon which the man in the stand is releasing to carry the intelligence of
the moment of the criminal's arrival at Tyburn.　In Scene the last, the
Lord Mayor's show turning the south-east corner of St. Paul's Churchyard
into Cheapside, I cannot find a trace of St. Paul's school.　Note the
extremely absurd appearance of the train-bands.　I don't think the royal
couple in the canopied balcony can be intended for the king and queen.
They are far too young ; moreover, Queen Caroline died long before
Industry and Idleness appeared.　The rather do I imagine the distinguished
pair to be intended for Frederick Prince of Wales and his consort.　There
may be in this a touch of the Hogarthian slyness.　The sign of the house
with the balcony is the King's Head.　You see his majesty's painted
countenance, crowned and periwigged, and through my glass he seems to
turn his eyes with a very sulky expression towards the son whom he hated.

which took its rise from a visit I took to France in the
preceding year." And from this short and not very
pleasant trip arose the print generally known as *The
Gate of Calais*. William proceeds to recall his impressions of French life and manners. It need scarcely be
said that he does not approve of them. Farcical pomp
of war; pompous parade of religion; much bustle with
very little business; poverty, slavery, and innate insolence, covered with an affectation of politeness; dirty,
sleek, and solemn friars; lean, ragged, and tawdry
soldiers; fishwomen who are "absolute leather:"—in
this uncompromising manner does William Hogarth of
Leicester Fields, in the parish of St. Martin, in the
county of Middlesex, painter—here is an "abuse of
specification" for you!—dispose of the magnificent
nation, which its well-beloved king, its sumptuous clergy,
its aristocratic military commanders, and its enlightened
philosophers, then indubitably imagined to be at the very
summit and apogee of European civilization.

As Hogarth was sauntering about Calais and looking
at the *Gate*, which was originally built by the English
during their long occupation, he thought he could
discern some traces of our royal arms sculptured on the
masonry. Proceeding to make a sketch thereof, he was
forthwith taken into custody by the soldiers of the
Maréchaussée; but not attempting to cancel any of his
sketches or memoranda, and, perchance, M. Dessein of
the Hôtel coming forward to vouch for his being a
painter and not a spy, the Commandant *de Place* did
not, in his discretion, deem fit to cause the captive to be
forwarded to Paris, but contented himself with placing
him under close arrest at his lodging, whence, when the

wind changed, he was despatched per packet-boat to
Dover. Hogarth's revenge for his churlish treatment
was amusingly characteristic. He painted a picture
and engraved a plate representing *Calais Gate*, with
tattered and hungry-looking French soldiers on guard ;
a greasy and unwholesome friar ; withered fishwomen, with
scapularies, and grinning like their own flat-fish ; cowled
monks and penitents in the background ; and a lean
French cook, carrying a mighty sirloin of beef, destined,
by the label attached to it, for "Madame Grandshire."
Perhaps she was Hogarth's landlady, and a jovial dame
who loved good eating. The cook hugs and fondles the
beef, but with a rueful twinge of muscle, as though it
were his unkind fate to cook beef, but not to eat it.

> As well-bred spaniels civilly delight
> In mumbling of the game they dare not bite.

In the right-hand corner crouches a cadaverous wretch
in tartan jacket and trews, whom Hogarth himself
describes as " a melancholy and miserable Highlander,
browsing on his scanty fare, consisting of a bit of bread
and an onion, and intended for one of the many that
fled from their country after the rebellion in 1745." In
the left corner, and the middle distance, Hogarth has
drawn himself, plump, spruce, and cheerful, in curly wig,
half-military roquelaure, and smartly cocked hat, with
pencil and sketch-book in hand. The lean paw laid on
his shoulder, and the tip of the halbert seen beyond
the perpendicular of the wall's angle, suggest that his
sketch is being disturbed by one of King Louis's
soldiers, and may have been the first thought for that
facetious diagram of abstract art which he afterwards
drew, and which purported to show "A sergeant with his

halbert on his shoulder and accompanied by his dog entering an ale-house." Three lines and a little cross stick suffice to indicate the event and the actors. A C is the section of the ale-house door; B F is the sergeant's halbert; D E is the dog's tail. *Voilà tout.**

Beer Street and *Gin Lane* are said to have had for their first idea the pair of pictures by Peter Breughel called, one *Lo Grasse*, and the other, *La Maigre Cuisine*. The moral of these pictures, one humorous, the other terrific, is just as applicable at the present day as a hundred and ten years ago. I have no space to descant upon them, nor on the *Inn Yard*, nor on the *Four Stages of Cruelty*, which are designed with as excellent a moral intention as that shown in *Industry and Idleness*, but are from their very nature always repulsive, and sometimes intolerably disgusting. The autopsy of Tom Nero, at Surgeon's Hall, is specially revolting. The dog gnawing the heart of the dissected criminal has been frequently treated as a gross and inexcusable exaggera-

---

* Mr. Pine, the well-known engraver, sat for the portrait of the Friar. He alleged that he did not know what use Hogarth intended to make of the sketch; but he was unmercifully quizzed in consequence, and, among his acquaintances, went by the name of "Friar Pine." The scarecrow figure of the French soldier was long used, as a rough woodcut, as a heading for English recruiting placards; and thus William Hogarth and Charles Dibdin were equally enabled, in different walks of art, to serve their country. The plate was chiefly engraved by C. Mosely; but the heads are evidently by Hogarth. Lord Charlemont was the purchaser of the original picture; but soon after it was sent home it accidentally fell down, and a nail ran through the cross at the top of the picture. Hogarth in vain attempted to repair the blemish, and at length he managed to conceal it by substituting a black crow, of hungry aspect, looking down on the beef.

tion ; but I have read ugly stories of a hyena and a vulture maintained for the same horrible ends at schools of anatomy within the last forty years.

The last capital work of Hogarth—executed, I mean, in the style to which he owes his renown—is the series entitled *Four Prints of an Election.* The first scene represents an "entertainment," or rather orgie, in the great room of the tavern of a provincial borough, the head-quarters of the contending political parties ; and while the "Blues" are gorging themselves to repletion, even to the point of impending apoplexy, necessitating the untying of cravats and the letting of blood, the "Buffs," or whatever may have been the opposing party's hue, are pelting them with stones and brickbats through the open window. The scene is crowded with figures ; is second only to the *Modern Midnight Conversation* in its vigorous arrangement of composition, and its tremendous scope and direction of humour, observation, and satire ; and offers a hundred points of detail susceptible of the most careful consideration, but on which to enlarge, at this crisis of my undertaking, would be useless. Let it pass with a barren mention. Let the remaining scenes of *Canvassing for Voters, Polling* and *Chairing the Member,* be just alluded to and dismissed. I can be, here, but the gentleman usher on the first landing, bawling out the name of the company to the groom of the chambers in the saloon above ; but time and opportunity may make amends.

Meanwhile I must go back a little to the "Forty-five," and there, taking up Hogarth the MAN, leave his WORK, and continue the thread of the TIME that yet remains to him. By the special Act of Parliament for which he had so doughtily battled, William had secured to himself the fair share of the emoluments accruing from his plates. Their popularity was enormous. He was for many years exclusively his own publisher ; but his works were bought much less as pictures than as graphic satires and lay sermons. The public taste for pictorial art in England was yet of the feeblest and most perverted nature ; and although William frequently received a commission for a single painting, he had much difficulty in selling his great series on canvas. In 1745 he devised an elaborate but too complex scheme for disposing of those of his pictures which remained unsold, by a kind of half-public auction. The ticket of admission to the sale was the etching of the *Battle of the Pictures*, in which he very tartly symbolized his contempt for the old masters, or rather for the spurious imitations of their productions, which then monopolized the patronage of the wealthy classes. The semi-auction was a more than semi-failure. The entire series of the *Rake's* and the *Harlot's Progress*, together with the *Four Parts of the Day* and the *Strolling Actresses*, brought, in all, no more than 427l. 7s. Hogarth was bitterly and cruelly disappointed. As a satirist, he had come at the nick of time ; as a painter, he had been born forty years too soon. Good man ! how his ears would have tingled to hear of the price paid for *The Awakened Conscience*, or *The Derby Day !*

About this time, also, importuned by well-meaning friends, he projected a *Happy Marriage*, as a companion to the *Marriage à la Mode;* but a besetting fear and more active horror of falling into the insipid and the inane, soon blotted out sketches for the *Matrimonio* *felice.* His reputation is the better, perhaps, for this reticence.*

Shortly before 1750 he purchased a small, snug house at Chiswick, at which he resided in summer-time; and he even set up a coach of his own, ensconced in which he and his wife made their pilgrimages in great state between the pleasant neighbourhood of the Mall and Leicester Fields. In the year '52, his scriptural piece of *Paul before Felix* was placed in the hall at Lincoln's Inn. Lord Wyndham had bequeathed 200*l.* for the execution of a picture by some approved master for the hall; and Hogarth's friend, Lord Mansfield, obtained the commission for him. The Honourable Society of Lincoln's Inn must have been well pleased with their artist, for they entertained him grandly at dinner in their hall. His large painting of *Moses before Pharaoh's Daughter*—in which a curly-headed, chubby little English urchin is being smiled upon by a smiling comely English lass, whose embroidered lappets are supposed sufficiently to denote her connexion with the Pharaohs and their dusky land of mystery and darkened knowledge : a blackamoor making love to her waiting-maid, and a rabbinical gentleman, apparently fresh from Houndsditch completing the tableau—he presented to the Foundling Hospital. Both

---

* There is a story fathered on Hogarth, assuming him to have been a very absent man, and narrating how, calling at the Mansion House, in his carriage, to visit the Lord Mayor, a violent storm of rain set in during his interview, at the conclusion of which the painter, quitting the municipal palace by another door to that at which he had entered, quite forgot that he possessed a carriage, walked home in the rain, and got wet through. Hogarth was the very reverse of an "absent" or *distrait* man ; and moreover, the story is told of half-a-dozen other equally celebrated personages who "flourished" both before and after his time.

these pictures were elaborately engraved under his superintendence and with his co-operation. According to his usual custom, he executed a whimsical etching as a ticket for subscriptions for the plate, and the subject of this—nobody in the world but Hogarth would have ventured upon such a one—was a deliberate burlesque upon the big solemn picture he had just completed. His intention is said to have been to show, by contrast, the difference between the real sublime and the low, coarse conceptions of the Dutch painters. He shows us a stumpy Paul, mounted upon a three-legged stool, and haranguing an ignoble Felix and an assembly apparently composed of pettifoggers from Thavies Inn and old clothesmen from Duke's-place, seated in an area mean and squalid enough for a Court of Requests. A hulking Angel with a Lifeguardsman's torso backs up Paul ; but the *Avvocato del Diavolo* is present in the shape of a tiny Callotesque demon, who is busily engaged in sawing away one of the supports of the three-legged stool. It is difficult to determine which is the funniest of the two *Pauls*, the one meant in earnest or the one meant in jest.

Dr. Warton took occasion, shortly after Hogarth's unfortunate *Horæ Paulinæ*, to remark in a note to his first edition of Pope, and on the line—" One science only can one genius fit "—that Hogarth was incapable of treating serious or dignified subjects. In a rage the painter proceeded to exhibit Warton and Warton's works from a most degrading point of view ; but through the interference of Garrick and Dr. John Hoadley, a reconciliation was brought about. In a subsequent edition Warton retracted his stricture, and paid William a very handsome compliment.

Well, he has been dead a hundred years and over. Criticisms, strictures, can do this valiant Englishman no harm now. It dims not one laurel-leaf of his real and glorious chaplet to admit that Warton, " scholiast" of my second essay—first severe, next complimentary—had some justice on his side from the first. Hogarth was *not* capable of the dignified in art. He could be serious indeed ; terribly and truly serious. Hang up the gambling-house scene, the duel in the bedroom scene, the harlot's death scene, or *Gin Lane*, by the side of Scheffer's *Faust and Mephisto on the Blocksburg*, of Delaroche's *Cromwell looking on the body of Charles I.*, of Décamp's *Morte*, of Edwin Landseer's *Shepherd's Chief Mourner*—and William Hogarth will keep his ground for solemn truth, for sober tragedy, for the reality, the domesticity of grief and terror. But can all the pictured Cæsars that ever fell at the base of Pompey's statue, or the Jaels that hammered nails into Siseras, or the Judiths that chopped off Holofernes' heads—can all the Apollos that ever destroyed Pythons or flayed Marsyases, equal in tragic terror a Body that is lying on a bed covered with a sheet, or a coffin-lid leaning against a door whence, yesterday, hung the silk dress of a fair woman ? I maintain, for the last time, that Hogarth could be serious, and that he could be alike dramatic, tender, and terrible ; as in my limited comprehension I can realize the notions of tenderness or of terror. I grant his lack of dignity, just as I admit his deficiency in appreciation 'of poetic, ideal beauty. No women can be fairer than his ; but they are flesh and blood, not marble. His tragedies were best told in succinct nervous prose. When on his firm-treading foot he placed the cothurnus, he stumbled. When he attempted blank verse he stammered and broke down, and those who best loved the man could ill suppress a smile at his rugged delivery and his ungainly accents. I ask again, does all this matter now? His worst scriptural pictures are but errors : they are ungraceful and prosaic, but they are yet too powerful ever to be contemptible. Had he painted three hundred instead of three or four unsuccessful works, his failures would not—should not mitigate against the endurance of his fame. They would not deprive him of the place among great men due to one who was as powerful a satirist as Juvenal, and not malevolent ; as keen as Swift, but not cruel ; and in his humble honest man's creed as pious (and as plain-spoken) as Hugh Latimer. Forget or remember his failures in the grand style as you will. Those failures will never wither the wreaths which posterity continues to hang on his tomb. Do failures dim the diadem of Dryden because he wrote rhyming tragedies as well as the *Ode on St. Cecilia's Day*? Does it matter if De Balzac wrote *Jeanne la Pâle* and *Dom Gigadas*—a whole cloud of worthless novels, before *Le Père Goriot* and *Eugénie Grandet*? Does *Swellfoot the Tyrant* stand in the way of the *Revolt of Islam*? and what does a hurried and inaccurate *Life of Napoleon* weigh against *Waverley* and the *Bride of Lammermoor*?

I suppose that the *Analysis of Beauty* must be reckoned among Hogarth's failures. He wrote this now often-mentioned but seldom-studied treatise as a kind of defiance to the scholarly critics whose censures galled him, even as a burlesque writer twitted on his ignorance by learned but dully mediocre adversaries might devote himself to the study of Greek, and produce

20—2

a commentary on Simonides or a new translation of Aristophanes. The *Analysis*, as an argument, certainly went to prove that a waving or serpentine line is a beautiful line. Beyond this it proved nothing. The fairest criticisms on the work itself are condensed in the oft-quoted remark of Nichols, that " the sources of beauty are so various and complicated, that every attempt to reduce them to any single principle, except that of association, has proved nugatory, and has foiled the ability of the most ingenious."

The publication of the *Analysis** brought nothing

---

* The manuscript of the *Analysis* was submitted for correction to Hogarth's friend, Dr. Morell ; and, after that gentleman's decease, to the Rev. Mr. Townley, the Head Master of Merchant Taylors' School. The work was originally published in quarto, and Hogarth engraved a strange frontispiece for it, treating *de omnibus rebus* in art matters. There is a caricature of Quin in the character of Coriolanus ; Desnoyer the ballet-dancer ; a beau in court costume, made first in the likeness of George III. as a young man, but subsequently, "by desire," altered to the Duke of Kingston ; the Venus de' Medicis, Apollo ; busts, cranes, anatomical *écorchés*, a whole row of ladies' corsets of various design, and legions of strange whims and oddities besides. Walpole, Beattie, Lamb have written on the *Analysis*, but without being able to make much of it. Indeed, it is very puzzling reading. Hogarth talks of "parsley leaves," well composed nosegays, "common old-fashioned stove grates," Indian figs, torch thistles and candlesticks, and other incongruous matters. But the Hogarthian common-sense is not entirely absent. Witness this passage : "Nor can I help thinking but that churches, palaces, hospitals, prisons, dwelling and summer-houses might be built more in distinct characters than they are, by contriving orders suitable for each ; whereas, were a modern architect to build a palace in Lapland or the West Indies, Palladio must be his guide, nor would he dare to stir a step without his book." Again, "What are all the manners, as they are called, of even the greatest masters, which are known to differ so much from one another, and all of them from nature, but so many strong proofs of their inviolable attachment to falsehood, converted into established proof in their own eyes by self-opinion. Rubens would in all probability have been as much disgusted at the dry manner of Poussin, as Poussin was at the extravagant of Rubens." Hogarth is a firm

but troublesome and irritating squabbles to a man now (1752) fifty-five years old, and who should have been safely moored in the haven of competence and peace. A German translation of the work by one Herr Mylius was prepared under the inspection of the author, and published in London. Another German translation, by Vok, appeared at Berlin in 1754. There are two or three translations of the *Analysis* in French : and in 1761 a version in Italian was produced at Leghorn.

Very long since I mentioned that Hogarth presented the casts and models bequeathed to him by Sir James Thornhill to the Society of Artists, who held their drawing-room in St. Martin's Lane. To the scheme of a Royal Academy, however, which began to be mooted in 1755, he offered a more than negative opposition, " as tending to allure many young men into a profession in which they would not be able to support themselves." This was a tradesmanlike view of the question fit for the old apprentice of Ellis Gamble ; but Hogarth qualified

defender of the three-legged stool. How pleasing, he says, is the idea of firmness in standing conveyed to the eye by the three elegant claws of a table ; the three feet of a tea lamp, or the celebrated tripod of the ancients ! He might have added a painter's easel, a camp-stool, or a pile of soldiers' muskets to his catalogue. While enthusiastic in his admiration for the Laocoon, he censures the absurdity of dwarfing the proportions of the children in order to bring the group within the pyramidal form of composition. He is happy when he calls the pine-apple one of Nature's " works of fancy," in contra-distinction to such plain work-a-day esculents as apples, and potatoes, and cabbages. He insists on intricacy as one of the elements of pleasure in art. " Wherein," he asks, " would consist the joys of hunting, fishing, shooting, and other diversions without the frequent turns, and difficulties, and disappointments, that are daily met with in the pursuit. How joyless does the sportsman return when the hare has not had fair play ! how lively, and in spirits even, when an old cunning one has baffled and outrun the dogs ! "

his discouragement, arguing against the creation of a mob
of artistic mediocrities by "degrading what ought to be
a liberal profession into a purely mechanical one." The
Royal Academy have certainly borne some portion of
Hogarth's warning in mind during the last half-century,
by teaching as few young men to draw as possible.

The last plate of the *Election* (Chairing) was not
completed until 1758. In the interval between this year
and 1755 Hogarth had published nothing of importance.
He contributed the inimitably droll frontispiece to
"Kirkby's *Perspective*," showing the true and the false
applications of that science; and he engraved an odd
conceit, called *Crowns, Mitres, and Maces*. Between '55
and '57, however, he was fortunate enough to get a
lucrative commission from the churchwardens of St.
Mary Redcliffe, Bristol, for three oil paintings of sacred
subjects : viz., *The Annunciation, The High Priests and
Servants sealing the Tomb*, and *The Three Maries*. He
went down to Bristol, and resided there some considerable time while the pictures were in progress; and a
correspondent from that western city—to whom, not
being able to decipher his signature, I hereby take the
opportunity of returning my sincere thanks—has been
good enough to forward me the fac-simile of Hogarth's
receipt for the amount of the commission—500*l.*

In 1757, William was elected a councillor and hono-
rary member of the Imperial Academy of Augsburg;
and, notwithstanding old King George's hatred for
"boetry and bainters," he condescended to overlook
Hogarth's libel on the Footguards, and appointed him
sergeant-painter to the king. The office was worth 200*l.*
per annum ; and it must be recorded to the honour of

John Thornhill, the marine painter, Sir James's son, and Hogarth's fast friend, who had succeeded his father in the office, that he resigned it in favour of his illustrious colleague and companion. In 1758, Hogarth gave the public a capital portrait of himself sitting at his easel and painting the *Comic Muse;* as also a humorous etching called *Character : or, the Bench,* containing the portraits of most of the eminent judges of the day. In 1759, he published one of the best of what I may call his " one act comedies," the *Cockpit Royal.*

1759 gave birth also to that famous fresco picture of his, the *Sigismunda.* It is said that it was painted in absurd emulation of Correggio. Hogarth himself says, that as the sum of four hundred pounds had been paid for a picture of *Sigismunda,* falsely attributed to Correggio, but really the work of a Frenchman, he saw no reason why he should not produce a version of the woe of Count Guiscardo's widow which should be worth as much money. Lord Charlemont had given him four hundred pounds for a sentimental picture, and now Sir Richard, afterwards Lord Grosvenor, commissioned a *Sigismunda* for the same price. The work was completed, but the critics concurred in abusing the performance. Sir Richard demurred from *Sigismunda* at any price. An angry correspondence between the patrician and the painter followed ; but the days of Joshua Morris and the *Element of Earth* were gone, to return no more. Hogarth did not go to law about his picture. He believed in its merit strongly ; but he was growing old, and querulous, and weary. He agreed to the cancelling of the bargain. The noble Grosvenor kept his money, and Hogarth his picture. *Sigismunda* was unlucky from first to last. To vindicate its excellence, Hogarth determined to have it engraved, but he hesitated to undertake so large a work himself. His old coadjutor Ravenet was willing, but he was under articles to Boydell. Then Grignion took it in hand, and got through the preparatory etching ; but Hogarth became dissatisfied, and withdrew the plate from him. Basire followed, and outlined the face "after the manner of Edelink." He, too, gave it up, and our poor old artist, in despair, issued advertisements, stating that he would engrave *manu proprio* the much-vexed widow. This was in January, '54 ; but he never lived to transfer *Sigismunda* to copper. To his widow he left strict injunctions never to part with the picture for a sum less than five hundred pounds. In this, as in all other behests Jane Hogarth obeyed her lord, and she faithfully kept *Sigismunda* — no purchaser offering the required price—until her death. At the sale of her effects in 1790, the unlucky portrait was at length knocked down to Alderman Boydell for fifty-six guineas ; but better financial fate was reserved for it. It was made one of the prizes in the Shakspeare lottery ; was sold by Mr. Christie in 1807 for four hundred guineas, and was exhibited at the British Gallery in 1814. Poor William could never bear to speak with patience of the criticism lavished on his attempt at the sublime—all provoked by a sale of questionable old masters, belonging to the courtier-connoisseur, Sir Luke Schaub. "The most virulent and violent abuse," he writes, "was thrown on it from a set of *miscreants* with whom I am proud of being *ever at war*. I mean *the expounders of the mysteries of old pictures.*"

The end was drawing nigh. The illustrious man was old. He was obstinate. He was testy. But one more event of moment remains to be recorded in his career :— his quarrel with WILKES and CHURCHILL.

Hogarth had ever, as you know, been a Church and State man ; a Tory Brunswicker, so to speak ; and demagoguism, nay liberalism, were to him only a carica- ture of papistry and Gallicism. He had been convivially friendly for some time with the notorious editor of the *North Briton*, but seldom was attraction visible in bodies so naturally fitted for repulsion. The decided democratic turn taken by Wilkes as a politician at the commence- ment of George III.'s reign, contributed to estrange him from Hogarth ; the breach widened ; and, as *will* happen, even in purely political disputes, the painter began to remember something of the private character of the leveller. He began to be shocked at this hideous, profligate, witty, worthless satyr ; a demoniacally-minded man it would seem, but, like Mirabeau, permitted by Providence to appear and flourish for a season, that he might give utterance to some eternal constitutional truths. Hogarth, the decorous, rate-paying citizen, husband, and king's sergeant-painter, began to see beneath the flaming cap of liberty the Asmodeus linea- ments of the Monk of Medmenham. It is but just to confess that he commenced the attack on Wilkes. In a print called *The Times* (the second under that title), he drew Wilkes in the pillory, with a rueful countenance, empty pockets, and a scroll inscribed " Defamation " above his head. Wilkes retorted by a severe but not undignified admonition to Hogarth in the *North Briton* (No. 17). Forthwith Hogarth etched that peculiarly abhorrent portrait of Wilkes sitting in a chair, with the cap of liberty on a pole. The Wilkites could not forgive the scathing indignation that stamped as it were on adamant and for ever the frightful squint, the horned Pan's leer of their leader. Charles Churchill, ex-parson and ex-gentleman, Wilkes's fellow-railer, crony and boon companion, threw himself, fiercely panting for fisticuffs, into the quarrel. He published his cruel and unmanly *Epistle to William Hogarth*, in which he sneered at the artist's works, at his life, at his wife, at his avarice, at his age, at his infirmities—in which he dubbed him "dotard," and bade him "retire to his closet." I think William Hogarth might have well replied in the superb lines of Ben Jonson apostrophizing himself :—

> Leave things so prostitute,
> And take th' Alcaic lute,
> Or thine own Homer, or Anacreon's lyre ;
> Warm thee by Pindar's fire.
> *And tho' thy nerves be shrunk, and blood be cold,*
> *Ere years have made thee old,*
> Strike the disdainful heat,
> So loud to their defeat,
> As curious fools, and envious of thy strain,
> Shall blushing own no palsy's in thy brain.

Hogarth had passed his sixty-third year, but he was no dotard, and no palsy was in his brain. For Alcaic lute, and Anacreon's lyre, and the fire of Pindar, Hogarth had, for all support, his graver and etching-needle. He went to work, looked up an old copper, blocked out a portrait of himself, with his dog Trump by his side (*vide* portrait in South Kensington Museum), slightly altered Trump, and for his own effigy substituted a caricature of Churchill as the *Bruiser, or Russian Hercules*—in other words, as a slavering, growling bear, with the torn

canonicals of a clergyman, a pot of porter by his side,
and a great ragged staff in his paw—each knot inscribed
with "lye." This satire was not very ill-natured. It
was a good knock-down blow, but not a stab with a
poisoned dagger as Churchill's *Epistle* was. Had Hogarth
chosen to be malicious, he might have overwhelmed both
his opponents with intolerable infamy. In one vignette
he might have touched upon certain traits in the character
of the patriot who wrote the *Essay on Woman* which
would have made the world loathe *Liberty Wilkes* as
though he had been a cagot or a leper. But so far he
refrained to advance. He did not tell half what he
knew or what he thought of the clever, meteoric ruffian
Churchill—the shooting-star that emitted such an unsavoury odour when it fell. Nor could Hogarth tell his
clerical enemy—he had not the gift of prophecy—that
both were squabbling on the verge of a grave half dug;
that one, Hogarth, was to die in peace and honour in
the arms of the woman who loved him, and to leave
a grand and unsullied name which remote posterity will
not let die; that another, Churchill, was to end bankrupt,
drunken, alone, forlorn, in a mean town on the seashore,
not to be remembered in this age save with a qualified
admiration in which curiosity that is almost pruriency
has the better part. For the time, Hogarth had the
worst of the controversy. His foes were younger and
active, and the mob were on their side. Churchill's
Epistle is undoubtedly as clever as it is wicked; but has
it aught but a galvanized existence now? and is not
every touch of William Hogarth living, vigorous, vascular,
to this day?

The Wilkites used to boast that they killed Hogarth.

A year before his death, indeed, Churchill again alluded
to the character Hogarth might draw

. . . . . were Hogarth living now.

The "Bruiser" habitually spoke of him in the past tense,
a conceit borrowed from Swift's attack on Partridge, the
almanack-maker. Hogarth, however, lived full two years
after the Wilkes and Churchill warfare. He produced
that grand rebuke to the frenzied revivalism of his time,
called "Credulity, Superstition, and Fanaticism." But
he had long been ill, and more and more sensible of a
gradual bodily decay. The last year of his life was
occupied in retouching his favourite plates, with the
assistance of several engravers whom he took with him
to Chiswick. Still he was merry and convivial, and
entertained his friends at his modest, hospitable table ;
but with a sad presentiment that the end was coming.
He drew and wholly engraved the last, the most pathetic
of his works—"*Finis ; or, the Bathos.*" It is the end of
all things. Time with clipped wings, broken scythe,
cracked hour-glass, has smoked his last pipe. The word
Finis curls in the last puff from his lips. Around him
all lies in ruins. The bottle is broken ; the broom is
worn to the stump ; the bell is cracked ; the bow un-
strung ; Phœbus and his horses are dead in the clouds ;
the ship is wrecked ; the signpost of the World's End
tavern tumbles down ; the moon is on the wane ; the
crown is in pieces ; the playbook lies opened at *Exeunt
omnes ;* the purse is empty ; the musket is shattered ;
the clock has stopped ; the gibbet falls ; the skeleton is
gone ; the chains drop. A statute of Bankruptcy is taken
out against Nature.

" Nothing now remains but this," said the old man, and drew a painter's palette, broken.

The print of *The Bathos* bears the date of the third of March, 1764 ; Hogarth never touched pencil or graver after its completion. He was, notwithstanding his growing weakness, cheerful to the last ; saw friends the day before his death, and ate a hearty dinner on the very day. On the twenty-fifth of October, 1764, he was removed from his Villa at Chiswick to his house in Leicester Fields, and there, the same night, and in the arms of his wife, he died. I need scarcely say that he was buried at Chiswick, and that the pathetic and affectionate epitaph on his tomb was written by his friend, David Garrick. Hogarth died in competence, but by no means in wealth. The most available jointure he could leave to his widow were the stock and copyright of his engravings, and these were deemed of sufficient value to be made chargeable with an annuity of 80*l*. to his sister Anne. Mrs. Hogarth survived her husband five and twenty years, dying on the 13th. November, 1789.

Here I pause. What more I have to say of the great Englishman who has been my theme in these pages during the last nine months, would fill very many and closely printed pages, in addition to those you already have. But of my essays on Hogarth, in this place, there is satiety, and I cease. I have endeavoured to touch upon the chief points in the painter's career, from his birth to his death, to notice his principal works, and as many of his minor productions as the space at my command would warrant. I am conscious of the commission of many errors and inaccuracies in the performance of my task ; but I humbly hope that the

opportunity will be afforded to me, at no distant date,
of correcting my blunders elsewhere. This work—
trivial as its results may be—has not been pursued
without difficulty ; it is not concluded without reluctance ;
but the remembrance of kindness and encouragement
from troops of friends, the majority personally unknown
to me, who have cheered me in my progress, softens the
sigh with which I rise from the labour of sixty-seven
happy nights—nights when the fruits of long years'
study of Hogarth and his time have been put to paper.

FINIS ; OR, THE BATHOS.